REGIONAL COOPERATION IN SOUTH ASIA

REGIONAL COOPERATION IN SOUTH ASIA

A Study of Political and Economic Dimensions of SAARC

NIDHI SHARMA

KALPAZ

ISBN : 978-93-5128-034-7
Price : ₹ 950

First Published 2014

Published by

Kalpaz Publications
C-30, Satyawati Nagar,
Delhi-110052
Ph. : 9212142040
E-mail: kalpaz@hotmail.com

Laser Typesetting : Rudra Computer Graphics, Delhi
Printed at : G. Print Process, Delhi

Cataloging in Publication Data—DK
Courtesy: D.K. Agencies (P) Ltd. <docinfo@dkagencies.com>

Sharma, Nidhi.
Regional cooperation in South Asia : a study of political and economic dimensions of SAARC / Nidhi Sharma.
p. cm.
Includes bibliographical references (p.) and index.
ISBN 9789351280347

1. South Asian Association for Regional Cooperation. 2. South Asian cooperation. 3. South Asia—Economic integration. 4. South Asia—Politics and government. I. Title.

DDC 338.954 23

Contents

Preface 9
Acknowledgements 11
List of Tables 13
List of Graphs 15
Acronyms 17

1. Concepts and Theories of Regional Integration **19**
Meaning of Regional Integration • Regional Integration : Concept • In the words of Philips de Lombarde and Luk Van Langenhove • According to Hans Van Ginkel • Regional Integration Initiatives should Fulfill at Least Eight Important Functions • Moves towards Regional Integration • Economic Implications • Economic Implications of Regional Integration • Investment Diversion Effect • Political Implication of Regional Integrations • Political Motives behind Regional Integration • So, Integration is Political • Regional Integration Theory • Political Approaches of Integration • Economic Approaches to Regional Integration • Optimal Currency Area with Stationary Expectations • OCA with International Risk Sharing System • Recent Regional Integration Agreements • Regional Integration and Globalisation • In what way is Regionalism a Response to Globalisation? • Role of W.T.O. and Regional Integration • WTO Provisions on Regional Integration Arrangements • The Enabling Clause • The Role of South Asian Association of Regional Cooperation (SAARC) and Regional Integration in South Asia • Conclusion.

2. Regional Cooperation in South Asia and SAARC: Historical Development and Evolution **59**
Origin of SAARC • Charter of South Asian Association for Regional Cooperation • SAARC Regional Centers • Areas of Cooperation • SAVE COMMITTEE • Promoting people to

people contact • Non-Governmental Organisations (NGOs) • SAARC LAW has been engaged in • Recognised Bodies of SAARC • Cooperation with Inter National Organisation • The SAARC Secretariat • Conclusion.

3. **An Introduction to SAARC Nations, SAARC Summits, Declarations and its Growth in South Asia since 1985** **92**
The Historical Background of South Asia • Political History of South Asian Countries • Profile of SAARC Member States • Agreements Convention and Declaration of SAARC Summits • Agreement on South Asian free trade Area (SAFTA) • SAARC Standard • Charter of the SAARC Development Fund (SDF) • Agreement on Establishing the SAARC Food Bank • Conventions • Declaration • Conclusion.

4. **Political Dimensions of SAARC** **133**
Political Conflicts and Relationship Among SAARC Nations • Afghanistan as a New Member of SAARC and its Relationship with South Asian Nations • India and Afghanistan • Pakistan and Afghanistan • Relations between Other SAARC Members • Role of India in SAARC : (Political Dimension) • Effects on Indo-Pak Relations • Cooperation Trouble between India and SAARC Members • India's Renewed Commitment • Political Challenges • Ways to Overcome Impediments • Confidence-Building Measures • Achievements of SAARC (Political Dimension) • Factors Leading to Development of SAARC • Role of Observer Nations • SAARC and the United States of America • Conclusion.

5. **Economic Dimensions of SAARC** **178**
Growth Rates of SAARC Countries • Economic Profile of SAARC Nations • The Economic Agenda of SAARC • Principles of SAPTA • From SAPTA To SAFTA • Challenges and Prospects for SAFTA • Developmental Mechanism of SAARC • Focused Areas: • The Millennium Development Goals (MDGs) • Taking SDGs Forward • Trade in Energy Resources • Information Exchange • Joint Research and Development • Sharing of Technology• Training of Personnel • Regional Economic Cooperation Among SAARC Countries • SAARC Trade Fairs • Impediments or Challenges to Further Enhancing Economic Cooperation • Ways to Overcome Impediments • Achievements

of SAARC (Economic Dimension) • SAARC and Other International Forums • SAARC and European Union (EU) • Comparison between SAARC and EU • SAFTA and NAFTA (The North American Free Trade Agreement) • WTO Negotiations and SAARC • SAARC and United Nations Organisation.

6. Overview **279**
SAARC TRADE • Review of Literature.

Bibliography **297**
Index **307**

Preface

Regional integration offers several benefits, for instance greater economic integration, frequent and easier people to people contact sustainable peace and development at the regional level. Regional cooperation in South Asia, initiate under the platform of the SAARC. This book analyses the present political and economic dimensions of SAARC. The SAARC forum has made significant attempts towards political and economic cooperation (through SAPTA and SAFTA), through various funds (SDF, SADF, SAARC - Japan special fund), through intra-SAARC trade and through various political agencies. From a structural point of view, SAARC has expanded not only by including Afghanistan as a new member, but also by opening its space to new observers from outside the region.

As SAARC has completed more than 25 years of its existence, during these two and half decades it had faced various impediments on its way to success and had proven its success in overcoming through various political and economic obstacles gracefully.

This work analyses that if South Asia has to play a leadership role in the new world that is taking shape, then it must undertake specific initiatives within a new policy paradigm for pursuing peace and overcoming poverty. However this requires that government should move out of a mind-set that regards an adversarial relationships with a neighbouring country as the emblem of patriotism, affluence of the few at the expense of many, as the hallmark of development, individual greed as the basis of public action and mistrust as the basis of inter-state relations. We have arrived at the end of the epoch when we could hope to conduct out social, economic and political life on the basis of such a mindset. Now, the people of South Asia have started recognising that they have a new tryst with destiny. They are affirming that their security and well being lies not in interstate conflict but in peace and cooperation for the bright future of SAARC and South Asia. There is a need to promote South Asian regional cooperation to promote common goals, meet common needs and resolve common problems is highly desirable. The establishment of SAARC itself is a very significant achievement, against the background of the tumultous interstate relations in the past among the major countries of the region.

SAARC, as the only regional instrument available to carry South Asian nations along cannot be neglected or undermined; instead it has to be endowed with greater vigor and a sense of purpose.

Nidhi Sharma

Acknowledgements

I would like to express my sincere gratitude to certain people without whose help and encouragement it would have been difficult to complete my book. I extend my sincere gratitude and thanks to my co-operative and cordial teacher, Prof. Nisar-ul-Haq for his constant encouragement, I am especially thankful for his constructive criticism, and suggestion, which made it not only possible to see this book in the present form but also added new dimensions to this work.

My special thanks are due to the library staff of Dr. Zakir Husain Library, J.N.U. Teen Murti Library, SAARC Documentation Centre, for allowing me to avail their valuable collection. I am thankful to my friends who have been the real source of my strength and encouragement. I am grateful to my family members for their consistent support. I am grateful to my Ma and Papa for their constant inspiration in completion of my book. I extend my special thanks to my elder sister and younger brother for their kind support which they have rendered in the completion of my work. I am also thankful to my husband and my family for their kind support.

Last but the most, I am grateful to almighty for his blessings.

Nidhi Sharma

List of Tables

1.1. Political Approaches to Regional Integration 34
1.2. Economic Approaches to Regional Integration 34
2.1. SAARC Summits 66
3.1. ESAR: Strategy Programmes in South Asia 96
3.2. Comparative Data of South Asia (2007-08) with Other Regions 106
4.1. Political System in SAARC Nations 144
4.2. Chronology of Major Conflict in South Asia 149
5.1. Growth rates of SAARC countries 179
5.2. Select Economic Indicators of SAARC Countries 187
5.3. SAPTA Rules of Origin 191
5.4. Tariff Concession under SAPTA 192
5.5. TLP Across FTAs in South Asia 193
5.6. Rules of Origin of FTAs in South Asia 194
5.7. Comparative Negative Lists Across FTAs in South Asia 195
5.8. Trade restrictions under SAFTA 196
5.9. Bilateral Trade restriction under SAFTA 200
5.10. Bilateral and Regional Agreement Except SAFTA 201
5.11. Technical Assistance Framework of Asian Development Bank 210
5.12. ADB Lending Assistance to South Asia 216
5.13. SAARC Development Goals (SDGs) 2007-2012 219
5.14. Present Status of SAARC Goals in South Asia 223
5.15. SAARC-Japan Special Fund in South Asia Countries 224
5.16. Foreign Direct Investment (FDI) Inflows to South Asian Countries ($ millions) 227
5.17. Intra SAARC Trade during (2000-2011) 240
5.18. EU's Trade Balance with SAARC 260
5.19. SAARC's Trade Balance with EU 262
5.20. Some of SAARC's Activities 265
5.21. Some of BIMSTEC's Activities Sectors and Subsectors 267
5.22. A Comparison among EU, SAARC, ASEAN and BIMSTEC 268
5.23. SAFTA and NAFTA (Integration Indicators) 272

List of Graphs

3.1. Percentage share of World Bank projects in South Asia having ICT components 95
5.1. Growth rate of Nepal 180
5.2. Growth rate of Afghanistan 181
5.3. Growth rate of Bangladesh 181
5.4. Growth rate of Maldives 182
5.5. Growth rate of Pakistan 183
5.6. Growth rate of Sri Lanka 183
5.7. Growth rate of Bhutan 184
5.9. SAARC country shares of regional gross domestic product, 2010 186
5.10. EU's trade balance with SAARC 261
5.11. SAARC trade balance with EU 263

Acronyms

ADB	Asian Development Bank
AFTA	Asian Free Trade Area
APEC	Asia Pacific Economic Cooperation
ASEAN	Association of South East Asian nations
ASEM	Asia Europe Meeting
BIMSTEC	Bay of Bengal Initiative for Multi Sectoral Technical and Economic Cooperation
CEEC	Central and Eastern European Countries
CEPA	Comprehensive Economic Partnership Agreement
COE	Committee of Experts
CTBT	Comprehensive Test Ban Treaty
CTH	Change in Tariff Heading
DVA	Domestic Value Addition
ECSC	European Coal and Steel Community
EFTA	European Free Trade Association
EU	European Union
FDI	Foreign Direct Investment
FTAA	Free Trade Areas of the Americas
GATT	General Agreements on Tariffs and Trade
GCC	Gulf Cooperation Council
GDP	Gross Domestic Product
GMS	Greater Mekong Sub region
HS	Harmonised Commodity Description and Coding System
ICT	Information and Communication Technology
IGG	Inter Governmental Group
IMF	International Monetary Fund
IPA	Integrated Program of Action
ISACPA	Independent South Asian Commission for Poverty Alleviation
IORARC	Indian Ocean Rim Association for Regional Cooperation
LTTE	Liberation Tiger of Tamil Elam
MDG	Millennium Development Goals

MFN	Most Favored Nation
MNE	Multi National Enterprises
NAFTA	North America Free Trade Agreement
NNWS	Non Nuclear Weapons State
NTB	Non Tariff Barriers
NTM	Non Tariff Measures
OCA	Optimum Currency Area
ODA	Official Development Assistance
OIC	Organisation of Islamic Countries
PTB	Para Tariff Barriers
PTM	Para Tariff Measures
QR	Quantitative Restrictions
RIA	Regional Integration Agreements
RIPA	Regional Integrated Program of Action
ROO	Rules of Origin
RTA	Regional Trading Agreements
SAARC	South Asian Association of Regional Cooperation
SADC	Southern Africa Development Community
SADF	South Asian Development Fund
SAFTA	South Asian Free Trade Agreement
SAGQ	South Asian Growth Quadrangle
SAIC	SAARC Agricultural Information Centre
SAPTA	SAARC Preferential Trading Agreement
SARSO	South Asian Regional Standards Organisation
SASEC	South Asian Sub Regional Economic Cooperation
SAVE	SAARC Audio Visual Exchange
SCCI	SAARC Chamber of Commerce and Industry
SDC	SAARC Documentation Centre
SDG	SAARC Development Goals
SDR	Special Drawing Rights
SECSCA Asia	Sub Regional Economic Cooperation in South and Central Asia Program
SHRDC	SAARC Human Resource Development Centre
SIC	SAARC Information Centre
SMC	SAARC Ministerial Council
SMRC	SAARC Meteorological Research Centre
SPC	SAARC Payment Council
SRMTS	SAARC Multimodal Transport Study
STC	SAARC Tuberculosis Centre
TLP	Tariff Liberalisation Program
TRAINS	Trade Analysis and Information System
TRIMS	Trade Related Investment Measures
WTO	World Trade Organisation

1

Concepts and Theories of Regional Integration

In the present global economic regime based on the WTO (GATT) and IMF system, which has sustained the world economy since World War II; regionalism, through which neighbouring countries seek to strengthen their economic and political relations by entering into some form of "regional integration" has become a major trend, this trend was triggered by the economic union market integration. In both developed and developing countries customs union and free trade areas continue to increase and expand. Today, they account for a considerable amount of world trade[1].

Meaning of Regional Integration

The word region stems from the Latin word *regio* which denotes "the direction point of the compass" but later develops by its association with another word *regere*, which means to direct or rule. One can define regions as — territorially based subsystems of the international system[2].

In the most general sense, integration refers to the unification of a number of hitherto independent units into a larger whole.

Integration as such, is then a process, describing the degree of unity in a system. A clear example of the integration is the formation of a state, the merging of previously independent units into a recognisable political entity, capable of independent action[3].

Regional Integration : Concept

Regional Integration is a process in which states enter into a regional agreement in order to enhance regional cooperation through regional institution and rules. Its objectives could range from economic to political initiatives, although it has become a political economy initiative where commercial purposes are the means to achieve broader social - political and security objectives.

Past efforts for regional integration have often focused on removing barriers to free trade in the region, increasing the free movement of people, labour, goods and capital across national borders, reducing the possibility of regional armed conflicts and adapting cohesive regional stance on policy issues, such as the environment, climate change and migration. Such an organisation can be organised either on supranational or inter-government decision-making institutional order, or a combination of both[4].

There have been several efforts made at regional integration including ASEAN, NAFTA and Mercosur. Perhaps the most well-known and development attempts at regional integration has been the European Union, which in some policy areas has moved beyond an inter-governmental approach to decision making at a federalist or super–state level.

In the Words of Philips de Lombarde and Luk Van Langenhove

Regional integration as a worldwide phenomenon of territorial system that increase the interactions between their components and creates new forms of organisations, co-existing with traditional forms of state led organisations at the national level.

According to Hans Van Ginkel

Regional integration refers to the process by which states within a particular region increase their level of integration with regard to economic, security, political and also social and cultural issues.

In short, regional integration is the joining of individual state within a region into a larger whole.[5]

Hence, regional integration refers to processes of complex social transformations characterised by the intensification of relations between independent sovereign states. It creates new forms of organisation, co-existing with traditional forms of state led governance at the national level. The processes of regional integration that emerged after the Second World War, were originally mostly about trade and economics, but it has become clear that, since the 1980s, with the so-called '**new-regionalism**' wave, regional integration can be seen as a multi-dimensional process that implies, next to economic cooperation, also dimensions of politics, diplomacy, security, culture etc.

Trade and economic integration remain the central aspect of the ongoing integration schemes. And in today's globalising world, there seems to be a growing tension between the quest for global free trade (as managed through WTO) and the fact that trade liberalisation is more often regionally than multilaterally organised. Indeed the number of regional integration initiatives is steadily increasing. About 250 regional trading agreements are currently in force[6].

Regional Integration Initiatives should Fulfill at least Eight Important Functions

- The strengthening of trade integration in the region.
- The creation of an appropriate enabling environment for private sector development.
- The development of infrastructure programmes in support of economic growth and regional integration.
- The reduction of social exclusion and the development of an inclusive civil society.
- Contribution of peace and security in the region.
- The building of environmental programmes at the regional level.
- The strengthening of the region's interaction with other regions of the world[7].

Aims and Objectives of Regional Integration

(1) Trade and Income

- To enhance the competitiveness of their firms in global markets.
- To create an expanded and secure market for the goods and services produced in their territories. To reduce distortions of trade.
- To modernise their economies in order to expand the supply and improve the quality of available goods and services, with a view to enhance the living conditions of their populations.

(2) Investment

- To ensure a predictable commercial framework for the production activities and investment.
- Pre-requisite for the stimulation of domestics, regional and foreign direct investment and the expansion, growth and the development of the economies of each member state and the region as a whole.
- A stimulus to the development of national economies by expanding investments and production opportunities, trade and foreign exchange earnings.

(3) Development

To ensure in particular that these arrangements encourage the development of the less advanced members of the custom union and the diversification of their economies.

(4) Democracy and Human Rights

- To involve the people of the region centrally in the process of development and integration, particularly through the guarantee of democratic rights to them, observance of human right and the rule of law.

- To strengthen democracy and respect for human rights, sustainable and balanced economies and social development to combat poverty and promote greater understanding between cultures.

(5) Regional Cooperation and Coordination

- To establish a firm foundation for common action to promote regional cooperation in the spirit of equality and partnership and thereby contribute towards peace, progress and prosperity in the region.
- To foster coordinated action by the parties in the international economic scenario.

(6) Regional and Global Integration

- To contribute to the harmonious development and expansion of world trade and provide as a catalyst to broader international cooperation.
- To contribute to hemispheric integration.[8]

Moves towards Regional Integration

In recent years, the moves towards regional integration have been more and more active, with countries seeking to strengthen their ties with other countries. In Europe, when the treaty on the European Union (EU) took effect in November 1993, the EU was created, which enlarged and built upon the Economic Commission. The enlargement of the European Union took place on January 1, 1995 by accession of three new countries; Austria, Sweden and Finland, which were former members of the European free trade association (EFTA). Meanwhile, the September 1993 signing of the side agreements to the North American Free Trade Arrangement (NAFTA) launched the free trade arrangement in North America in January 1994. Also in the Americas, certain countries in Latin America initiated the Southern Common market treaty (MERCOSUR) in January 1995. On the other side of the Pacific, the Asian Free Trade Area (AFTA) began lowering tariffs among its members in January 1993, and while expanding the range of items covered, they have agreed to begin negotiations on the access to service areas. The AFTA members have also agreed to make efforts towards the acceleration of the integration process with a view towards full implementation of AFTA by the year 2000[9].

One of the trends that have recently been observed is to create mechanisms for broader regional cooperation. This includes

(1) Enlargement of existing regional integration, including the FTAs between the EU and the Central and Eastern European countries (CEEC), the FTA to be setup between the EU and the Mediterranean

countries and the creation of a Free Trade Area of the Americas (FTAA).

(2) Linkage between regional integration organisations, such as economic cooperation, including the creation of a future FTA between EU and MERCOSUR.

(3) Continent based regional cooperation that may not necessarily be seeking to create a FTA or customs union, such as Asia-Pacific Economic Cooperation (APEC) and the Asia Europe Meeting (ASEM).

The APEC is some form of regional cooperation that does not immediately seek to establish custom unions or FTAs. The APEC is founded on an open regionalism that seeks not only to reduce the barriers for trade among its member economies but also to make the result of these efforts available to other non-region economies as well. In November 1994, an unofficial summit of the leaders of the APEC economies was held and a joint declaration was issued **"setting a goal of free and more open trade and investment by the year 2010 in the developed countries and 2020 in the developing countries" (the Bogar Declaration)**. At the Manila meeting in November 1996, all members submitted specific Individual Action Plan (IPA). All members (including new participating members in 1998, i.e., the Russian Federation, Vietnam and Peru) submitted revisions of their plans at the Vancouver meetings held in November 1997 and at the Kuala Lumpur meeting in November 1998 and steps were therefore taken towards liberalisation and facilitation have been taken[10].

Economic Implications

"Trade Creation Effect" and "Trade Diversion Effect"

Regional integration expands markets and promotes competition by eliminating barriers to trade among constituent countries as well as having a **"trade creation effect"** that improves the economic welfare of the members. With regard to countries outside the region, the creation of an expanded regional market as a whole can be expected to have a positive side effect of an "**increase trade opportunity**". On the other hand, **the positive trade creation effect** can also in fact, be overshadowed by a negative "**trade diversion effect**" if the elimination of barriers to trade between members of the region causes trade that had been conducted with efficient non regional countries to be diverted to less efficient regional countries[11].

Economic Implications of Regional Integration

Impact on countries which are constituent of the trade pact and countries outside from these two effects differ according to the contents and the policies of the agreement and the time that had elapsed. In general it is the positive **"trade diversion effect"** in the case of constituent countries, although one cannot deny the possibility that the reverse may also hold. Imports from outside countries, on the other hand tend to be placed it a competitive disadvantage to imports from constituent countries because RTAs usually raise barriers to trade relatively, if not absolutely.

Thus regional integration may affect outside countries negatively. However, by increasing the productivity and making the constituent countries highly competitive, it may lead to elimination of the barriers and the world-wide trade liberalisation in the future. Still generally, the reduction on tariffs through the multilateral efforts in the round has tended to decrease the level of discrimination against outside countries through preferential margins, new rules and policies that discriminate against and disadvantaged outsiders can be seen. Given below are concrete examples of measures found in some RTAs that may violate GATT/WTO principles and disciplines.

(a) Movement towards stricter preferential rules of origin.
(b) Conditional rules do not apply tariffs on certain products, that are applicable only to certain corporations, but that are not applied to new entrants or outsiders.
(c) Increase of tariff rates imposed on outside countries just before a regional integration agreement has been signed.

Integration should be pursued in such a way that outsiders can enjoy the positive effects of market expansion while the negative effects of trade diversion are minimised. In this respect APEC, "**an open regional integration**" does not have negative impact on outside countries because it does not have trade diversion effects on them[12].

Investment Diversion Effect

Interest has recently been growing in the "**investment diversion effect"** of regional integration as well. In 1984, the European Union received only one thirds of the direct investment that the United States received but by 1989 it was at the same level.

To foreign companies, the single, unified market that regional integration creates is also an attractive market for investment and the larger the integrated market, the greater the scale merits and therefore, the attraction of locating there. However, in as much as investment resources are limited, this has the effect of diverting investment away from other countries. Naturally, investment decisions are part of a company's business judgment and the investment diversion effect should be seen as the result of this. But if regional integration brings with it trade policies that discriminate against products from outside the region then it may distort the investment pattern between regions[13].

Political Implication of Regional Integrations

Countries often form trade blocs for non-economic reasons, such as national security, peace and that helps in developing political and social institutions. These are public goods and are so unlikely to be efficiently provided in the absence of some form of intervention, such as an RIA. The political objectives can be important for regional integration agreements, but it is still desirable that they will be achieved efficiently and the policy makers will pay heed to their economic costs.

Political benefits such as peace and security can sometimes swamp the simple material considerations that usually determine economic policy. And because such benefits are typically shared by only a limited number of countries usually neighbours it makes sense to pursue them on a regional basis rather than on a multilateral basis. These political concerns are thus relatively more important in analysing regional integration agreements than for some other international issues. The formation of regional integration agreements may be an effective way to deal with security, tensions between neighbouring countries, and the argument is essentially that mutual trade fosters peace between countries and that regionalism fosters trade. For a regional integration agreement, it is designed to enhance security, the optimum external tariff declines over time and as integration deepens.

Joining a regional integration agreement with large democratic countries can help a developing country achieve or up hold democracy if the RIA imposes "club rules" such as democracy and civil rights on its members. The size and location of the partners matters because larger partners are generally able to impose greater costs on recalcitrant members than are smaller ones, and because a democratic partner country is likely to be far more concerned about a possible spillover (such as migration) from events in a sizable and nearly developing country than from elsewhere.

A concern for many regional integration agreement members is whether increased regional integration will weaken the nation state. For small and even medium size countries pooling sovereignty and undertaking collective action can enhance the effectiveness of the state by helping solve economic problems, by strengthening countries against third- country security threats, and by increasing international influence by lowering negotiation costs or increasing bargaining power in dealings with the world[14].

(1) Regional Integration as a Means of Reducing Frictions between Antagonistic Neighbours

The idea is that trade can be an important force for creating and maintaining peaceful relations between countries. Since forming a regional integration agreement almost always increases trade between the partners, there seems to be a good chance that the pacific effects of trade would extend to this particular form of trade relationship, as more trade means greater economic interdependence between the countries involved. With the increase in interaction between the peoples and governments of the two countries, more familiarity with the neighbours' goods and services and greater understanding of their cultural, political and social institutions is achieved. All this is likely to increase trust. Secure trading relations will reduce the likelihood of war by increasing security of access to the partner's supplies of strategic raw materials and would reduce the threat of trade embargo[15].

(2) Regional Integration Agreements as Promoters of Peace

Trade relations, including RIAs and especially deeper arrangements, might assist political relations between member countries by developing means for avoidance and management of intramural conflict. The negotiations between leaders of neighbouring countries that are required to form and operate an RIA tend to generate trust between them. This helps them identify with each other, understand each other problems and interpret each other actions. Trade Talks allow political and economic elites to form coalitions for subsequent collaboration and consensual action.

Wallace (1994:4) argues that the "most striking phenomenon of formal European Integration has been the interpenetration of national administrations with ministers and officials from different governments in close and continuous contact".

Srinivasan (1994:7) argues that greater economic interdependence among South Asian countries would help defuse tensions among them stating that "promoting freer movement of goods, services, people and capital in the region might also facilitate the resolution of political and territorial disputes".

(3) Regional Integration Agreements and Social and Political Pressures

The formation of an RIA is sometimes seen as a means of preventing or reducing the spread of civil disturbances or civil war from neighbouring nations and/or of controlling migratory flows. Similarly both the United States and Mexico have been concerned about the possibility of occasional social strife and violence in Mexico spreading northward, and both hoped that NAFTA, by facilitating access to the US markets, would help improve Mexico's economic situation and reduce the social strife. Implicit in this hope is that NAFTA will increase Mexican economic welfare.

Closely related is the manifest desire of rich countries to stem large scale migration from poorer countries even if it does not immediately threaten political and social stability. This too has played a role in the formation of RIAs, including NAFTA and the EU's European Agreements with the countries of Central and Eastern Europe (OECD 1995).

Whether RIAs do help solve immigration problems depends on whether trade and migration are complements or just substitutes. Standard trade theory holds that they are substitutes, so that increased trade integration is likely to reduce income or wage differentials and decrease labour migration flows. However, more recent analysis, and some empirical results have shown that North South trade and migration may be complements, so that integration may not lower migration, especially of unskilled labour.

(4) The Role of Regional Integration in Strengthening Democracy and Political Institutions

RIAs can be useful tools for improving political institutions. Trade blocs with strong club rules can help anchor democratic reforms in member countries Membership in a Regional Integration agreement can increase the likelihood of achieving or upholding democracy, especially, if the bloc includes large democratic developed countries. Newer or less politically advanced countries may gain from joining an RIA that includes at least one large developed country if accession is part of the strategy of pursuing political, economic, or social reforms (or preventing backsliding) when such moves would not be feasible without the conditionality embodied in the RIA's club rules. Those rules often include democracy and human rights.

The EEC had no formal democracy requirement, although by convention and practice it was understood that from the mid-60s such a condition existed, at least for new members.

The EU agreements with Mediterranean countries also include respect for human rights and the rules of law.

Conditions regarding democracy and human rights will be truly effective only if the penalties for violating them are severe and their enforcement is credible. The enforcement of club rules depends both on the value of belonging to the bloc and on the credibility of the threat of action.

First, new members who in joining a large bloc, obtain significant benefits including access to a large markets and greater bargaining power with the rest of the world are unlikely to break the rules and so risk of losing these benefits. Admittedly, parties that pose threats to democracy may not be moved by such considerations, but ordinary economic agents will be, and so the conditions will increase the difficulty of building support for insurrection.

Second, the credibility of the threat of action is likely to be greater if violation of club rules by new members entails a large cost to be on the other members. That cost may be direct and economic or indirect and political, such as a demonstration effect.

The effectiveness of club rules is likely to vary with the nature of the membership. RIAs between small low- income countries, which typically trade very little with each other, are less able to impose significant costs on recalcitrant by ejecting them. Choosing large important partners improves the chances that club rules will be enforced. Because a country is likely to be more concerned about the social and political conditions of a nearby than of a far off country, enforcement of club rules is likely to be more effective in RIAs between neighbours than in those between distant partners[16].

(5) Regionalism and the Nation State

Joining an RIA necessarily requires surrendering some immediate control over policy making and losing some political autonomy, if only over tariffs on the partner's exports. Some RIAs however, go deeper than this and create institutions for joint decision making. For example, as the EU's integration has deepened, decision making has increasingly moved away from the national capital to Brussels and much of the current debate is shaped by the belief that some form of political unification must eventually follow the creation of an integrated economic unit. But such integration need not result in the suppression of the nation as an organisational framework or in the loss of effective sovereignty.

On the contrary, by pooling sovereignty, members of an RIA may be able to preserve and enlarge it and thus strengthen the concept of national identity and integrity. Nation state can strengthen themselves by creating a united front against external pressures or by joining forces in international negotiations.

(6) Regional Integration to Deal with Outside Threats and Regional Hegemony

The normal approach to external security threats is for countries to form alliances independent of any trade preferences. It is possible, however to start with a trade pact, based on "hopes that economic union between the weak and the powerful might be established strong enough to depend on, against aggressions from the outside" nations that feared being absorbed forcibly by larger states have united to forestall such coercion. ASEAN was partially motivated by a perceived need to stem the threatened spread of communism in South East Asia.

(7) Regional Integration and Negotiations with the Outside World

Regional cooperation can strengthen the voices of small nations. These countries often face severe disadvantages in dealing with the rest of the world because of their low bargaining power and high negotiation costs. Bilateral and multilateral negotiation often require substantial financial resources, time and expert knowledge, which are limited in small countries. As the world has become more integrated and the number of issues to be dealt with in the international arena has grown the incentives for small countries to cooperate with their neighbours has grown.

Small countries can substantially reduce these negotiation costs and at the same time increase their market and negotiating power by pooling their resources and acting together to articulate shared interests. This is more likely to come about :

(1) If their interests are similar.
(2) If the cost of international negotiation is high.
(3) If a large number of issues need to be dealt with.

These steps can be politically difficult, especially if the group is large and the countries differ widely. The coalition also needs to devise ways of responding to offer and setbacks in negotiations; for it is quite certain that they will not achieve all that they hope for initially. Setting up a secretariat and formulating suitable institutional rules for decision making may help in these process but require significant time and resources upfront.

Finally, the objective of strengthening negotiating and bargaining power is not confined to the formation of blocs by small countries.

Whalley, argues that this idea was shared by the countries involved in the creation of the EEC in the late 1950s, which felt that together they would have much greater leverage in negotiations with the US than they would individually[17].

(8) Regional Integration is more Political than Economic

Regional integration is more political than economic because it meets political needs, such as security or enhanced bargaining power, and it satisfies influential lobbies. Indeed the purpose of integration is often political and the economic consequences whether good or bad are side effects of the political pay-off. The most successful regional integration today has been the European Union.

However, there is another and a more reason to worry because those economic effects that are most apparent — larger markets and economic of scale happens to be favourable, other effects that make the net economic impact of integration ambiguous, but these are often overlooked in political discourses.

So, regional integration is good politics, because it is "Sound bite Economics". This is seriously misleading the illusion of gain collides with the reality of large costs and major redistributions.

The combination of political payoffs and sound bite economics is tempting and goes far to explain the popularity of regionalism.

Regional integration may also be good economics, but the impetus for integration has usually not been the economics.

Sometimes, good politics delivers bad economics, the political payoff may nevertheless be worth it. If a country can substantially increase its security or lack of it in a democracy by forming a regional integration scheme, then it may be willing to accept a few hundred million dollars of costs as being worthwhile. But sometimes the political benefits are ephemeral and the economic costs are high. We show that the economic effects can vary enormously depending upon the characteristics of the country, the countries it chooses as partners and the detailed design of the integration arrangement[18].

Political Motives behind Regional Integration

1. Integration for Security

(a) Intra Regional Security

The politics that most concerned President Hallstein and his colleague in building the European Union was security. Security also played an important role in the southern cone. The political impetus to European and southern cone integration was based on the belief that increasing trade would reduce the risk of intra-regional conflict. Similar motives are found in the creation of the ASEAN to reduce the tensions between Indonesia and Malaysia.

Political scientists suggest that negotiations between political leaders on trade issues gradually build trust, so that elites learn to form cross national coalitions for subsequent collaboration. They considered the economic integration would make it "materially impossible" meaning, that interlocking of steel, coal and other strategic industries would leave countries unable to wage war against each other.

Thus regions that are economically highly integrated may tend to have less internal conflict. It seems an obvious step from this result to the proposition that policies that promote trade within a region will increase intra-regional security. If so, regional integration may provide a first best solution and external trade barriers must fall over time and follow a deep integration. Sometimes economic integration power paves the way for full political integration so that the risk of internal conflicts is greatly reduced.

(b) Extra Regional Security

The political impetus for regional integration is sometimes not intra-regional security, but the need to unite to face a common external threat. The underlying idea is that common action in the economic sphere makes common action for security easier and more credible. The country perceived as a potential threat is typically the regions' hegemony.

2. Integration for Bargaining Power

By joining together, the weak can become strong. Through integration small countries can bond together to increase their bargaining power in trade negotiations.

The classic example of regional solidarity exerting economic power is that of the Organisation of Petroleum Exporting Countries, (OPEC). The OPEC government is not strictly regional and does not involve economic integration, but it does illustrate what solidarity can achieve its objective was not to increase trade among its members but rather to coordinate a restriction in oil export volumes, equivalent to a coordinated increase in export taxation. Hence it was certainly a trade agreement. This was a successful bargaining strategy in what it raised the price of oil.

3. Project Cooperation

Countries can benefit greatly from cooperation when they share resources such as rivers, fishing grounds, hydroelectric power or rail connections or when they join to overcome problems such as pollution and transport bottlenecks. Failure to cooperate in these areas can be very costly. For instance, the uncoordinated exploitation of the Aral Sea by the five central Asian riparian countries resulted in one of the world's worst environmental disasters, with the sea's desiccation, destruction of the ecosystems, the pollution of surface and ground water and more.

However finding equitable ways to share the burdens and benefits of cooperation can be difficult. Countries sometimes find themselves unwilling to cooperate because of national pride, political tensions, lack of trust, high coordination costs among a large number of countries or the asymmetric distribution of costs and benefits. Regional cooperation agreements are typically harder to achieve than national ones, they must be self-enforcing because of the absence of regional courts or authorities to enforce them. The fact that these agreements must by self-enforcing reduces the set of feasible cooperative solutions and their benefits. International Organisations, such as the World Bank with high international credibility, expertise in dealing with the complex issues involved, and have the ability to mobilise financing having often helped achieve an agreement where it might not have been possible otherwise.

Regional integration agreements can help because the tie of collaboration and frequent policy level contact can raise the degree of trust among the parties. Moreover, regional agreements also help by putting more issues on the table and embedding them in a wider agreement, both of which lower the size of compensatory transfers required and make it easier to reach an agreement.

4. Integration for Lock in to Reform

The agreements so far have all had to do with international relations, but integration can also help domestically as a government seeks to implement its political agenda. Reform plans can often be thwarted by the mere possibility that they will be reversed. Adjusting to reform typically involves investments but these investments will not be made unless investors are confident that reform will persist. Confidence in the persistence of the reforms may be low, particularly if the country has no track record of reform; and worse, a history of reversing reform. If the investments are not made, then government is likely to face increasing pressure to reverse the reforms. To escape from this trap governments often need institutions that enable them credibly to lock into decisions. These are sometimes referred to as commitment mechanism.

For trade liberalisation, regional agreements are a well-designed piece of commitment mechanism because they are built upon reciprocal preferences.

Regional groups also sometimes use their potential as commitment technologies to lock into economic policies other than trade and the most important example of this is probably NAFTA. Although, NAFTA was ostensibly about trade policy, its underlying motivation was the desire on the part of both the Mexican and US governments to lock in the broad range of economic reforms that the Mexican government had undertaken in the preceding years. The implicit agreement was that if Mexico maintained its policies it would have access to the US market and also would have a more general claim on US assistance. One motivation for the US government was that it had a strong interest in encouraging Mexican economic growth in order to curtail Mexican emigration to the United States. By making the Mexican reforms more credible it hoped to raise the Mexican growth rate.

Regional trade agreements have worked as a commitment mechanisms in practice. Most agreements involving high income countries have survived, by successfully locking in their policies among developing countries. Among developing countries the record is less good, a number of regional agreements have collapsed or never moved far from paper to practice. When regional trade agreements have been used as the foundation of other types of commitment they have had some important successes.

5. Lobbying for Integration

Government's policy making is likely to be shaped by the competing demands of different lobbies which are why firms invest heavily in lobbying bureaucrats and politicians. Some interest groups will have much more influence than others will paradoxically, if the benefits of a policy change are spread very wide, no single beneficiary has an incentive to spread resources by lobbying. In contrast, if the benefit is concentrated, then it pays the few beneficiaries to spend heavily. Because of this, lobbies tend to promote policies that cause transfers from the many to a few, and this usually means that it is the producers groups that dominate the lobbying scenes. Usually also, producers competing against imports are more powerful than exporter from a statue quo with trade barriers, the import substituting producers are already in business, while export sector may be relatively small and undeveloped.

To producer groups, regional integration may appear as an attractive option, particularly compared to unilateral non-preferential liberalisation.

First it limits the increase in international competition to which the countries industries are subjected to, since liberalisation is only with the partner countries.

Second, the agreement is reciprocal with the have country obtaining improved market access in partner countries markets.

Since these markets also may be protected from competition from the rest of the world; it may be possible to make quite large profits.

Political economy reasons may therefore make it easier for countries to liberalise trade on a regional basis than unilaterally, or through the multilateral process, thus for a government seeking trade reform, regional integration may be seen as the only politically feasible way to liberalise its economy and perhaps also as the first step in a process of further liberalisation.

So, Integration is Political

Trade policy gets shaped by the political needs of governments and by the political pressures exerted by well-funded lobbies. Adding a regional dimension to trade policies, meet some political needs and changes lobbying opportunities. Sometimes the political needs met by regionalism are highly valuable, such as the lock in to democracy or to reform policy. Regional integration can also serve as an efficient tool to enhance security among member countries, as has occurred in some of the largest regions. However, with the political effects can lead to something to be unexpected or the opposite of the aspirations, as when regional preferences would create such unfair redistributions that they provoke conflict[19].

Regional Integration Theory

Theories of integration have mainly been developed to explain European Integration. Europe was the region of the world, where regional integration started in the early 1950s with the European Coal and Steel Community (ECSC) in 1952. Earnest Haas theorised his experience in "the Uniting of Europe" in 1958. The main theoretical contribution was the concept of spillover. Later Lindberg used this concept to study the early years of the European Economic Community (EEC), which started its existence in 1958[20].

The theoretical approaches to regional integration can be divided into two groups.

1. Political Approaches to Regional Integration.
2. Economic Approaches to Regional Integration.

Table 1.1 Political Approaches to Regional Integration

Theory	*Main Focus*	*Method*	*Timing of Integration*	*Objective of Integration*	*External Effect of Integration*
Functionalism	Supranational Institution	Normative Dynamic	Assumed (After War)	Peace through prosperity	N/A
Neo Functionalism	Political Actors at Supra and Sub national levels.	Positive, Dynamic	N/A	Welfare Maximisation (Assumed)	N/A
Intergovernmentalism	Heads of Governments	Positive, Dynamic	Explained (As convergence of member state preferences)	Welfare and Power Maximisation	N/A

Source : The logic of regional integration- By Walter Mattli.

Table 1.2 Economic Approaches to Regional Integration

Theory	*Main Focus*	*Method*	*Timing of Integration*	*Objective of Integration*	*External Effect*
1. Customs union theory	Markets (goods and services)	Positive, Static	N/A	Improvement of national income	Indirectly addressed
2. Optimal Currency Area Theory	Markets (goods and factors)	Positive, Static	N/A	Full employments and payments equilibrium.	N/A
3. Fiscal Federalism (Casella Approach)	Interaction of markets and Excludable public goods	Positive, Dynamic.	Explained	Improvement of market efficiency.	N/A

Source : The logic of regional integration- By Walter Mattli.

Political Approaches of Integration

1. Functionalism

David Mitrany, the main proponent of functionalism, wrote in a 1943 essay entitled **'A working peace system'** that "the problem of our time is not how to keep nations peacefully apart but how to bring them actively together". He proposed a solution which he called the pragmatic functional approach. It breaks away from the traditional link between authority and a definite territory by ascribing authority to activities based in areas of agreement. Peace "is more likely to grow through doing things together in workshops and market place rather than by signing pacts in chancelleries". Co-activity rather than national co-existence defines the ideal of peace. Mitrany put his faith "not in a protected peace but in a working peace".

This functional method projects a gradual process towards peace and prosperity. Every function is left to generate others gradually; in every case the appropriate authority is left to grow and develop out of actual performance. A fundamental aspect of the functional method is that "sovereignty cannot be transferred effectively through a formula, only through a function. By entrusting an authority with a certain task, carrying with it command over the requisite powers and means, a slice of sovereignty is transferred from the old authority to the new, and the accumulation of such partial transfers in time brings about a translation of the true seat of authority". This is the logic of "**peace by pieces**". Functional cooperation does not start from the political but from the low key economic and social planes such as the joint management of scarce resources, unemployment, commodity price fluctuations, labour standards and public health.

"Any political scheme would start a disputation; any working arrangement would raise a hope and make for confidence and patience". Through gradual functional developments and through the provision of common services, the system may in time even build up solid foundations for closer political association.

To summarise, the assumptions and propositions of functionalism are as follows: political divisions are a source of conflict among nations. These divisions can be transcended only gradually by seeking out areas of mutuality and establishing a **"working"** web of international functional institutions, managed by technical elites, in which and through which the interests of all nations are gradually integrated. Power and welfare, politics and economics are separable. Areas of functional cooperation are likely to be found in the **"low politics"** areas of economic and social life. Prosperity through global economic integration is the guarantor of a stable and peaceful international system. Economic unification will ultimately lead to political unification.

The weakness of functionalism is apparent. First, it is not properly speaking a theory of integration but rather a normative method. It describes a way that should be pursued to attain Peaceful Coexistence. However it fails to specify fully the conditions under which such a scheme is feasible.

Second, even a positive rendering of its main theme, that integration is in fact sought to secure peace, is not fully compelling.

Both neo-functionalism and inter-governmentalism refines a prior and simpler theory, **functionalism** which shaped the thinking about political integration among scholars and policy makers from the end of the First World War until the 1950s. Functionalism assumed that the sheer existence of a mismatch between the territorial scale of human problems and of political authority generates pressures for jurisdictional reform. David Mitrany, the principal functionalist thinker after the Second World War, believed that the welfare benefits of supranationalism would impel reform.

Later, scholars elaborated explanations from a more detached scientific standpoint. They retained the functionalist insight that regional integration is a response to the collective benefits of extending the territorial scope of jurisdictions, but they were well aware that the mismatch between collective welfare and the structure of authority does not speak for itself[21].

2. Neo-functionalism

Neo-functionalism restates the assumptions of functionalism, it refines its analytical tools, elaborates sketchy ideas and intuitions evoked by passing and embeds earlier concepts into an analytical framework that proposes to study not international but regional integration. In a significant departure from functionalism, it shifts its analytical focus from the technology, a working peace system, to the utilitarian dimension of the functional method. This enables it to shed the normative and utopian ballast of its predecessor, thus gaining analytical clarity and powerful implications. The logic of integration was first systematically analysed and elaborated by **Ernst Haas, the chief exponent of neo-functionalism, in his pioneering study 'The Uniting of Europe'**. This work and a collection of later contributions share a common neo-functional framework. The approach is concerned with explaining "how and why nation states cease to be wholly sovereign, how and why they voluntarily mingle, merge and mix with their neighbours so as to lose the factual attributes of sovereignty while acquiring new technologies for resolving conflicts between them". More precisely, neo-functionalism describes a process — "Where by political actors in several distinct national settings are persuaded to shift their loyalties, expectations and political activities towards a new and a larger centre whose institutions possess or demand jurisdictions over the pre-existing states".

Neo-functionalism's Main Analytical Attributes are Summarised Below

1. Political Actors : The process whereby the 'participants' in the policy making process, from the interest group to bureaucrats and statesman begin to develop new perspectives, loyalties and identifications as a result of their mutual interactions.

2. The Motives : One of the important contributions of neo-functionalism is the introduction of a unambiguously utilitarian concept of interest in politics that stands in sharp contrast to the notions of unselfishness or common good that pervades of functionalist writing. Assumptions of goodwill, harmony of interests or dedications to the common good need not be postulated to account for integration. Ruthless egoism does the trick by itself. As Haas puts it "the **'good Europeans'** are not the main creators of community, the process of community formation is dominated by nationally constituted groups with specific interests and aims, willing and able to adjust their aspirations by turning to supranational means when this course appears profitable". The supranational actors are likewise not immune to utilitarian thinking. They seek unremittingly to expand the mandate of their own institutions and have a more influential say in community affairs.

3. The Process : Three related concepts lie at the core of the dynamics of integration: functional spillover, political spillover and upgrading of common interests.

(a) Functional spillover is based on the assumption that the different sectors of a modern industrial economy are highly interdependent and that any integrative action in one sector creates a situation in which the original good can be assured only by taking further actions in related sectors, which in turn creates a further condition and a need for more action, and so forth. This process is described by Haas as **"sector integration"** because it gets its own impetus towards extension to the entire economy even in the absence of specific group demands.

(b) Political spillover describes the process of adaptive behaviour that is the incremental shifting of expectations the changing of values and the coalescing at the supranational level of national interest groups and political parties in response to sectoral integration. Neo-functionalism does not postulate an automatically cumulative integrative process.

Again in Haas words, "the spillover process though rooted in the structure and motives of the post-capitalist welfare state is, far from automatic and functional contents tends to be autonomous; lessons learned in one organisation are not generally and automatically applied in others or even by the same group in a later phase of its life". In other words, neo-functionalism identifies certain linkage mechanisms but makes no assumptions as to the inevitability of actors' response to functional linkages.

(c) Upgrading common interests is the third element in the neo-functional description of the dynamics of integration. It occurs when the member states experience significant difficulties in arriving at a common policy while acknowledging the necessity of reaching some common stand to safeguard other aspects of interdependence among them. One way of overcoming such deadlock is by swapping concessions in related fields. In practice, the upgrading of the parties, common interests relies on the services of an institutionalised autonomous mediator. This institutionalised swapping mechanism induces participants to refrain from vetoing proposals and invites them to seek compromises, which in turn bolsters the power base of the central institutions.

4. The Context : The context in which successful integration operates is economic, social and technical, and it is nominally a political. Here Haas seems to accept a key assumption of the predecessor to his theory 'functionalism' which posits that functional cooperation must begin on the relatively low key economic and social planes. However economic and social problems are ultimately inseparable from political problems. Haas thus replaced the dichotomous relationship between economic and political in functionalism by a continuous one: The supranational style stresses the indirect penetration of the political by way of the economic because the 'purely' economic decision always acquire political significance in the minds of the participants 'technical' or 'controversial' areas of cooperation, however might be so trivial as to remain outside the domain of human expectation and actions vital for integration.

The areas must therefore be economically important and endowed with a high degree of 'functional specificity'.

The advent of the first major economic commission crisis in 1965 initiated by de Gaulle's adamant refusal to proceed with certain aspects of integrations, he deemed contrary to French interests, triggered a crescendo of criticism against neo functionalism. The theory, it was claimed had exaggerated both the expansive effect of increment within the economic sphere and the gradual politicisation effect of spillover. Critics further castigated neo functionalists for failing to appreciate the enduring importance of nationalism, the autonomy of the political sector and the interaction between the international environment and the integrating region.

This move was unfortunate, for the growing inapplicability of the approach did not mean the framework was wrong.

With the revival of European integration in the mid-1980s, neo-functionalism regained popularity in the international relations literature as a framework for explaining the process of integration, particularly in the legal domain. Several of its analytical categories boast enduring relevance, notably the focus on sub-national actor and its emphasis on the role played by supranational institutions in catalysing the processes of integration. Nevertheless, neo-functionalism has shortcomings. For example, it being by stating that supra nationality is the only method available to states to secure maximum welfare, but it fails to give a theoretical account of the link between welfare maximisation a regional integration.

It then focuses on institutional arrangements within a region on in which economic transactions take place, but it leaves these transactions mostly unexamined. Further, the framework never fully specifies the condition under which societal demands for integration becomes accepted at the national level. The approach simply assumes that if there is a problem cutting across frontiers and there is felt need, actors at the sub-nationals and supranational levels will mobilise resources and the problem will be solved. This somewhat naive view is the result of inadequate attention to the preferences of governments and a lack of understanding of the nature of collective action problems that impede progress towards integration.

3. Intergovernmentalism

It holds that integration can best be understood as a series of bargains between the heads of the governments of the leading states in a region. These political leaders, jealous of their national sovereignty, carefully circumscribe any sacrifice of sovereignty that may become necessary in order to attain common goals. Big states exercise a de facto veto over fundamental changes in the rules of integration. As a result "bargaining tends to converge towards the lowest common denominator of large state interests". Small states are often bought off with side payment offered by the big ones.

The emphasis of inter-governmentalism on heads of states as central players are a key difference it and neo-functionalism. There is ample evidence to suggest that governments do indeed play an important role in integration. But as a theory of integration, inter-governmentalism suffers from several shortcomings. By focusing only on episodes of interstate bargaining the theory cuts into ongoing social process and produces what Paul Pearson calls "snapshot view of integration that is distorted in crucial respects".

Defining events that precede interstate bargains are over looked, discounted or treated in an adhoc fashion and events that follow italics of bargains appear to be irrelevant. Thus the theory implies for example that the implementation of interstate agreement is easy and automatic.

This is hardly a plausible proposition considering that the majority of integration schemes have failed at the implementation stage.

Furthermore, a theory that focuses only on major interstate decision or "celebrated intergovernmental bargains" risks suffering from a particular type of selection bias — Selection on the dependent variable.

Such a theory offers no range of possible outcomes but only a constants event, "celebrated bargains" it is thus difficult to test. Inter-governmentalism argues that the 'ups' of integration, that is the big decisions, are the result of convergence of the preferences of the leading states. By implications, a slow down or halt of the integration process must similarly reflect converging preferences.

However, a theory that explains the mean during the course of integration is solely in terms of shifting. Preferences offer few ways of assessing its validity. A more challenging approach would be to seek to explain varying integration out comes by examining how changes in external factors and constraints affects integration, given fixed preferences of the member states. It is only when this approach fails that we can conclude with confidence that changes in outcomes are best explained by shifts in member-state preferences[22].

4. Liberal Inter-governmentalism

Later Andrew Moravcsik developed 'liberal inter-governmentalism' during the 1990's to explain the process of integration in Europe, suggesting the combination of a liberal theory to explain national preference formation and an intergovernmental theory of interstate bargaining to explain substantive outcomes. Later he added a third stage, institutional choice, where pooling and delegation of sovereignty are mainly seen as a way to create "credible commitments"[23].

Economic Approaches to Regional Integration

Economic integration refers to trade unification between different states by the partial or full abolishing of customs tariffs on trade taking place within the border of each state. This is meant in turn to lead to lower prices for distributors and consumers (as no customs duties are paid within the integrated area) and the goal is to increase trade.

The framework of the theory of economic integration was laid out by Jacob Viner (1950) who defined the trade creation and trade diversion effects; the terms introduced for the change of inter-regional flow of goods caused by changes in customs tariffs due to the creation of an economic union. He considered trade flows between two states prior and after their unification and compared them with the rest of the world.[24]

1. Customs Union Theory

Customs union theory is neither dynamic nor concerned with institutions. It thoroughly discounts the importance of the political or common policy dimension of regional integration. It looks narrowly at markets of goods and considers the welfare implications of discriminating mergers of such markets.

The seminal contribution to the customs union theory is Viner's **'the customs union issue'.** According to Viner the creation of a customs union involves the elimination of intra area trade barriers and the equalisation of tariffs on imports from non-member countries. Trade creation effects arise of the output of inefficient industries is replaced, after the removal of tariffs, by cheaper imports from more efficient industries in a member state of the union. Trade creation makes a country better off because the lower price on newly imported goods increase the consumer's surplus and permit production gains. However, the union's common external tariff against third countries could have a trade diversion effect. The agreement is as follows — let us assume that the third countries were the lowest cost suppliers prior to the establishment of a customs union. The imposition of the common tariff puts these suppliers at a competitive disadvantage after the creation of the union. Thus the tariff may discourage imports from the countries outside the union and encourage import from less efficient sources of supply within the integrated area. The resulting trade diversion reduces a country's economic welfare the net welfare effect of a custom union is an empirical question and diverted as well depending on the amount of trade created and diverted as well as on differences in unit costs. The degree of trade diversion is likely to be small where the members of a union have extensive trade with each other and a low common tariff on imports from non-member countries. The welfare effects of a custom union will also depend on transportation costs, the lower the transportation costs among member countries the greater the net gains from integration.

Viner has defined it by adding two further motives for the creation of customs unions. The first motive is strategic and considers the impact of integration on the terms of trade. The argument is as follows — if non-member countries are producers of competitive goods with high price elasticity of demand, then the price of their exports is taking a fall after the imposition of a common external tariff. The resulting terms of trade gain to the union may offset the welfare loss due to trade diversion. Empirical studies have found support for the terms of trade argument.

The second motive refers to changed preference. Some countries are assumed to have a preference for domestic industrial and agricultural production per se, rather than for a straight maximisation of national income. It is argued for example, that countries at a comparative disadvantage opt for more domestic production to satisfy nationalist strategies that are not implemented by means of taxes and export subsidies. A possible answer is that export subsidies outside agriculture don't conform to international trading agreements, whereas customs unions are compatible with trade (GATT) and now World Trade Organisation (WTO). In short, constraint on the use of first best domestic policies may help to explain the formation of custom unions[25].

2. Optimal Currency Area Theory

In economics, as optimum currency area (OCA) is also known as optimal currency region (OCR), is a geographical region in which it would maximise economic efficiency to have the entire region to share a single currency. It describes the optimal characteristics for the merger of currencies or the creation of a new currency. The theory is used after to argue whether or not a certain region is ready to become a monetary union, one of the final stages in economic integration.

An optimal currency area is often larger than a country. For instance, part of the rationale behind the creation of the **'Euro'** is that the individual countries of Europe do not each form an optimal currency area, but that Europe as a whole does form an optimal currency area. The creation of the **'Euro'** is often cited because it provides the most modern and largest scale case study of the engineering of an optimal currency area, and provides a comparative before and after model by which to test the principal of the theory.

The theory of the optimal currency area was pioneered by economist Robert Mundell. Credit often goes to Mundell as the originator of the idea, but others point to earlier works done in the area by Abba Lerner.

Mundell came up with models in his theory :

1. Optimal currency area with stationary expectations.
2. Optimal currency area with international risk sharing system.

Optimal Currency Area with Stationary Expectations

The four often cited criteria for a successful currency union are :

1. Labour mobility across the region. This includes physical ability to travel (visas, workers' rights etc.) lack of cultural barriers to free movement (such as different languages) and institutional arrangements (such as the ability to have superannuation transferred throughout the region) (Robert A Mundell). In the case of the Eurozone, while capital is quite mobile, labour mobility is relatively low, especially when compared to the US and Japan.

2. Openness with capital mobility, price and wage flexibility across the region. This is so that the market forces of supply and demand automatically distribute money and goods to where they are needed. In practice this doesn't work perfectly as there is no true wage flexibility.

In the case of the Euro zone, while capital is quite mobile labour mobility is relatively low, especially when compared to the US and Japan.

1. Openness with capital mobility and price wage flexibility across the region. This is so that the market force of supply and demand automatically distributes money and goods, as there is no true wage flexibility. The Euro zone members trade heavily with each other (Inter European trade is greater than international trade) and most recent

empirical analyses of the 'Euro effect' suggest that the single currency has increased trade from five to 15 per cent in the Euro Zone when compared to trade between non Euro countries.

2. A risk sharing system such as an automatic fiscal transfer mechanism to redistribute money to areas sectors which have been adversely affected by the first two characteristics. This usually takes the form of taxation redistribution to less developed areas of a country. This policy, though theoretically accepted is politically difficult to implement as the better off regions rarely give up their revenue easily.

Theoretically, Europe has no bail-out clause in the stability and growth pact, meaning that fiscal transfers are not allowed, but it is impossible to know what will happen in practice.

3. Participant countries have similar business cycles when one country experiences a boom as recession, other countries in the union are likely to follow. This allows the shared central bank to promote growth in downturns and to contain inflation in booms.

While Europe scores well on some of the measures characterising an OCA, it has lower labour mobility than the United States and similarly cannot rely on fiscal federalism to smooth out regional economic disturbances. Also, its Gini coefficient of 31 should have a stabilising effect in comparison, the USA has a Gini index of 46.9 (a lower measure indicates a more even distribution of wealth).

This theory has been most frequently applied in recent years to the Euro and the European Union. Despite the prominence of the EU as the primary case study of an OCA, money have argued that the EU does actually not meet the criteria for not constitute an optimal currency area and therefore the Euro should be a suboptimum union of currencies. However it is hoped that the creation of the Euro will in itself help encourage the conditions enumerated by Mundell.

The primary criticism of Mundell's Theory is that the area that has optimal condition for a single currency is one that already has a single currency, a circular argument. Furthermore many existing currency areas do not fulfill these requirements.

OCA with International Risk Sharing System

Here Mundell tries to model how exchange rate uncertainty will interfere with the economy.

Supposing that the currency is managed properly the larger the area, the better. In contrast with the previous model, asymmetric shocks are not considered to undermine the common currency because of the existence of the common currency. This spreads the shocks in the area because all regions share claims on each other in the same currency and can use them for dumping the shock, while in a flexible exchange rate regime, the cost will be concentrated on the individual regions, since the devaluation will reduce its buying power.

So, despite a less fine turned monetary policy the real economy should do better.

A harvest failure, strikes, or war, in one of the countries causes a loss of real income, but the use of a common currency (or foreign exchange reserve) allows the country to run down its currency holdings and cushion the impact of the loss, drawing on the resources of the other country until the cost of the adjustment has been efficiently spread over the future. If on the other hand, the two countries use separate monies with flexible exchange rates, the whole loss has to be borne alone, the common currency cannot serve as a shock absorber for the nation as a whole except in so far as the dumping of inconvertible currencies on foreign markets attracts a speculative capital inflow in a favour of the depreciating currency[26].

Robert A. Mundell is found in both sides of the debate about the Euro. Most economists cite preferentially the first (stationary expectations) and conclude against the Euro, yet Mundell advocates this one, and conclude in favour of the Euro.

Rather than moving towards more flexibility in exchange rate with in Europe the economic argument suggest less flexibility and a closer integration of capital markets.

These economic arguments are supported by social arguments as well. On every occasion when a social disturbance leads to the threat of a strike and the strike to an increase in wages unjustified by increases in productivity and then to devaluation, the national currency becomes threatened.

Long run costs for the nation as a whole are bartered away by government for what they presume to be short run political benefits. If instead, the European currencies were bound together disturbances in the country would be cushioned with the shock weakened by capital movements[27].

Neither customs union theory nor optimal currency area theory is concerned with explaining changes in the rules and policies that govern economic regions. In this sense, these two theories are static and fail to shed light on the process of deepening and enlarging communities. Their focus is on market relations political and supranational institutions in the process of integration are assumed away. This is hardly a satisfactory state of affairs, for the implications of regional integration go beyond trade in goods, services and factors. As recently acknowledged by three respected economists, regional economics arrangements, almost by definition, entail the imposition of some common rules of conduct for participating countries and a set of reciprocal commitments and obligations. The importance of this political dimension of regional integration may well exceed that of the more direct implications having to do with trade flows.

Robert Lawrence has similarly noted that, most theorising about regionalism in economics considered these arrangements in the context of a traditional paradigm in which trade policy is characterised by changes to barriers at the border. Regional arrangements are modeled either as customs union or as free trade area. But although the removal of internal border barriers is certainly an important feature, focusing only on these barriers overlooks much of what regional arrangements are about.

The traditional perspective is at best incomplete and at worst misleading. In many cases these emerging arrangements are also meant to achieve deeper integration of integration competition and investment. Once tariff are removed, complex problems remain because of differing regulatory policies among nations.

Thus, to understand regional integration, it is of critical importance to analyse how these complex problems are solved and to assess the political consequences of such solutions.

(3) Fiscal Federalism and Economic Integration

Fiscal federalism theory is an offshoot of public finance theory that analyses the special fiscal problems which arise in federal countries, drawing on the literature on public goods, taxation and public debt incidence and various parts of location theory. It examines the reasons for the assignments of authority over various parts of fiscal policy to different level of procurement, and considers the efficiency implications of migration from one jurisdiction to another, as well as the role of intergovernmental revenue transfers and their most desirable form in a federal structure.

Many of the issues discussed in fiscal federalism are relevant to the study of regional institution-building. Particularly in the European case where free trade and capital mobility, along with steps towards monetary union have raised the question of the desirability of fiscal capital, labour, consumers and taxpayer (individual or corporate) implies that regional differences in taxation and in supply of public goods can induce migration of each of these categories. This raises the potential for fiscal spillovers across borders creating incentives for fiscal policy coordination and thereby raising the problem of determining the appropriate levels for fiscal public decision–making. The forms of coordination which can be attained range from simple interstate agreements to mutually adapted centralised policies depending on the scope of spillover, the cost of enforcement of an agreement, and the extent of economics of scale from centralisation.

Allocated efficiency through coordination is not the only objective of policy–makers; another concern is the achievement of distributional goals. Mobility of tax payers reduces the ability of the local governments to use taxes and transfers to redistribute income locally. This raises a need for centralised redistributive policies. Finally economic integration is likely to raise questions as to how the winners will compensate the losers. The ensuring need for compensatory mechanism is bound to widen the fiscal responsibility of the central authority in a region.

The contribution of the fiscal federalism literature to economic integration is not limited to the identification of the appropriate policy focus within a larger economic space. It has also triggered more general reflections on the link between the evolution of private markets and the creation of new institutions. The work of Alessandra Casella is particularly noteworthy in this context.

Casella seeks to understand how the development of market integration is likely to shape the geometry of market integration, is likely to shape the geometry of public goods provision within a region. Her work links concepts and ideas developed in public finance with recent work on international trade and economic geography. It, thus, connects well the club size with characteristics of economic markets.

Casella uses institutions and jurisdiction interchangeably and defines them as "clubs whose member jointly decide on, finance and enjoy an excludable public good".

Her argument can be summarised as follows — the widening of market requires centralised regional institutions to achieve coordination and reduce transaction costs. However, as integration deepens the difference in economic roles and needs within the region becomes more marked, giving rise to demand for a broad range of public goods.

"Jurisdiction must be redrawn to satisfy the requirements of unified, more competitive, more sophisticated markets. What emerges is 'functional federalism'. That is, a regime where individuals and members states organise themselves into a pattern of overlapping jurisdictions, with each jurisdiction responsible for the provision of a specific class of public goods. These jurisdictions have variable membership depending on the scope of policy under consideration and they represent a highly decentralised system of economic organisation"[28].

Recent Regional Integration Agreements

The EU has played a large role in the recent surge of activity, with the implementation of the single market programme in 1992, enlargement of its membership and numerous agreements with other countries. These agreements account for two-thirds of the agreements notified to GATT/ WTO since 1990 and included the European Economic Area, the Europe agreements with the countries of Eastern Europe, the EU - Turkey customs union, and the development of a Mediterranean policy potentially incorporating regional agreements with most countries on the southern and eastern shores of the Mediterranean.

In Latin America, MECOSUR was formed in 1991 and the group of three in 1995. The Andean Pact and Central American Common Market (CACM) were resurrected in 1991 and 1993, respectively.

In the Sub-Saharan Africa, the blocs in West Africa were reformed and reorganised. The Southern Africa Development Community (SADC) developed out of an earlier defense based Organisation, SADC Conference, and was supplemented for many of its members by the cross-border initiative. The East African Cooperation sprang up where the East African community had failed.

The Middle East witnessed the development of the Gulf Cooperation Council (GCC) and in 1997 Arab League members agreed to cut trade barriers over a ten years period. In Asia, the association of South East Asian Nations (ASEAN) countries developed 25 years of political cooperation into a free trade area in 1992, with the formation of the ASEAN free trade area. The South Asian Association for Regional Cooperation was established in 1985 and in 1997 it set to transform itself into the South Asian Free Trade becoming in terms of the population it represents, the world's largest regional agreement.

New ground was broken in 1994 when the Canada- US Free Trade area was extended to Mexico through NAFTA. For the first time a developing country joined industrial countries as an equal partner in a trade bloc designed to bolster economic development in all three economics. Links between high income and developing countries were also being forged in the Asia-Pacific Economic Cooperation (APEC), established in 1989—a looser organisation, committed to trade liberalisation on a non-preferential basis by 2010 for industrial country members and 2020 for developing countries[29].

Regional Integration and Globalisation

Regional cooperation processes are increasingly relevant factors in the states' affairs and global dynamics. The European Union, despite its problems in upgrading its institutional design and motivating its people is the key to explaining the sustained peace and prosperity of former antagonists. Since the end of cold war, a plethora of new regional projects, mixing economic, political, security and socio-cultural goals have sprung up all around the world[30].

In what way is Regionalism a Response to Globalisation?

The preferential trading arrangement among developing countries means that regional integration was actually a prelude to globalisation. In new circumstances regional integration may still play such a role. But the newer reasons for regional integration suggest that it is a very loop-sided response.

While it may help protect a market which is being threatened by the response to globalisation, namely by forestalling contingent protection in the export market, it cannot protect one's own markets from foreign competition. In so far as opposition to globalisation comes from import competing as the most favoured nation concessions granted in multilateral trade negotiation cannot be withdrawn. It can only be a response to the extent that it strengthens exporting interests— interests that, may act as a counter-balance to the interest in the import competing industries.

The main benefit from globalisation arises from the better allocation of the world's resources as it allows for specialisation based on economic logic. Global rules provide a certainty that it reduces transaction costs. One of the benefits of MFN treatment and having only a few tariff rates is the simplification of administration and a possible reduction in corruption. Complex rules of origin that give special treatment to various products negate the benefit that tariff simplification brings out.

The analysis in the theoretical literature concludes that a three-block trading system is the worst scenario from the view print of world welfare and therefore raises the question whether preferential trading arrangement can be considered a move towards free trade or a move away from free trade.

The Chinese economy expands and because of the substantial size of its trade, the threat of these bloc situations could become imminent. But such a situation is still more likely a couple of decades away and trade analysts hope that tariffs would have been reduced to such insignificant levels that preferential treatment losses its meaning[31].

Role of WTO and Regional Integration

The instruments we have for international policy on regional integration is the WTO, and this section explores how it manages regional integration and whether its rules could be reformed to help it do better.

RIAS are officially sanctioned by conditional exception the GATT's rules on non-discrimination. The conditions imposed on regional integration agreements formation doubtless constrain and mold the pattern of regional integration in the world, but they are neither adequate nor adequately enforced to ensure that regional integration is economically beneficial for either its members or countries.

The responsibility for good outcomes falls on the governments themselves, they cannot tie their own or each other's hands sufficiently tightly in the WTO to prelude the possibilities of signing harmful regional integration agreements.

The world trade system works pragmatically and consensually. The GATT was created in 1947 as a temporary body to assist countries in trade liberalisation. Its role was to codify and record a series of tariff reductions that its members wished to make and provide a structure to give credibility to those reductions. It discouraged the reversal or nullification of tariff cuts by restricting policies that impose duties on all adhoc bases, such as antidumping duties and emergency protection and equivalent policies such as internal taxes on imports. It also defined important mechanics of trade such as the valuation of trade for customs purpose. A key concept of the GATT, indeed the corner stone of the present world trading system is nondiscrimination between different sources of the same imported goods, which is achieved by requiring members to give each other MFN treatment, except in specified circumstances, with an assurance of nondiscrimination. When 'A' negotiates a reduction in one of 'B's tariffs, it knows that the commercial value of its efforts will not be undermined by 'B' then offering 'C' an even lower tariff. This in turn, makes 'A' more willing to 'buy' the concession by reducing one of its own tariffs on 'B' and so encourages trade liberalisation.

The World Trade Organisation (WTO) which was created in 1995 to oversee the GATT and certain others agreements is more legalistic, but still focuses heavily on pragmatic and mutually acceptable solution to problems. The WTO administers a set of rules for behavior not a set of outcome. It is concerned with meeting agreed obligation and rights rather than with economic outcome per se. The WTO has undoubtedly been an underlining force for economic good, but its role has not been defined in those terms.

The WTO is rather more far reaching through its greater breadth and its (single under taking) under which members must subscribe to virtually all its rules, rather than as previously, treat some as optional extras, it has constrained governments more tightly. Nevertheless, the WTO can still be effective only if it proceeds more or less by consensus[32].

WTO Provisions on Regional Integration Arrangements

Appendix 1. Articles XX1V of GATT

4. The contracting parties ... also recognise - that the purpose of a customs union or of a free trade area should be to facilitate trade between the constituent territories and not to raise barriers to trade.

5. (a) With respect to a customs union ... the duties and other regulation of commerce imposed at the institution...shall not on the whole be higher or more restrictive than the general incidence of duties and regulations of commerce applicable in the constituent territories prior to the formation of such union.

(b) With respect to a free trade area the duties and other regulations of commerce maintained in each of the constituted territories and applicable at the formation of such free trade area... shall not be higher or more restrictive than the corresponding duties and other regulations of commerce existing in the same constituent territories prior to the formation of the free trade area.

(c) Any interim agreement....shall include a plan and schedule for the formation of such a customs union or of such a free trade area within a reasonable length of time.

7. (a) Any contracting party deciding to enter into customs union or a free trade area, shall promptly notify the contracting parties and shall make available to them such information.

8. (a) A custom union shall be understood to mean the substitution of a single customs territory for two or more customs territories, so that (I) duties and other restrictive regulations of commerce (except, where the necessary those permitted under articles IX, XII, XIII, XIV, XV and XX) are eliminated with respect to substantially all the trade in products originating in such territories.

(b) A free trade area shall be understood to mean, a group of two or more customs territories in which the duties and other restrictive regulations of commerce (except where necessary as those permitted under article XI, XII, XIII, XIV, XV and XX) are eliminated on sub substantially all the trade between the constituent territories in products originating in such territories.

The Enabling Clause

1. Notwithstanding the provisions of Article 1... contracting parties may accord differential and more favorable treatment to developing countries, without according such treatment to other contracting parties.

(c) The provisions of Paragraph 1 apply to the... regional or global arrangements entered into almost less developed contracting parties for the mutual reduction or elimination of tariffs and, in accordance with criteria or conditions which may be prescribed by the contracting parties for the mutual reduction or elimination of non-tariff measures on products imported from one other.

The Uruguay Round Understanding on the Interpretation of Article XXIV

2. The evolution of the duties and other regulation of commerce... shall... be based upon an overall assessment of weighted average tariff rates and of customs duties collected... For this purpose, the duties and charges to be taken into consideration shall be the applied rates of duty. It is recognised that for the purpose of the overall

assessment of the incidence of other regulation of commerce for which qualification and aggregation are difficult, the examination of individual measures, regulations, products covered and trade flows affected may be required.

3. The "reasonable length of time" referred to in Article XXIV (5) C should exceed ten years only in exceptional cases[33].

Advantages and Disadvantages of Regional Integration

Regional integration aims to improve economic outcomes for all participants involved, alt[illegible] practice not all participants achieve the same degree of benefits. Oftentimes, economic integration is a process whereby nation promotes free trade and usually creates institutions to streamline economic cooperation; it is followed by political integration as well. For example, it is followed by political integration as well. For example, today's European union is a product of the European Community, which itself was a product of the European Coal and Steel Community of 1954, a largely economic regime that eventually led to evolution towards political integration with the latter two.

1. In theory regional integration is hailed as a way to maximise economic outcome for all participants, but in practice some problems do arise. Some of these problems include, but are not limited to :
   - Determining whether or not all participants have equal say in policies set by the regional institutions that oversee cooperation.
   - Determining how to deal with economic disruptions and or redistribution of resources. Economic problems might affect participants unequally, such that some states will be net recipients of some form of aid while others will be net lenders of aid. One might look at NATO as an example of a multi-state institution where one major participant the United States is the primary donor of aid while most other states within NATO are recipients of that aid which is principally economic and military.

In fact, such redistributive issues are typical of all institution where a certain benefit is sometimes a public good and is available for all but which usually requires little contribution by most. Benefits gained within a regional institution are not strictly 'public goods' in that the institution may, by norms, procedure or by–laws, prevents some participants from obtaining the goods, while the use of a finite resource such as economic aid is rival because one state's receipt means less for the rest. However, problems similar to those that involve strictly defined public goods also plague collective goods in the case of multi-state institutions.

Perhaps the most prominent collective goods problems may be regarded as the "free rider" problem — states, because inducements to cooperate or threats to punish may be low, fail to provide for the collective benefit. Therefore essentially "passing the buck" to other states, and most frequently to the most economically powerful participants.

Citizens of large states like France, Great Britain and Germany frequently complain that smaller states are not paying their 'fair share' of the costs of the European Union. Meanwhile smaller states may complain that they are overlooked or even disregarded because of their economically weaker states.

Some forms of regional integration achieve monetary union, whereby a singular currency is issued within the region and where a central bank has monetary authority. Although delving into this aspect is beyond the scope, there are numerous at least theoretical problems concerning monetary union. One of the most prominent concerns unequal monetary expansion or contraction resulting from unequal growth patterns in individual states. Although such problems were very real aspects prior to the European monetary union of 1999, today the most pressing problems have to do with unequal growth patterns in the participants states.

2. Beyond economics, political integration might give rise to a whole set of problems :
   - It includes determining a method of resolving political problems and crises, the form, control and oversight of some form of regional managing board and or political apparatus.
   - Immigration management, border crossing, policing and national defense coordination.
   - Political integration is more problematic on some levels than economic integration, as it necessitates some form of coordination and uniformisation among states with disparate cultures and languages. It is frequently more advantageous that the participants are homogenous, preferably on economic as well as political culture levels.
   - States that are most efficient in certain processes can trade with those in which they are comparatively less efficient. This ensures that participants specialise principally in those goods and services where they are most efficient. This is not only advantageous within the zone of integration as it helps lower costs to consumers but also outside the zone. Participants can coordinate economic activity at least in theory as to promote gains for the zone abroad.

On many levels, we consider the European Union as an independent singular entity even though of course it consists of politically independent and sovereign units. Therefore one must always keep in mind that unlike an integrated "model" such as the United States where the control authority is supreme by law, regional zones and institutions consist of participants who are not strictly bound by law. It is always a possibility that in the future a member will secede permanently. In this sense, one can view each states' participation as by treaty and not by law. Although most states do not easily relinquish the requirements set forth in a treaty, they can reject some or all of its requirements, therefore making it all the more difficult to attempt to impose via some central authority, responsibility that is not desired by participants.

The Role of South Asian Association of Regional Cooperation (SAARC) and Regional Integration in South Asia

The South Asian region is unique demographically, racially, religiously, economically, socio-culturally and politically. A large segment of world population inhabits in South Asia. South Asia is also confronting both the positive and negative economic and cultural dimensions of globalisation while coping with gross inequities in the distribution of developments benefits within society[34].

The region is also marked by the reflection of hostility between India and Pakistan with Jammu and Kashmir as the major bone of contention and this in spite of the vociferous claims of the political elites on both sides for normalisation of relations though peaceful negotiations which have been held any number of times with full sound and fury signifying just nothing.

In South Asia religion, in its perverted form and the inter religion relationships are still a potential forced rupture the social fabric as it has been frequently seen in India, Pakistan, Bangladesh and Sri Lanka in terms of communal rioting and displacement of people.

However, the phenomenon ethnicity and ethnic conflicts within each South Asian State and between the states has occupied the centre-stage of political discover during last couple of decades[35].

The South Asian countries have undertaken extensive reforms of their economies to integrate themselves more intensively with the world economy. As a result, the proportion of trade in their national incomes has risen from 22 per cent to nearly 30 per cent over the 1990s. The increasing global integration enables them to benefit from the emerging international specialisation, obviate the constraints on their development by the size of domestic markets and absorb spill-over of knowledge and technological developments taking place in rest of the world.

Besides unilateral moves towards liberalisation of policy regimes, trade liberalisation has also been facilitated by WTO Agreements under which the South Asian countries have undertaken considerable commitments.[36]

The global trend towards a free trade and the formation of intra-regional blocs spurred South Asia into action and in 1985, the South Asian Association for regional cooperation, was formed by seven South Asian countries as a forum for the discussion of intra-regional issues, particularly the improvement of relations between the very large India and her smaller neighbours. The South Asian Association for Regional Cooperation aims to promote peace, trade and development among its members. In 1995, SAARC Preferential Trading Agreement SAPTA was inaugurated for bilateral reduction tariffs and non-tariffs barriers on specified commodities on reciprocal basis, but with special treatment given to least developed countries (LDC). The eventual objective was for SAPTA to become SAFTA by 2001 based on multilateral tariff reductions. But SAARC had been brought to a standstill due to the worsening relations between India and Pakistan, caused by nuclear tests conducted in 1988 and the Kashmir despite in 1999. In the meantime SAPTA failed to yield the desired benefits to the members particularly the LDC's. The slow progress of the SAARC forum prompted the members to pursue bilateral and other regional and sub-regional groupings centered primarily on India. India concluded bilateral FTA with Nepal, Bhutan and Srilanka discussions are in progress for secular agreements with Maldives and Bangladesh. At the same time, Bangladesh is also discussing bilateral FTA with Srilanka and Pakistan. In 1997 BIMSTEC was formed to foster socio - economic cooperation among Bangladesh, India, Srilanka and Thailand. The Principal are contained in the "Bangkok Declaration". In 1997, Myanmar was admitted in to BIMSTEC and earlier this year Nepal and Bhutan also joined the bloc. There were two other initiatives known as "South Asian Growth Quadrangle (SAGQ)" comprising of Bangladesh, Nepal, Bhutan and parts of India and the "Kumming Initiative".

In 2000, Asian Development Bank (ADB) under a technical assistance program established South Asia Business Forum under South Asia sub regional economic cooperation (SASEC) as the request of the participating countries to support the official level SAGQ initiative in the light of the successful Greater Mekong Sub Region (GMS) cooperation. The initiative envisages integrating resource rich areas of Yunnan Province of China, Northern Myanmar, Northeast India, Bangladesh, Nepal and Bhutan into an Asian communication network which is interlinked with the networks of West and Central Asia as well as Europe with the potential of Bangladesh emerging as hub.

Two recent developments have rekindled hopes for accelerating the regional cooperation.

Following improvement in relation between India and Pakistan, the seven member countries of SAARC signed a Free Trade Agreement at the Islamabad summit in January 2004 to go into effect from January 1, 2006. The other development was the signing of Free Trade Agreement by the seven BIMSTEC members[37].

One of its major goals is to create a South Asian Economic Union by 2020. The adoption of South Asian Free Trade Agreement Framework treaty in 2006 has given new dynamism to the association and should further stimulate intraregional trade and integration. The European Union is eager to enhance trade and investment links with this fast developing region. The European Union strongly supports SAARC and believes that increased regional co-operation will not only boost trade but also prevent internal conflicts from spilling over national borders in line with its commitment to the Doha Development Agenda, the European Union views trade related technical assistance and capacity buildings programmes as crucial tools that could help transform South Asian economies. These mechanisms can support SAARC member states by improving their ability to trade while promoting constructive development work in the region.

Consequently, the European Commission has offered to share its own expertise in trade and economic integration with SAARC[38].

All the South Asian countries are witnessing impressive growth. The South Asian region is witnessing a democratisation surge, which will strengthen developmental politics and stimulate cooperative drive. One of the most important developments has been the softening of Indo-Pak relations with accent on opening trade, commerce and people to people contacts.

One hopes that growing economic engagement between these traditionally hostile neighbours will lead the greater mutual confidence and understanding between them. An improved Indo-Pak relationship will surely advance the SAARC. SAARC has expanded adding Afghanistan as a full member and nine other countries as observers. Among observers are countries like China, US, Iran and Japan. The presence of such observers will stimulate competition and economic dynamism. There is also a radical change in India's approach to SAARC. From a reluctant participant it is gradually emerging as an active leader. These developments will positively help in making SAARC more effective and purposeful[39].

Conclusion

This chapter has shown that a process of regional integration is not necessarily a novel feature of contemporary global politics. Development of regional identities and formal integration mechanism has been a widespread and persistent feature of twentieth century politics. Theories of international politics have often been divided not merely over how to explain these developments – in terms of power balancing defensive mechanism as a transformation of political and economic relation between societies, but in terms of understanding how global socio-economic change poses challenges to established identities and practices.

Concern for how regional integration might affect the world order is regularly expressed as concern for the western multilateral trading regime maintained by GATT/WTO rules and procedures. The rise of regional trading blocs have been invariably seen in terms of the US, EU and Japan may increase potential for trade conflict or 'wars' and undermine compliance with global rules and institutions.

Regional economic groupings by their very nature involve some degree of preferential economic and trading relationship. In recent years, global politics has witnessed strategically oriented, retaliatory and aggressive trade politics on the part of developed countries EU-US trade friction has increased far beyond the 'chicken wars' of the early 1960's and 1990. Japan successfully challenged the EU within the GATT/ WTO for unfair trading practices.

In an increasingly globalised world economy it is a persuasive argument that regional trade blocs are the only alternative to a hegemonic 'vacuum' where one powerful state is unable or unwilling to ensure compliance with global rules.

The globalisation process emphasises rapid Trans-nationalisation of capital, trade, information and technology. The world has become smaller. However human resources and social customs are less often transnational phenomena. Globalisation dominated by Western Corporate identities is often perceived as a threat to local customs and communities. Regional integration may be seen as mechanisms to protect and enrich 'local' identity and values.

In this chapter the example of regional integration in contemporary world politics have been described. Regional integration has helped to redefine socio-political relations at the local level, and in some cases it has been proved intrinsic to pacification and domestication of traditional interstate relations.

A major feature of the new world order will be de-linking of local and regional conflicts, on the one hand and the stabilisation of conflict in the system as a whole.

From such a perspective, regional integration is not merely a utilitarian device to reconcile state interests, to overcome local security dilemmas, or defend local identities and practices against global challenges, but it may be in the post-cold war period comprise significant world order stabilising mechanisms[40].

References

1. WTO Annual Report, Press/85. (The WTO Secretariat), Regional Integration, Part-II, 8 Dec., 1997.
2. Files- Educational module on regional integration, p. 1.
3. *Ibid.*
4. Wikipedia- online encyclopedia, http://www. regional integration.htm/.
5. *Ibid.*

6. Lombarde de Philippede- Assessment and measurement of regional integration, Rouletdge Publications Warwick's studies in globalisation, New York, 2006, p. 9.
7. Wikipedia, online encyclopedia, http://www.regional integration.htm/.
8. Maurice.W. Schiff, L. Alan Winters, Regional integration and development, A co-publication of Oxford University Press, Washington D.C. 2003, p. 8.
9. W.T.O. Annual Report- Press/85. (The W.T.O. Secretariat), Regional Integration, part-III, December, 8-1997
10. *Ibid.*
11. W.T.O. Annual Report, Press/85 (The W.T.O. Secretariat) part-II, Regional Integration, 8 December, 1997.
12. *Ibid.*
13. *Ibid.*
14. Maurice W. Schiff, L. Alan Winters, Regional Integration and Development, The World Bank Publications, 2003, p. 22.
15. Maurice.W. Schiff, L. Alan Winters, Regional Integration and Development, The World Bank Publications, 2003, p. 187.
16. *Ibid.* p. 200.
17. *Ibid.* p. 205.
18. Regional integration agreement-PDF Acrobat, p. 11.
19. Regional Integration Agreement- PDF Acrobat-Politics and policy making.
20. Finn Laursen: Comparative Regional Integration, Theoretical Perspectives, Ashgate Publishing Ltd, Hampshire, England, 2003, p. 3.
21. Liesbet Hooghe and Gary Marks-A Post functionalist theory of European Integration from Permissive Consensus to constraining Dissensus-British Journal of Political Science-Cambridge University Press, Vol. 39, Part-I, 2009.
22. Walter Mattli-The logic of regional integration, Europe and beyond, The review of theoretical approaches to integration, p. 21, Cambridge University Press, 1999, U.K.
23. Finn Laursen Comparative Regional integration: Theoretical Perspectives, published by-Ashgate Publishing Limited, Hampshire, England, 2003, p. 4.
24. Wikipedia-online encyclopedia-http://www.economicintegration.htm/.
25. Walter Mattli-The logic of regional integration- The review of theoretical approaches to integration, p. 31, Cambridge University Press, 1999, U.K.
26. Mundell, 1973-Uncommon Arguments for common currencies, p. 115.
27. Robert A Mundell, 1973-A Plan for European Currency, pp. 147, 150.
28. Walter Mattli-The logic of regional integration- The review of theoretical approaches to integration, p. 31, Cambridge University Press, 1999, U.K.
29. Regional integration agreement, PDF Acrobat. http://www.regionalintegration agreement.htm/
30. Fawn Rick, International Affairs-Journal, International relations theory, globalisation-the regional, regionalising the global, Vol. 85, Sep. 2009, p. 1045.

31. International studies, Journal-Vol. 41, Regional Trading Arrangements in the Era of Globalisation: An Indian Perspectives, 2004.
32. Regional Integration Agreement- PDF Acrobat, http://www.192341 regional integration.pdf/
33. *Ibid.*
34. Sareen T.R.- Socio-economic and Political Development in South Asia, Vol. 3, Isha Books, 2004. p. 42.
35. Singh Gopal - South Asia, Democracy, discontent and societal conflicts, Anamika Publishers and Distributers, 1998, p. 516.
36. Sareen T.R. Socioeconomic and Political Development in South Asia, Vol. 2, Isha Books, 2004, pp. 7-8.
37. Bangladesh Country Note: Promoting Regional Integration in South Asia: http// www.siteresources.worldbank.org/INT SOUTH ASIA/Resources/ Bangladesh.final.pdf.
38. European Commission- External Cooperation Programs, http://ec.europa.eu/ europaid/where/asia/regional-cooperation/support-regional integration/ SAARC-en.htm.
39. Sukh Deo Muni and Jaithley Rajshree: The changing dimension: SAARC http://www.2008/8:SAARC.htm/
40. John Baylis and Steve Smith- The globalisation of World Politics-An introduction to international relations, Oxford University Press, 1997, p. 423.

2

Regional Cooperation in South Asia and SAARC: Historical Development and Evolution

The South Asian Association for Regional Cooperation (SAARC) comprises the eight countries of South Asia: Bangladesh, Bhutan, India, the Maldives, Nepal, Pakistan, Sri Lanka and Afghanistan. Afghanistan joined SAARC in 2007 as an eighth nation during 14th SAARC Summit held in New Delhi. It is an association based on the consciousness that in an increasingly interdependent world, the objectives of peace, freedom, social justice and economic prosperity are best achieved in the South Asian region by fostering mutual understanding, good neighbourly relations and meaningful cooperation among the member states which are bound by ties of history and culture.[1]

The setting up of the South Asian Association for regional cooperation (SAARC) marked the beginning of regional cooperation in South Asian. It has been described as one of the most important developments of 1980s is this region. Its establishment is backed by the concept of regional integration, which has been defined by Earnest Haas *"the process whereby political actors in several distinct national settings are persuaded to shift their loyalties, expectations and political activities towards a new larger center whose institutions possess or demand jurisdiction over pre-existing nation-states"*. This is a process that links several nations of a region in collective decision-making system. Regional organisations enable nation-states in a particular region to minimise their conflicts and promote cooperation. Cooperation among states is promoted by common factors which may be geographic, ethnic, linguistic, religious, civilisational, politico-historical or social economic. The greater the interaction, the better are the chances of success of cooperative endeavours.

Origin of SAARC

In South Asia it was only in 1977 that the idea of a regional organisation was first floated by the then Bangladesh President Zia-ur-Rehman. It was with the yearning to bring some measure of stability and peace and to improve the subhuman conditions of eternal poverty and misery. It has been argued that compulsions of domestic conditions of economic chaos made Zia-ur-Rehman suggest a regional organisation for economic cooperation.

The South Asian Association for Regional Cooperation (SAARC) was established in December 1985 at a summit of seven heads of states or governments, of South Asian Countries, held at Dhaka. India and Pakistan, the two major actors of the region, were initially reluctant to join SAARC proposal found ready acceptance by Sri Lanka, Nepal, Bhutan and Maldives. But Pakistan felt that an association where India would play a major role was not in its interest. The feeling in Pakistani circles was that India would dominate by sheer weight size of everything – land, economy, military, industry, power, infrastructure, science and technology. However, India wanted to avoid playing a local big brother. India also had a lurking doubt that the principle of bilateralism, which it had so zealously guarded, may lose its significance and the forum may be used to raise bilateral issues which would be against the principle of regional cooperation. However, reluctance of both India and Pakistan was soon overcome by the desire for social, economic and cultural cooperation within the region.

Inspired by the then President Zia-ur-Rehman, who had mooted the idea of SAARC while touring India, Pakistan, Nepal and Sri Lanka in 1977, the Government of Bangladesh circulated a working paper, titled "Regional Cooperation in South Asia" advocating regional cooperation in economic, technical, scientific, social, cultural and education fields.

It was circulated in 1980 and it suggested that meetings at foreign secretary level should examine prospects of regional cooperation. From 1977 to 1981 consultative and preparatory work had been done. The proposal was formally submitted to concerned governments in May 1980 by President Rehman. The first meeting of Foreign Secretaries was held at Colombo in April 1981. It was followed by six more such meetings in other capitals. Foreign ministers of seven countries also held a number of meetings, before the Dhaka Summit.

An Integrated Programme of Action (IPA) was adopted in 1983 at the Foreign Ministers meeting in New Delhi. The programme was announced through the New Delhi Declaration. During negotiations, leading to Dhaka Summit (1985), it was agreed that SAARC would actively try for greater regional cooperation on the basis of sovereign equality of states, protection on the basis of territorial integrity, and non-interference in the internal affairs of each other. The cooperation was likely to grow in the economic, social and cultural spheres. Initially eleven areas of regional cooperation were identified. They were telecommunication, meteorology, transport, shipping, tourism, agricultural research, joint ventures, market promotion, scientific and technological cooperation, educational cooperation and cultural cooperation. There were areas which were quite vast to promote cooperation and seek regional unity.

The spade work for launching the SAARC was completed in the Foreign Ministers meetings held at Male in July, 1984 and Thimpu in May, 1985. It was decided to hold a summit of seven South Asian countries at Dhaka on December 7 and 8, 1985. The summit was presided over by Bangladesh President General H.M. Ershad. India was represented by Prime Minister Rajiv Gandhi. The other heads of states who attended Dhaka summit included President (Gen). Zia-ur-Haq of Pakistan, President J.R. Jayawardene of Sri Lanka, kings of Nepal and Bhutan and President M. Abdul Gayoom of Maldives. The Dhaka Summit was held in a very cordial atmosphere. Sri Lanka's President Jayawardene praised the role of Late Mrs. Indra Gandhi and Prime Minister Rajiv Gandhi in the establishment of SAARC and promotion of regional cooperation, despite tensions and bilateral disputes. Jayawardene went to the extent of suggesting that Rajiv Gandhi should be requested to lead the association. A 10-point Charter of South Asian Association for Regional Cooperation (SAARC) was adopted, and SAARC was formally launched. The Secretariat was temporarily located in Dhaka and Mr. Abdul Hasan was chosen as the first SAARC Secretary General. The Foreign Ministers later decided to establish the Permanent Secretariat at Kathmandu (Nepal), where it now functions.[2]

The Heads of State or Government at their First SAARC summit held in Dhaka on 7-8 December, 1985 adopted the SAARC Charter formally establishing the South Asian Association for Regional Cooperation (SAARC).

The charter contains the basic objectives, principles and general provision of SAARC.

Charter of South Asian Association for Regional Cooperation

We, The Head of State or Government of Bangladesh, Bhutan, India, Maldives, Nepal, Pakistan and Sri Lanka

1. Desirous of promoting peace, stability, amity and progress in the region through strict adherence to the principles of the UNITED NATIONS CHARTER AND NON-ALIGNMENT, particularly with respect for the principles of sovereign equality, territorial integrity,

national independence, non-use of force and non-interference in the internal affairs of other states and peaceful settlement of all disputes;

2. Conscious that in an increasingly interdependent world, the objectives of peace, freedom, social justice and economic prosperity are best achieved in the South Asian region by fostering mutual understanding, good neighbourly relations and meaningful cooperation among the Member States which are bound by ties of history and culture;
3. Aware of the common problems, interests and aspirations of the peoples of South Asia and the need for joint action and enhanced cooperation within their respective political and economic systems and cultural traditions;
4. Convinced that regional cooperation among the countries of South Asia is mutually beneficial, desirable and necessary for promoting the welfare and improving the quality of life of the peoples of the region;
5. Convinced further that economic, social and technical cooperation among the countries of South Asia would contribute significantly to national and collective self-reliance;
6. Recognising that increased cooperation, contacts and exchanges among the countries of the region, will contribute to the promotion of friendship and understanding among their peoples;
7. Recalling the Declaration signed by their Foreign Ministers in New Delhi on August 2, 1983 and noting the progress achieved in regional cooperation;
8. Reaffirming their determination to promote such cooperation within an institutional framework;

DO HEREBY AGREE to establish an organisation to be known as South Asian Association for Regional Cooperation herein after referred to as the ASSOCIATION, with the following objectives, principles, institutional and financial arrangements:

Article I
OBJECTIVES
The objectives of the Association shall be

(a) To promote the welfare of the peoples of South Asia and to improve their quality of life;
(b) To accelerate economic growth, social progress and cultural development in the region and to provide all individuals the opportunity to live in dignity and to realise their full potentials;
(c) To promote and strengthen collective self-reliance among the countries of South Asia;

(d) To contribute to mutual trust, understanding and appreciation of one another's problems;
(e) To promote active collaboration and mutual assistance in the economic, social, cultural, technical and scientific fields;
(f) To strengthen cooperation with other developing countries;
(g) To strengthen cooperation among themselves in international forums on matters of common interests;
(h) To cooperate with international and regional organisation with similar aims and purposes.

Article II
PRINCIPLES

(a) Cooperation within the framework of the association shall be based on respect for the principles of sovereign equality, territorial integrity, political interdependence, non-interference in the internal affairs of other state and mutual benefits.
(b) Such cooperation shall not be a substitute for bilateral and multilateral cooperation but shall complement them.
(c) Such cooperation shall not be inconsistent with bilateral and multilateral obligations.

Article III
MEETINGS OF THE HEADS OF STATE OR GOVERNMENT

The Heads of State or Government shall meet once a year or more often as and when considered necessary by the member states.

Article IV
ARTICLE IV CONSISTS OF THE INSTITUTIONAL SETUP OF SAARC COUNCIL OF MINISTERS

The council of ministers comprises the Foreign Ministers of member states. The council is expected to meet twice a year and may also meet in extraordinary sessions by agreement of Members States. Until now 32 regular sessions have taken place. The last session was held in Thimpu on 27th April 2010.

The council of ministers had to perform the following functions:
(a) Formulation of the policies of the association.
(b) Review of the progress of cooperation under the association.
(c) Decision on new areas of cooperation.
(d) Establishment of additional mechanism under the association as deemed necessary.
(e) Decision on other matters of general interest to the association.

Article V
STANDING COMMITTEE

The standing committee includes the foreign secretaries of member states.

The committee has held 37 regular session until now. The Standing Committee is authorised to setup Action Committees comprising member states concerned with implementation of projects involving more than two but less than all members states.

The Standing Committee is assisted by a programming committee (which is not a SAARC charter body) comprising senior officials to scrutinise the Secretariat Budget, finalise the Calendar of Activities and take up any other matter assigned to it by the Standing Committee. The Programming Committee has also been entrusted to consider and submit to the Standing Committee recommendations, for action on the Reports of the Technical Committees, SAARC Regional Centers and the SAARC Audio Visual Exchange (SAVE) Committee. Until now the Programming Committee had completed 38th session on 24th April 2010 in Thimpu.

The Standing Committee has to perform the following :

(a) Overall monitoring and coordination of programme of cooperation.
(b) Approval of projects and programmes, and the modalities of their financing.
(c) Determination of inter-sectoral priorities.
(d) Mobilisation of regional and external resources.
(e) Identification of new areas of cooperation based on appropriate studies.

2. The Standing Committee shall meet as often as deemed necessary.
3. The Standing Committee shall submit periodic reports to the Council of Ministers and make reference to it as and when necessary for decisions on policy matters.

Article VI
TECHNICAL COMMITTEES

1. Technical committees comprise of the representatives of members states. At present, there are seven Technical Committees functioning in various fields under the agreed areas of cooperation. The Technical Committees formulate specialised programmes and projects in their respective fields under the SAARC Integrated Programme of Action (SIPA). The last 5th meeting on Science and Technology of Technical Committee was held on 2 and 3 August, 2010 in New Delhi.

2. The Technical Committees shall have the following terms of reference:
(a) Determination of the potential and the scope of regional cooperation in agreed areas.
(b) Determination of financial implications of sectoral programmes.
(c) Formulation of recommendations regarding apportionment of costs.
(d) Implementation and coordination of sectoral programmes.
(e) Monitoring of progress in implementation.
(f) Formulation of programme and preparation of projects.
3. The Technical Committees shall submit periodic reports to the Standing Committee.
4. The chairmanship of the Technical Committees shall normally rotate among Member states in alphabetical order every two years.
5. The Technical Committees may, use the following mechanisms and modalities, if and when considered necessary:
(a) Meetings of heads of national technical agencies.
(b) Meetings of experts in specific fields.
(c) Contact amongst recognised centers of excellence in the region.

Article VII
ACTION COMMITTEES

The Standing Committee may setup Action Committees comprising Member States concerned with implementation of projects involving more than two but not all Member States.

Article VIII
SECRETARIAT

There shall be a secretariat of the association.

Article IX
FINANCIAL ARRANGEMENTS

1. The contribution of each member state towards financing of the activities of the association shall be voluntary.
2. Each Technical Committee shall make recommendations for the apportionment of costs of implementing the programmes proposed by it.
3. In case sufficient financial resources cannot be mobilised within the region for funding activities of the association, external financing from appropriate sources may be mobilised with the approval of or by the standing committee.

Article X
GENERAL PROVISION

1. Decision at all levels shall be taken on the basis of unanimity.
2. Bilateral and contentious issues shall be excluded from the deliberations.

In faith where off we have set our hands and seals hereunto.

Done in Dhaka, Bangladesh, on this the eighth day of December of the year one Thousand Nine hundred and eighty five.

SAARC SUMMIT

The highest authority of the Association rests with the Heads of State or Government, who meet annually at the Summit level.[3] Until now 17 Summits have been held:

Table 2.1: SAARC Summits

Summit	*Countries*	*Year*
1st	Dhaka	1985 (7-8 Dec.)
2nd	Bangalore	1986 (16-17 Nov.)
3rd	Kathmandu	1987 (2-4 Nov.)
4th	Islamabad	1988 (29-31 Dec.)
5th	Male	1990 (21-23 Nov.)
6th	Colombo	1991 (21 Dec.)
7th	Dhaka	1993 (10-11 April)
8th	New Delhi	1995 (2-4 May)
9th	Male	1997 (12-14 May)
10th	Colombo	1998 (29-31 July)
11th	Kathmandu	2002 (4-6 Jan)
12th	Pakistan	2004 (2-6 Jan)
13th	Dhaka	2005 (12-13 Nov.)
14th	Delhi	2007 (3-4 April)
15th	Colombo	2008 (27 July 3 Aug.)
16th	Thimpu	2010 (26-27 April)
17th	Maldives	2011(10-11 Nov)

At present SAARC has its headquarters at Kathmandu, Nepal. Its official language is English; its demonym is South Asia. It has 8 members (India, Pakistan, Bhutan, Bangladesh, Sri Lanka, Nepal, Maldives and Afghanistan) and 9 observers nations (Australia, China, European Union, Iran, Japan, Mauritius, South Korea, United States) respectively. The Present Chairman of SAARC is Mahinda Rajapaksa of Sri Lanka and Abdul Saleem of Maldives as its Secretary General. The total area of South Asia where SAARC functions is 5,130,746 km^2 with the GDP (PPP) of US$ 4,074,031 million and per capita of US$ 2,777.

SAARC Regional Centers

The SAARC Secretariat is supported by Regional Centers established in member countries to promote regional cooperation. These centers are managed by Governing Board comprising representatives from member states, SAARC Secretary General and the Ministry of Foreign/External Affairs of the host government. The Director of the centre acts as Members Secretary to the Governing Board which reports to the Standing Committee.

The third special session of the Standing Committee (Colombo, August 2001) entrusted the Secretary General to undertake a performance audit of all the Regional Centres in order to take stock of their practical output with regard to regional cooperation, to evaluate their mandates and to suggest ways and means of improving their functioning.

1. SAARC Agricultural Information Centre (SAIC), Dhaka, Bangladesh

SAIC, the first regional institution was established in Dhaka in 1988. SAIC serves to network relevant national information centres in member states with a view to exchanging regionally generated technical information to strengthen agricultural research and development activities SAIC has brought out several publications, which contain information on agricultural institutions in SAARC countries as well as on fisheries, forestry, livestock and crops.

The 17th meeting of the Governing Board held in Dhaka on 19-21 October 2003 reviewed, status of implementation of the decisions of its Sixteenth Meeting, completed programmes of 2002 and 2003 as well as current and ongoing programmes for the financial year 2004. The Board prioritised new programmes for 2004 for implementation in case of delay in the approval of its report, which are:

(i) Workshop on "Attempts and successes of ICT Road map to villages in the SAARC countries".
(ii) Continuing professional development programme.
(iii) Guide on Medicinal and Aromatic Plants (GMAP).
(iv) A Handbook on disease of fishes and crustoceans in the SAARC Region.
(v) Production of Interactive Multimedia CDs (IMM CDROMs). It also prioritised the programme "SAIC NET", during 2005.

2. SAARC Meteorological Research Centre (SMRC), Dhaka, Bangladesh

The SMRC was inaugurated on 2 January, 1995 in Dhaka. The centre concentrates primarily on the research aspects of weather forecasting and monitoring. In addition to monitoring weather phenomena, the centre is also engaged in developing a networking system among member states.

The centre's ongoing activities include collating data from national meteorological services and other up-to-date climatologically information for the complication of a Directory of Meteorological Professional and Technicians in South Asia; bringing out newsletters regarding its programmes; and collating required meteorological data from sources outside the region for its research programmes.

3. SAARC Tuberculosis Centre (STC), Kathmandu, Nepal

The STC was setup in 1992 in Kathmandu. The main objective of the STC is to work towards the prevention and control of Tuberculosis (TB) in the region by coordinating the efforts of the national TB programmes of member states.

It serves as the regional coordination centre for national tuberculosis control programmes in the region and functions as a centre for information exchange and related activities by collecting, collating, analysing and disseminating all relevant information regarding the latest developments and findings in the field of tuberculosis in the region and elsewhere. It is also working to establish a networking arrangement among the national tuberculosis programmes. Among its objectives are to initiate, undertake and coordinate research and training in technical biomedical, operational and other aspects related to tuberculosis control programmes in the region; to ensure adequate supply at low cost of anti-tuberculosis drugs another related supplies in all the member states; to monitor incidence prevalence and emergence of drug resistant strains of tuberculosis in the region, to promote action on issues relating to HIV related tuberculosis in the SAARC region; and to carry out any other functions related to tuberculosis at the directive of the technical committee on social development.

A project proposal for the enhancement of the STC's capacity to deal with HIV/AIDS related tuberculosis under the SAARC-CIDA Memorandum of Understanding has been prepared and a Regional Strategy on TB and HIV/AIDS control is being formulated.

The STC has developed a format for collection of information related to tuberculosis and HIV/AIDS from SAARC Member states. The centre also published a newsletter twice a year which includes its activities, special articles and technical information on TB.

The STC has been organising seminars, workshops and training programmes related to TB control. Experts and TB Programme Managers are kept informed about recent developments in the field of TB control in and around the region, including information from WHO.

The centre also organises meetings of National TB Programme Managers of the members states to discuss the problems faced during implementation of programmes.

4. SAARC Documentation Centre (SDC), New Delhi, India

The SDC established in New Delhi in May 1994 fulfills the need for ready access to information on SAARC and its member countries. At present it focuses on data in member states and international databases in the areas of biological, physical, chemical, engineering and life sciences as well as in developmental matters. The center undertakes several workshops, seminars and training courses in the fields of library science and information technology. A two-year Master Degree course on "Associate-ship in information science" has also been included in its regular activities.

5. SAARC Human Resource Development Centre (SHRDC), Islamabad, Pakistan

The SAARC Human Resource Development Centre (SHRDC) has been established in Islamabad with an objective to undertake research, training and dissemination of information on human resource development issues. At its second meeting, the Governing Board finalised the terms of reference, budget programme of activities, administrative/financial rules and other functional aspects of the centre. The third meeting, which was held in Islamabad in October 2002, proposed its programme budget along with institutional cost.

This meeting also identified for the first time programme activities to be undertaken during the year 2003. These activities include : development of a database in the areas of education, health, gender, poverty, children and environment; preparation of a directory of HRD institutions in SAARC countries; development of a SHRDC website; publication of a SHRDC newsletters; and holding of a training programme on poverty alleviation.

6. SAARC Coastal Zone Management Centre, Maldives

The establishment of a regional coastal Zone Management Centre was recommended in the SAARC study on the causes and consequence of Natural Disasters and the Protection and preservation of the environment (SAARC, 1992). More recently, Mr. Maumoon Abdul Gayoom, President of the Maldives, highlighted the importance of the establishment of a SAARC Regional Coastal Zone Management Centre in his inaugural address to the SAARC Environment Ministers' conference held in Male from 15-16 October 1997. At the conference, the SAARC Environment Ministers decided to conduct a feasibility study for such a centre, and welcomed the offer of the government to Maldives to undertake the study.

7. SAARC Information Centre, Kathmandu, Nepal

The SAARC Information Centre is a new addition to the Regional Centres and has recently been approved by the SAARC bodies. The first meeting of the Governing Board of the Centre will be held during this year in Kathmandu.

The SAARC Plan of Action on Media and Information adopted by the Information Ministers at their first meeting in Dhaka in 1998 calls for the establishment of a SAARC Information Centre. This was approved by the 10th summit. The successive meetings of various SAARC bodies have given due emphasis on the subject. In this context, while appreciating the SAARC Secretariat's efforts for dissemination of information on SAARC and taking note of the existing mechanisms for publicity and projection of SAARC activities within and outside the region, the SAARC Information Ministers in their second meeting urged the establishment of a SAARC Information Centre with a view of reaching to a wider audience in an effective manner.

The second meeting of the Heads of TV and Radio Organisations decided to hold on Expert Group Meeting in Pakistan in mid of 2003 to work out the technical details of the proposed centre. The Expert Group Meeting identified the objectives, scope and functioning details of the centre. Accordingly, establishment of the SAARC Information Centre in Nepal was approved by the council of minister at its twenty fourth session held in Islamabad in January 2004. At the initial stage, the centre would consist of production, research and training units.

8. SAARC Energy Centre, Pakistan

The cooperation in the energy sector will cover, planning, development, trade, transportation, information exchange, capacity building, encouraging private sector participation and international cooperation, including the following areas :

- Establishment of a SAARC Energy Centre in Pakistan.
- Facilitation of private investment in the energy sector.
- Accessing resources from international financial institutions for harnessing regional energy potential.
- Development of a regional energy database.
- Promotion of energy trade including establishment of regional energy grids.
- Exploration of vast coal resources using economic, clean fossil fuel technologies.
- Exchange of geological information for expediting fossil fuel exploration and development.
- Development of hydropower resource.
- Development of renewable and alternate energy resources. Particularly in the rural areas, for poverty alleviation.
- Sharing of best practices in energy sector including, rural electrification, CNG, solar, wind, bio-fuels and other technologies.

- Promoting energy efficiency and conservation.
- Human resource development in the energy sector and exchange of experts.
- Cooperating with regional and international organisations and learning from the experience of energy cooperation programmes in other parts of the world.

9. SAARC Disaster Management Centre, New Delhi, India

The centre would serve the member countries of the SAARC by providing policy advice and facilitating capacity development services inducing learning, research, training, system development, expertise promotion and exchange of information for effective disaster and risk reduction and management.

The centre will collect, compile, document and disseminate data, information, case studies, indigenous knowledge and good practices relating to disaster management particularly from the member countries. It will network with the national focal points of disaster management and with the concerned regional and international bodies. The centre will collaborate with other SAARC Centre to achieve synergies in programmes and activities. The following regional centre is in the process of establishment:

1. SAARC Cultural Centre, Sri Lanka.
2. Forestry Centre, Bhutan.[4]

Areas of Cooperation

The SAARC Integrated Programme of Action (SIPA)

At the time SAARC was established in 1985, the core of its work programme was the Integrated Programme of Action (IPA) consisting of a number of Technical Committees on agreed areas of cooperation. However, as the agreed Agenda of SAARC expanded, new areas were identified for regional cooperation. The IPA too expanded. Given the emphasis laid down at successive summits on the need to consolidate and streamline the IPA and make it more result oriented, a set of guideline and procedures was adopted in 1992 for rationalisation of SAARC activities. The objective was to focus more on activities that would yield the standing committee in 1996 reviewed the institutional mechanisms and activities of the Association. This included an evaluation of the mandate and functions of the Technical Committee and the role of the Secretariat.

An independent group of experts set up by the Secretary-General in 1997 also undertook an extensive review of the functioning of the IPA and made wide ranging recommendations. These were considered by the Standing Committee at its twenty-sixth session held in Sri Lanka in March 1999. It proposed a newly restructured SAARC Integrated Programme of

Action (SIPA), which was approved by the council of ministers in its twenty-first session.

Under the reconstituted, SIPA, the number of technical committee has been reduced from eleven to seven mainly through the amalgamation of different areas covered by the technical committee eliminating overlapping and duplication. The prime objective of the reorganisation has been to enhance clarity in terms of goals and targets of the activities as well as to improve their quality and efficacy.

The seven Technical Committees under SIPA now cover:

1. Agriculture and Rural Development.
2. Communications and Transport.
3. Social Development.
4. Environment, Meteorology and Forestry.
5. Science and Technology.
6. Human Resource Development.
7. Energy.

An inbuilt mechanism for automatic review of activities under SIPA has been provided. The review will be undertaken after every three years by an independent multidisciplinary Expert Group to be constituted by the Secretary General in consultation with Member States. The Secretary General is authorised to propose activities and programmes under SIPA and to make specific recommendations to the standing committee regarding the mobilisation of necessary resource for the approved activities. This enables the Secretary General to explore funding possibilities for specific activities from within the region and other acceptable source.

The Secretary General reports to the Standing Committee on the progress of the implementation of the SIPA both at its inter-summit and pre-summit Sessions.[5]

The Areas of Work Assigned to Respective Technical Committees are as follows:

1. Technical Committee on Agriculture and Rural Development

The two Technical Committees on Agriculture and Rural Development were merged into one as the Technical Committee on Agriculture and Rural Development. The reconstituted committee under the chairmanship of Nepal started functioning in 2000 and held two meetings. Following adoption of the regional integrated programme of action (RIPA) by the 24th session of the Council of Ministers in Islamabad in January 2004, India hosted the first meeting of the technical committee on Agriculture and Rural Development under RIPA in New Delhi on 22-23 June 2004. The meeting reviewed activities under the mandate of the Technical Committee during the year 2003-04. It discussed the theme paper namely **"Water Resources Management for Agriculture in SAARC**

Countries", it also discussed the draft TOR on establishing a **"SAARC Quadrangle Milk Grid"** and the concept paper on **"Exchange of Rural Development Volunteers in the SAARC Countries"** as well as follow-up of the decisions related to Agriculture and Rural Development emanating from the twelfth SAARC Summit and the 24th session of the council of Ministers.

India hosted the 2nd meeting of the SAARC Technical Committee on Agriculture and Rural Development in New Delhi from 27—28 June 2005, which reviewed the activities under the committee since its last meeting. It had discussion on its theme paper **"Water for Agriculture in SAARC Countries".** The meeting considered the report of the SAARC-FAQ Expert level meeting on food security, integrated pest management (IPM) and Transboundary Animal Diseases (TAD). The meeting also discussed Concept Paper on **"Exchange of rural development volunteers in the SAARC Countries."**

Subsequently, the preceding meeting of the 13th SAARC Summit, approved the three projects jointly identified with FAQ with some observation.

(a) Control of Transboundary animal diseases.
(b) Enhancement of integrated pest management.
(c) Regional strategy and regional programme for food security.

In future involvement of the world organisation of animal health (OIE) is also expected to help SAARC countries in their efforts to control transboundary animal diseases.

The member states recognising the importance of regional and sub-regional collective self-reliance with respect to food security, established a SAARC Food Security reserve through signing on agreement on establishing the SAARC Food Security reserve. The agreement came into force on 12 August 1988 provides for a reserve of food grains meet emergencies. The reserve has 241,580 tons of food grains in stock.

2. Communication and Transport

During the 9th SAARC Summit (Male, May 1997), the heads of state or government noted that inadequate communications facilities amongst the member states was a major hindrance to the closer economic cooperation. They stressed on the importance of developing infrastructure and adequate communications networks among member countries to reinforce the process of economic cooperation. In this regard, the first SAARC communication minister's conference was held in Colombo in May 1998. It adopted a Plan of Action of Telecommunication to give impetus to the telecommunication sector in the region. The second meeting of the communication ministers held in Islamabad in June 2004 adopted the SAARC Plan of Action in 2004. The ministers agreed to adopt the following SAARC Plan of Action on telecommunication:

(i) Telecom tariffs within the SAARC region should be reduced to the lowest extent feasible within the framework of cost orientation based on international benchmarks.

(ii) For the intra-regional tariffs within SAARC countries. Efforts should be made to utilise either direct links / transit facility within the region by 2005.

(iii) Member states should offer special rates for transiting / hubbing regional traffic and utilise the facilities of other member for their overflow traffic. For this purpose licensed international long distance operators should be encouraged to frequently negotiate agreements for offering lowest possible tariffs.

(iv) Intra-regional communications for the traveller and entrepreneur should be facilitated by promotion of country direct services, calling cards, cellular roaming and liberalised leased lines within the regulatory frameworks of the member states. Besides the plan envisages complete digitalisation of inter-country links, human resource development in telecom sector; development of rural services with affordable tariffs etc. The conference also considered the current situation in the SAARC member states on digital divide and decided that more concerted efforts were required to improve the situation. It urged the member states to share their successful initiatives for development of ICT within the region.

SAVE Committee

The SAARC Audio Visual Exchange (SAVE) Committee is one of the original areas agreed at the inception of the SAARC. It aimed at increasing the awareness of each other among the peoples of the region and disseminating information about member countries was established by the council of ministers at its third session (New Delhi, June 1987). The committee has been entrusted with the task of producing and implementing the SAVE programmes.

3. Social Development

The SAARC charter envisages acceleration of social progress through active collaboration and mutual assistance amongst member states in the field. Focus on social issues under the broad heading of health and population activities were one of the five original areas of cooperation identified by member states.

The association promotes social development in the region through cooperation in the following areas :

1. Gender related issues.
2. Children and youth.

3. Health and population activities.
4. SAARC social charter.

4. Environment, Meteorology and Forestry

Environment has remained as an important agenda in the SAARC process. Successive summits have under scored the need for intensification of regional cooperation in the area of preservation of environment and disaster management to ensure that development process in the member states were not undermined. Six SAARC ministerial meetings on environment have been held so far.

Soon after the establishment of SAARC, a technical committee on environment was formed in 1992 to coordinate regional cooperation in environment and related areas. One of the first tangible outcomes of cooperation in the field of environment saw the production of two studies as mandated by the leaders.

The leaders during the third SAARC Summit at Kathmandu in 1987 deeply concerned on the causes and consequences of natural disasters and the protection and preservation of the environment. Its main recommendations were endorsed by heads of state or government at their sixth summit in 1991 at Colombo. The recommendations outlined in the study are categorised below:

(a) Measures to protect and manage the environment.
(b) Measures and programme for strengthening disaster management capabilities.
(c) Implementation mechanisms for the measures outlined in the study.

The fourth summit in 1988 at Islamabad noted with serious concern on green-house effect and its impact on the region.

The fifth SAARC Summit in 1990 at Male noted with the satisfaction of methodology recommended for the study on the green-house effect and its impact on the region. During the seventh SAARC Summit in Dhaka in 1993, the leaders recognised that the completion of the study was a significant step forward in promoting regional cooperation in this vital area. The study has the following components:

(a) Regional measures in sharing experiences, scientific capabilities and information on climate change.
(b) Global collaboration in monitoring climatology, sea level rise, natural disaster, technology transfer and finance etc.

Cooperation in meteorology was earlier considered by the erstwhile technical committee on environment, meteorology and forestry. Under the restructured regional Integrated Programme of Action, the subject of meteorology comes under the purview of the technical committee on Science and Technology. Given the unique geography and meteorological phenomena of the region, meteorology has remained an important area of cooperation in SAARC. Initiatives in this area are focused on intensifying regional cooperation in harnessing advances in atmospheric sciences and on current climate issues. A particular emphasis is made on cooperation in monitoring and prediction of weather to lesser its adverse impact on socio-economic development.

A SAARC meteorological research centre was established in 1995 with a clear set of objectives to further regional cooperation in meteorology. It continues to cooperate in this field. Recognising the progress in technology and emerging trends, the centre has recently revised its objectives and goals.

5. Science and Technology

The heads of State or government, conscious of the vast potential being afforded by current advances in scientific research for the application of science and technology towards the well-being of the peoples of South Asia, agreed during the sixth SAARC summit in 1991 at Colombo, that scientific and technological cooperation should transcend national frontiers to derive the maximum benefit for the region. They emphasised that cooperation in the field of Science and Technology was of utmost importance in order to accelerate the process of development in South Asia. At the eighth summit in 1995 at New Delhi, some progress had been made towards establishment of networking arrangements, in the fields of bio-technology, genetic engineering, energy modeling techniques and low cost housing and building technologies, the leaders called for further acceleration of this process. The leaders at the tenth summit in 1998 at Colombo note that the development of regional self-reliance capability of South Asia in scientific research and development was essential, given a global context in which barriers to the free flow of technology still remained in place.

6. Human Resource Development

The significance of human resources in socio-economic development of the region has been recognised since the inception of SAARC. The leaders at the first SAARC summit in 1985 reaffirmed that their fundamental goal was to accelerate the process of economic and social development through the optimum utilisation of human and material resources to promote the welfare and prosperity of people and to improve their quality of life.

At the second summit in 1986, the leaders recognised that the needs of children should be given highest priority in national development planning.

The leaders recognised at the fourth summit in 1988 the offer of Pakistan to host the SAARC Human Resource Development Centre in Islamabad.

The centre undertakes research, imparts training and disseminates information on HRD issues and advises member states on HRD related policies and strategies.

SAARC countries have been cooperating in the development of various dimensions of human resource. Such cooperation stated as early as August 1992 in the fields of sports, art and culture. In 1998, the SAARC leaders decided to include education in the agreed areas of cooperation and a technical committee was formed to deal with the principal area requiring urgent attention in the region. This technical committee was re-organised in 1992. The further re-structuring of the SAARC Integrated Programme of Action (SIPA) in 1999 resulted in the creation of the technical committee on human resource development. This was reconstituted in January 2004 to deal with matters pertaining to education, skill development, arts, culture and sports. The technical committee met in March 2004 and made a number of concrete and result oriented recommendations for regional cooperation in the vital area of human resource development.

At the twelfth SAARC summit held in Islamabad in January 2004, the leaders underlined that investment in human resource development was critical for future development of South Asia. It was, therefore, essential to establish a network of centres of higher learning and training and skill development institutions across South Asia.

7. Energy

During the twelfth SAARC Summit, the council of ministers at its twenty fourth session approved the most recent restructuring of the SAARC Integrated Programme of Action. Under the new Regional Integrated Programme Action (RIPA), seven technical committees were reorganised. At the same time five new working groups were created. The idea of working groups is new in SAARC, working groups have been especially created to focus on five new and emerging areas namely, energy, tourism, ITC, intellectual property rights and bio-technology.

The working groups are intended to have higher profiles than the technical committees and to function along the lines of the committee on economic cooperation that has been functioning for over a decade now.

As early as its fifth session the standing committee approved the recommendation of the then technical committee on science and technology to hold a workshop on renewable energy. Since then, various activities were held in the energy sector under the auspices of the technical committee on science and technology.

The twenty-fifth session of the council of ministers in Islamabad on 20–21 July 2004 approved the report of the first meeting of the working group on energy (WORGEN) and recommended the following plan of action:

1. A South Asia energy forum at ministerial level may be formed under the SAARC umbrella for exchange of view on policy issues and cooperation.
2. The possibility of setting up a SAARC energy centre may be explored.
3. A study may be carried out on options, benefits and constraints of energy trade in the region.
4. Exchange of information and technical discussions are prerequisite for cooperation and may be encouraged by the respective governments.
5. Joint strategies may be evolved for global energy forums for the benefit of the member states.
6. Countries of the region may benefit from each other's experiences in institutional and pricing reforms in the energy sector.
7. In the long terms, transnational energy lines (electricity, gas and oil) could provide basis for an integrated and prosperous economic future of South Asia.
8. Special focus is required on energy availability in rural area, in including conventional and non-conventional forms of energy for economic development and poverty reduction.
9. Non-conventional and renewable sources of energy may be promoted through sharing of manpower, expert, know-how and training programmes.
10. Feasibility of establishing a regional fund for promoting non-conventional energy may be explored.
11. Energy efficiency and conservation may be promoted as a least cost option.
12. Cooperation on CNG use in transport may be promoted.
13. Lessons may be learnt from innovative projects in member states such as Nepal electricity rickshaw project, Bangladesh rural electrification cooperative societies etc.
14. A quarterly internet based SAARC Energy newsletter may be posted by the Secretariat based on the information provided by the member states.

The working group decided to pursue cooperation in all recommended areas:

(a) Exchange of energy information.
(b) Environment friendly energy.
(c) Creation of a regional power grid.
(d) Cooperation regarding renewable energy.

SAARC-ASEAN Cooperation in the Energy Sector

SAARC-ASEAN cooperation recently development between the two secretariats recommended the proposals of visit by the experts from the

SAARC region to relevant ASEAN institutions coordinated by the ASEAN Secretariat.[6]

Promoting People to People Contact

The second SAARC Summit at Bangalore in 1986 laid special emphasis on promoting people contact in the region and approved the following five initiatives in this regard:

(i) SAARC Audio-Visual Exchange (SAVE) Programme

The SAVE Programmes comprise of regular TV and radio programmes which are being telecast / broadcast on the 1st and 15th of each month respectively in all SAARC member countries SAVE Radio and TV Quiz Programmes are also being held at regular intervals and have evoked keen interest among the youth. The other programmes included joint productions on specific themes such as Environment, Disabled Persons and Youth. SAVE has provided to be an effective medium for promoting South Asian consciousness amongst the people of the region and for establishing people to people contact.

(ii) SAARC Documentation Centre

This centre has been established to provide ready access to reliable and up-to-date information on technical scientific and development matters.

(iii) SAARC Scheme for Promotion of Organised Tourism

The scheme was initiated with the over-all objective of people-to-people contact in the region and more specifically as a step to facilitate development of intra-regional tourism. Concessional air fare to the tourists travelling under the scheme is now under the consideration of the technical committee on tourism which is presently taking necessary action to ensure early implementation of the scheme.

(iv) SAARC Chairs, Fellowships and Scholarship Schemes

The SAARC Chairs, fellowships and scholarships schemes was instituted with the aim of providing increased cross-fertilisation of ideas through greater interaction among students, scholars and academics in the SAARC countries. The scheme has now been brought under the purview of the technical committee on education, culture and sports.

(v) SAARC Youth Volunteers Programme (SYVOP)

(a) The main objective of the SYVOP is to harness the idealism of youth for regional cooperation programmes by enabling them to work in other countries in the field of agriculture and forestry extension work SYVOP was brought under the purview of the technical committee on

Rural Development in 1989. Seven activities have so far been held in the member countries under this programme.

(b) Other initiatives taken by the organisation for promoting people-to-people contact include the following.

(vi) SAARC Visa Exemption Scheme

In order to further promote closer and more frequent contacts among the peoples of the region the SAARC Visas exemption scheme was initiated in 1988. The scheme became operational from March 1, 1992 and so far about 1600 visas that have been issued under the scheme. Currently, persons entitled to the scheme are the Supreme Court Judges, Members of the National Parliaments, Heads of national academic institutions, foreign/ permanent secretaries dealing with foreign affairs, SAARC Secretary General and directors of the SAARC secretariat, Presidents of National Chambers of Commerce and Industry and their accompanying spouses and dependent children below 18 years of age.

(vii) South Asian Festivals

The first South Asian Festival was held in India from 9 to 24 October, 1992 with popular participation from all member states. The festival which included performing arts, exhibitions and seminars was a unique event and served to enhance the interaction and strengthened the affinities among the peoples of South Asia. The festival also served to focus on the civilisational personality of South Asia manifested in the rich heritage of its art forms, architecture, literature, theater and films.

South Asian Festivals covering selected areas would be organised in future in member countries.

Non-governmental Organisations (NGOs)

SAARC has emphasised the need for strengthening inter-governmental efforts with increased people to people contacts through greater participation of NGOs including professional bodies in the private sector, to promote socio-economic and cultural development of South Asia. In this context, a set of guidelines and procedures for granting recognition by SAARC to regional Apex Bodies has been formulated.

While the following regional apex bodies have been welcomed / granted recognition by SAARC, applications for recognition from several other apex bodies of professionals such as architects, accountants, university cowmen etc. are presently under consideration :

(i) Association of SAARC Speakers and Parliamentarians

The Speakers of Parliaments of SAARC countries first met in Sri Lanka in June 1992 and resolved to setup an Association of SAARC

Speakers and Parliamentarians. They met in Kathmandu in November 1992 and the first South Asian Festival held in India (October 1992) with participation from all Member Countries was a unique event which focused on the rich cultural heritage of South Asia formally launched the "Association of SAARC Speakers and Parliamentarians" and adopted the Charter of the Association. The speaker's council which is the Apex Body of the association finalised and ratified the draft rules of the association prepared by the parliamentary secretaries general in January 1994. Since then they have met periodically and addressed issues of common interest of member countries. The heads of state or government at their seventh summit (Dhaka, April 1993) welcomed the initiative of the Speakers of Parliaments of SAARC countries in forming the Association.

(ii) SAARC Chamber of Commerce and Industry (SCCI)

The SAARC Chamber of Commerce and Industry (SCCI) were recognised by SAARC in December 1992. SCCI has established its headquarters at Karachi and national units in all SAARC countries. Mr. S.M. Inam was elected as the first President of SCCI. The establishment of SCCI is a significant development and it will act as a dynamic instrument of promoting regional cooperation in the areas of trade and economic relations.

The SAARC Chamber has been instrumental in disseminating the information about the content, scope and potential of the Framework Agreement on SAARC Preferential Trading Arrangements (SAPTA) among the business community in the region. For this purpose, it has organised various national seminars on SAPTA in the member countries. A regional seminar on SAPTA was also organised in Kathmandu in December 1994.

(iii) SAARC LAW

SAARC LAW is an association for persons of the legal communities of the SAARC countries, established in 1991 with its headquarters in Colombo was recognised by SAARC as a regional apex body in July 1994. In has been established with the twin objectives of bringing together the legal communities within the region for closer cooperation and developing law as a source towards social change for development. SAARC LAW has been convening periodic conference covering important areas of common interest to member countries.

SAARC LAW has been engaged in

(a) Exchange of personnel (lawyers, judges, academics).
(b) Establishment of a SAARC LAW library in each country.
(c) Harmonisation of laws which offer mutual assistance within the judicial process.
(d) Publication of SAARC LAW magazine.

(e) Establishment of a SAARC Arbitration centre.

SAARC FUNDS

1. South Asian Development Fund

A panel of experts, in order to establish South Asian Development Fund, was formed under the chairmanship of H.E. Lyonpo Dawa Tshering, the Foreign Minister of Bhutan. The panel of experts consisting of eminent persons from the SAARC region held three meeting and the chairman had exploratory consultations with the potential donors. Later on, it was decided to establish on Inter Governmental Group (IGG) on South Asian Development Fund (SADF) to define the size, structure, resources and operational modalities of the proposed fund and also to examine the relationship of the fund with the SAARC fund for regional projects including the possibility of their merger. A consultant appointed by the Secretary General submitted his report which was considered by IGG at its second meeting held at the SAARC Secretariat in October 1994. The meeting recommended that South Asian Development Fund (SADF) may be established with the merger of the SAARC fund for regional projects (SFRP), the SAARC regional fund (SRF) and for social development and infrastructure building. This recommendation has been since approved by the 15th session of the council of ministers at New Delhi in 1995. The council approved the recommendation of the Standing Committee which included convening a meeting of the Group of Experts. At present South Asian Development Fund is a $300 million funding mechanism which was set up at the 15th Summit in Colombo in 2008 and this can become a visible achievement of SAARC in coming years.

2. SAARC Japan Special Fund

SAARC- Japan Special Fund has been established, under which the government of Japan has agreed to finance activities/programmes relating to SAARC region. Letters were exchanged between the General Secretaries and the Japanese Ambassador in Kathmandu on 27 September, 1993 confirming the acceptance of the Memorandum on the Guidelines for the Fund.

The fund established entirely with the contribution of the Government of Japan consists of two components the allocation under component I — is to be used to finance selected programmes/activities identified and managed by the member states. Component – II would be for the programmes / activities identified and managed by the Government of Japan.

3. SAARC Fund for Regional Projects (SFRP)

The SAARC Fund for regional projects was established in 1991 to make available credit on easy terms for the identification and development of projects having a regional character. The fund is managed by the Council for SAARC Fund for Regional Projects (CSFRP) comprising representatives of the development financial institutions of SAARC member states. Until now 13 projects have been undertaken which cover hydropower, sericulture, dairy products, medicinal cultivation and herbs etc.

4. SAARC Regional Fund (SRF)

The SRF aims at expediting the implementation of approved programmes / projects under IPA which remain unimplemented due to financial constraints. It would be administered by members states themselves. The sources of the fund would be grants from donor countries, international agencies and organisations, and private sector donations. The projects / programmes that would qualify for funding are programme costs of SAARC regional institutions, costs of programme component of networking arrangements, developments projects of scientific and technical in nature; projects involving high costs, long-term training programmes and programmes of any nature to be identified in future by member states.[7]

Recognised Bodies of SAARC

The following bodies enjoy the status of SAARC Recognised Bodies :

1. South Asian Association for Regional Cooperation of Architects (SAARCH)

SAARCH was founded in 1991 in Colombo with the objective of assisting the development of national architectural bodies within the South Asian region and providing opportunities for conferences of architects to discuss professional matters. It was accorded SAARC recognition in May 1997.

The Seventh SAARCH conference was held in Kathmandu in October 2002. The theme of the conference was "Heritage Conservation and Architecture of Tourism in the SAARC countries". The SAARCH Secretariat is located in Sri Lanka.

2. Association of Management Development Institutions (AMDISA)

AMDISA was established in June 1988 for promoting management education and training, and fostering management development activities in the South Asian region. It has brought under its umbrella the leading institutions of public and private sector, involved in teaching, training and research in management and development oriented fields. It seeks to combine the best elements of public and private sector management norms and techniques. It was accorded SAARC recognition in May 1997. Its general office is located in India.

3. SAARC Federation of University Women (SAARCFUW)

SAARCFUW was established in July 1995 in Colombo with the objectives of bringing together the university women of the region to promote mutual understanding and cooperation and to contribute to the social upliftment in the region. It was accorded SAARC recognition in May 1997. At present, it has national chapters in Bangladesh, India, Nepal, Pakistan and Sri Lanka. The secretariat of SAARCFUW rotates among the national chapters holding the chair.

4. SAARC Association of Town Planners

The main objective of the Association is to promote coordinated town planning in the region. It was accorded SAARC recognition in July 1998. At present, its country chapters are in the Bangladesh, India, Pakistan and Sri Lanka. Its headquarters is located in Colombo.

5. SAARC Cardiac Society

The main objective of the society is to foster cooperation and exchange of information in the field of cardiovascular sciences including research, training and rehabilitation programmes. It was accorded SAARC recognition in July 1998. It has country chapters in Bangladesh, India, Nepal, Pakistan and Sri Lanka. Its headquarters is located in Dhaka. The society has developed several guidelines pertaining to primary and secondary prevention of coronary heart diseases.

6. SAARC Teacher's Federation (STF)

STF was recognised by SAARC in January 2002. Since its recognition the activities have been identified for STF and member organisations with special emphasis on the role of the teaching community in social development. It's headquarters is located in Kathmandu with a relating secretariat.

7. Foundation of SAARC Writers and Literature (FSWL)

FSWL and its affiliated chapter have been working to foster people-to-people contacts in the region especially amongst the writers and intellectual of South Asia. FSWL was recognised by SAARC in January 2002. It's headquarters is located in New Delhi.

8. Federation of State Insurance Organisations of SAARC Countries (FSIO)

FSIO is engaged in strengthening cooperation among the state sector insurers in the SAARC region, and also in promoting cooperation with international organisations for the development of insurance industry. FSIO was recognised by SAARC in January 2002.

In view of the ongoing process of liberalisation and privatisation of insurance business in the SAARC region, FSIO has decided to expand its scope to include private insurers operating in SAARC countries in addition to state insures organisation. Its headquarters is located in Colombo. It rotates its chair.

9. Radiological Society of SAARC Countries (RSSC)

The establishment of the Radiological Society of SAARC countries is a step forward to further pursue the foundation of the scientific bond amongst SAARC countries. The RSSC is geared towards the development and advancement of the radiological science among member countries through education and scientific research. The RSSC is expected to form a specialised group to monitor and coordinate the implementation of programmes and policies pertaining to the radiological science in the region. RSSC was recognised by SAARC in January 2002. Its headquarters is located in Colombo.

10. SAARC Surgical Care Society (SSCS)

SSCS is formed to promote understanding and cooperation among the surgeons, surgical associations, colleges, societies and organisations in the SAARC countries. The society aims to develop and promote cooperation in all matters related to surgical practice, education and research, to interchange information and ideas about surgical interventions and to facilitate activities consonant with the SAARC Charter. SSCS was recognised by SAARC in January 2002. Its headquarters is located in Kathmandu.[8]

COOPERATION WITH INTERNATIONAL ORGANISATION

1. UNCTAD

SAARC- UNCTAD Memorandum of Understanding on the Trade Analysis and Information System (TRAINS) was signed in February 1993. The global aim of TRAINS is to increase transparency in international trading conditions and thus facilitate trade. This was the first agreement of cooperation to be signed by SAARC with an international organisation. Under this agreement, UNCTAD provides the SAARC Secretariat, an updated copy of TRAINS CD-ROM containing latest data on trade control measures prevailing in development and developing countries. The SAARC Secretariat in turn updates trade control measures prevailing in the SAARC member states on a regular basis and forwards the same to UNCTAD Secretariat, on computer floppies for incorporation in the updated versions of TRAINS CD-ROMS.

SAARC Secretariat has now data on trade control measures prevailing in 50 countries including most of the SAARC member countries. The largest of UNCTAD is to include latest trade control measures of 100 countries of the world in this PC-based information system. This information is available to SAARC member states on request.

2. ESCAP

A Framework Agreement for cooperation between SAARC and ESCAP was signed in February 1994. The Agreement provides for cooperation on development issues through joint studies, workshops and seminars and exchange of information and documentation in poverty alleviation, human resource development, trade promotion, foreign direct investment, environmental protection and prevention of drug trafficking, infrastructure development etc.

SAARC Secretary General has attended two consultative meeting of the executive heads of sub-regional organisations in Asia and the Pacific and ESCAP in Bangkok in 1994 and in Jakarta in 1995. The Secretary General also participated in the meeting of eminent persons on human resources development organised by ESCAP Secretariat in Bangkok in November 1994.

3. UNICEF

A Cooperation Agreement between SAARC and UNICEF, was signed on December 1993. The Agreement envisages cooperation in implementing the relevant SAARC decisions relating to children through an annual agenda which induce joint studies, exchange of documentation and monitoring of implementation.

In regard of the cooperation agreement, the SAARC Secretariat and the UNICEF Regional Office for South Asia have been holding regular consultations, which have covered progress in the implementation of summit directive on children and the recommendations of the council of ministers, standing committee and the relevant technical committee. The consultations focus on all child related issues including the annual review of the situation of children in the SAARC countries; implementation of the Colombo resolution on children; Plan of Action to mark 1991 - 2000 AD as the SAARC Decade of the Girl Child; the serious threat faced by girl children in Especially Difficult Circumstances (GCEDC), the mid-decade goals on children emanating from the world summit for children (1990) and certain aspect and of the United Nations convention on the rights of the child. The regular interaction between SAARC and UNICEF has facilitated better understandings of problems faced by children in South Asia and regional policies and strategies to meet these challenges.

4. Asia Pacific Telecomm Unity (APT)

A Memorandum of Understanding (MOU) was signed by SAARC Secretary General and Executive Director of Asian Pacific Telecommunity (APT) on 4 February, 1994. The MOU envisages cooperation between the two organisations to promote the growth of telecommunications in order to accelerate economic and social development in the region SAARC and APT will exchange information, publications and documents on their respective activities in this field. They will also exchange technical and operational details of plans for improvement of national, regional and international telecommunication network. Collaboration is also envisaged in planning and development of networks, transfer of technology promoting international standards, development of human resources and application of telecommunications in sectors such as health, education, environment, transport and tourism.

5. United Nations Development Programmes (UNDP)

A memorandum of understanding (MOU) between SAARC and UNDP was signed by the SAARC Secretary General and Administrator of UNDP in July 1995. The MOU embodies a general agreement for broad-based collaboration with the aims and purposes of promoting sustainable human development for attaining poverty elimination, preservation and protection of environment, regeneration of natural resources, employment creation, and the goals of women in development; undertakes periodic consultation for joint activities; publishing studies on priority concerns and exchanging relevant reports.

6. United Nations International Drug Control Programme (UNDCP)

SAARC Secretary General and International Drug Control Programme of United Nations signed an MOU on 18 August, 1995 to coordinate their efforts in combating drug trafficking and drug abuse in the region. The memorandum envisages mutual consultation and exchange of information between the two organisations, the two organisations have agreed to seek each others technical cooperation in pursuing their respective drug control activities in areas of drug supply and demand reduction to assist in the development and implementation of such activities as human resource development; improving regional cooperation on drug intelligence through the SAARC Drug Offences Monitoring Desk; legislation; financial investigation, money laundering; precursor control; the establishment of a networking arrangement among existing institutions in drug abuse prevention etc.

7. Colombo Plan

SAARC has also entered into cooperation arrangement with the Colombo Plan Bureau for promotions on the role of SAARC NGOs in anti-narcotic activities. Efforts are also underway to establish a working relationship between the SAARC Secretariat and the Colombo Plan Bureau on training facilities in the region.[9]

8. Economic Commission (EC)

A Memorandum of Understanding (MOU) was signed between SAARC and Economic Commission (EC) on 10 July 1996 in Brussels. The MOU envisages cooperation between the two organisations on exchange of information, training programmes, technical assistance and any other areas jointly agreed to. Its primary objective is to draw upon the expertise of the Economic Commission in areas such as the Single European markets from which the process of regional economic cooperation within SAARC could benefit.

The areas that have been identified for areas of cooperation are facilitating access into the single European market, implementing the EU's GSP Scheme including cumulative rules of origin, drawing on the EU experience for the SAFTA Process and evolving common standards and harmonisation with international obligations including certification, testing etc.

9. Association of South East Asian Nations (ASEAN)

Consultations between SAARC and the Association of South East Asian Nation (ASEAN) at the ministerial level were initiated in New York in 1997 on the sidelines of the UN General Assembly Session. The areas for cooperation being discussed between the two organisations include regular consultations on UN and multi-lateral issues including on elective posts, sharing of expertise and experience including on poverty alleviation programmes, common approaches against terrorism, academic exchanges, programmes to combat HIV/AIDS, encouraging cooperation between ASEAN and SAARC chambers of commerce, encouraging people to people contract and closer Secretariat to Secretariat consultations.

10. Canadian International Development Agency (CIDA)

A Memorandum of Cooperation between SAARC and Canadian International Development Agency was signed on 2 July, 1997 to promote cooperation and mutually beneficial interactions in areas such as poverty eradication, economic cooperation and trade, social and human resources development and sustainable economic growth and development.

A workshop on NAFTA / SAFTA was organised by the SAARC Secretariat in Collaboration with CIDA in December 1998. The workshop facilitated the sharing of relevant experiences of the North American Free Trade Area (NAFTA) for the creation of a free trade area in South Asia.

Cooperation between CIDA and SAARC in the field of health is proceeding with the involvement of the SAARC Tuberculosis Centre in Kathmandu.

11. International Telecommunications Union (ITU)

The Memorandum of Understanding was signed between SAARC and International Telecommunications Union (ITU) in March 1997, providing a framework agreement for ensuring closer cooperation and coordination of efforts between SAARC and ITU. The areas covered by the MOU include development of telecommunications and telematic services as well as improvement of the quality of voice and non-voice telecommunications services in the region and improvement in the productivity and efficiency of the telecommunications organisations and networks in the region.

12. United Nations Fund for Women (UNIFEM)

A Memorandum of Understanding (MOU) was signed between SAARC and United Nations Fund for Women (UNIFEM) on 30 December, 2001 in Kathmandu. Under the MOU, SAARC and UNIFEM agree to help member states strive towards the goals of Gender Equality based on the empowerment approach in terms of the Beijing Platform for Action (BPFA) and the Beijing plus Five Outcome Document and encourage mutual learning and cross fertilisation among developing countries for effectively tackling the challenges posed by gender discrimination and promoting women's human rights and women's participation.

13. World Health Organisation (WHO)

SAARC and World Health Organisation (WHO) signed a Memorandum of Understanding (MOU) in August 2000 to mutually cooperate in agreed ways to help member countries strive toward the goal of health for all. The MOU envisages collaboration between WHO and the SAARC Tuberculosis centre in Kathmandu and other institutions in South Asia, particularly those active in the field of malaria, tuberculosis and HIV/AIDS.

Under the MOU, the two organisations promote research analysis and dissemination of information with view to enhance technical cooperation and human resources development including programmes for women resources development including programmes for women and children and mobilising innovative action in favours of the under privileged. The STC has been organising activities on cross border issues and conducting training courses on TB, HIV, Malaria and Kalaazar.

14. United Nations Environment Programme (UNEP)

The third special session of the Standing Committee in Colombo in August 2001 authorised the Secretary General to develop common projects with United Nations Environment Programme (UNEP) in the areas of sharing of expertise for the development of collective approaches for the protection of bio-resources and capacity building and training with a view to facilitate implementation of Multilateral Environment Agreements (MEAs).

SAARC and UNEP have since initiated consultations on evolving joint programmes in these areas.

15. South Asia Cooperative Environment Programme (SACEP)

The twenty-eighth session of the Standing Committee in Kathmandu in August 2002 requested the Secretary General to discuss with South Asia Cooperative Environment Programme (SACEP) suitable modalities of cooperation between the two organisations.

Accordingly, the Secretariat has since initiated discussions with SACEP in developing a cooperation agreement spelling out a broad outline of modalities of cooperation between the two organisations.

The SAARC Secretariat

The SAARC Secretariat was established in Kathmandu on 16 January 1987. Its role is to coordinate and monitor the implementation of SAARC activities, service the meetings of the association and serve as the channel of communication between SAARC and other international organisations. The Secretariat has also been increasingly utilised as the venue for SAARC meetings.

The Secretariat comprises the Secretary General, seven Directors and the General Services staff. The Secretary General is appointed by the council of ministers upon nomination by a member state on the principle of rotation in alphabetical order.

The Present Secretary General is Abdul Saleem of Maldives. The Directors are appointed by the Secretary General upon nomination by member states for a period of three years. In special circumstances, the term may be extended by the Secretary General for a period not exceeding another full term, in consultation with the member state concerned.[10]

Conclusion

The establishment of SAARC in South Asia aims to bring stability to South Asia by enhancing regional cooperation. SAARC is the first formal initative that sought to bring the countries of South Asia to the same platform with the aim of promoting the welfare and quality of life of its people through accelerated economic growth, social progress and cultural development in the region. SAARC aims to strengthen cooperation of member countries with other developing countries, to strengthen cooperation among the member countries in international forum on matters of common interests and to cooperate with international and regional organisation with similar aims and purposes.[11]

References

1. Goel O.P., India and SAARC engagements – Vol. 2, Isha Books, p. 1.
2. Khanna V.N., Foreign Policy of India – Vikas Publishing House, p. 238.
3. Goel O.P., India and SAARC Engagements Vol. 1, Isha Books, p. 83.
4. Report- SAARC Documentation Centre, http://www.sdc.gov.in//htm.

5. Goel O.P., India and SAARC Engagements, Vol. 1, Isha Books, 2004, p. 7.
6. http://www.sdc.gov.in/aboutsaarc.htm.areasofcooperation.
7. http://www//southasianassocationforregionalcooperation.htm.
8. Goel O.P. – India and SAARC Engagements, Vol. 1, Isha Books, p. 66.
9. //http://www./saarcdocumentationcentre.htm.
10. Goel O.P. India and SAARC Engagements, Vol. 2, Isha Books, p. 74.
11. Khan Rafi Shaheen, Regional Integration,Trade and Conflict in South Asia, p. 17.

3

An Introduction to SAARC Nations, SAARC Summits, Declarations and its Growth in South Asian Region Since 1985

South Asia is a region generally known as a cluster of geographically proximate countries that share common historical bonds, cultural and social identities, economic, political and strategic interests, with a desire to live in harmony and cooperation. As a term, 'South Asia' has been in use only for the past five decades or so. It is in the 'Indian sub-continent' that the term has been in longer usage. The political division of the Indian sub-continent brought about at the time of the British withdrawal in 1947 gave rise to the use of the term South Asia for the Indian sub-continent.[1]

South Asia covers three per cent of the world's land surface, contains 22 per cent of the world's population and shares one per cent of the world's trade. It is a sub-region of Asia, comprising the modern states of Bangladesh, Bhutan, India, Maldives, Nepal, Pakistan and Sri Lanka. Despite rapid economic growth during the 1990s, the nations in the region have the lowest per capita incomes in the world.

South Asia is in turmoil today, as it actually had been since 1947-48 when the British colonial rulers decided to quit the major part of the sub-continent. The partition of India into two dominions - India and Pakistan on the basis of two-nation theory is still clearly reflected in a hostile India. Pakistan has relations with Jammu and Kashmir as the major bone of contention; and this in spite of the vociferous claims of the political elites on both sides for normalisation of relations through peaceful negotiations which have been held many times with full sound and fury signifying just nothing.

In South Asia 'religion' is in its perverted form and the inter-religion relationships are still a potential force to rapture the social fabric as it has been frequently seen in India, Pakistan, Bangladesh and Sri Lanka in terms of communal rioting and displacement of people. However, the phenomenon of ethnicity and ethnic conflicts within each South Asian state and between the states and has occupied the center stage of political discourse during last couples of decades.

'Regionalism' on the other hand has two dimensions in South Asian countries, one demand for a separate state within a parent nation state and the other demand for secession. Demand for Uttarakhand, Bodoland, Gorkhaland and Jharkhand fall in the first category whereas the demand for Azad Kashmir, Khalistan, Independent Assam, Nagaland, Mizoram fall in the second category.

Tamils are demanding Tamil Elam in Sri Lanka and the Malarias, the Baluch; the Pathans are demanding secession in Pakistan.

Another issue which has assumed significance is about the gender question in South Asian countries. Women constitute roughly fifty per cent population and because of the patriarchal nature of the society and also because of social traditions, practices, rituals and religious commandments, they are still being suppressed.[2]

In South Asia, the levels of social development, though improved since the 1960s, have started to stagnate or even decline. This decline had been caused by problems which were common to all social sectors across the region. These included: weak planning and budgeting: inadequate and irregular supply of key inputs required for regular and quality service delivery; lack of trained staff aggravated by recruitment bans; weak supervision, monitoring and accountability leading to poor governance; extensive gender biases, resulting in low coverage of female population and absence of any involvement of clients in the design and management of services. Underlying all these issues were lack of political commitment and in adequate focus on social services.

The most important challenge faced by South Asia is to use the forces unleashed by globalisation to improve human development. The region needs to make sustained effects in the areas of education, improve economic management and enhance regional and global integration.[3]

From the beginning of 1990's all the South Asian countries were under the fascination of a new liberal environment characterised by three words - liberalisation, privatisation and globalisation (LPG). Besides the discriminatory agreements like GATT and WTO, the global market forces are trying to marginalise the role of the state.

Over the past decade the South Asian countries have undertaken extensive reforms of their economies to integrate themselves more intensively with the world economy. As a result, the proportion of trade in their national incomes has risen from 22 per cent to nearly 30 per cent over the 1990s. The increasing global integration enables from them to benefit from the emerging international specialisation, obviate the constraints on their development by the size of domestic market and absorb spill-over of knowledge and technological developments taking place in the rest of the world.

Beside unilateral moves towards liberalisation of policy regimes, trade liberalisation has also been facilitated by WTO Agreements under which the South Asian countries have undertaken considerable commitments. The 1990s also saw a significant move towards freeing intra-regional trade with the agreement like SAPTA and SAFTA, apart from bilateral free trade agreement between some of the South Asian economies. As a result exposure of the South Asian economies to international trade and investments has increased substantially by the end of the twentieth century.

The liberalisation of the financial and capital market has in a similar manner linked the performance of the capital markets of South Asian with global capital markets.[4]

Information and Communication technology have also provided a new set of tools to solve mighty development problem faced by region like South Asia. Recent trends have given high expectations about the applicability of such technologies. However, current uses are not necessarily focused towards human development.

In order to effectively use ICTs in human development in the region, there should be a shift in paradigm in the thinking about ICTs. This includes rethinking of government policies, integrating ICT policies with economical goals, combining ICTs with other development tools and active participation by normal people.[5]

However, the developing countries in South Asia recognise the potential of ICTs for development of their economies and communities. But the use of ICTs for development has to address the digital divides in the countries of South Asia ICT projects must take into account the initial high costs and must be implemented effectively for long-term sustainability. Many ICT projects lack the self-sustaining base after the experimental phase usually because they are funded by international agencies that stop funding after a period of time and the user communities are too poor to continue with it.[6]

But still ICT development in South Asia is in the developing phase. Many ICT programmers and policies have been adopted by South Asian nations until now.

In the contemporary international scenario, South Asia occupies an important position in the context of nuclear proliferation, as it is inhabited by two non-declared nuclear weapon states. Reviewing the clauses and

Graph 3.1 - Percentage Share of World Bank Projects in South Asia Having ICT Components

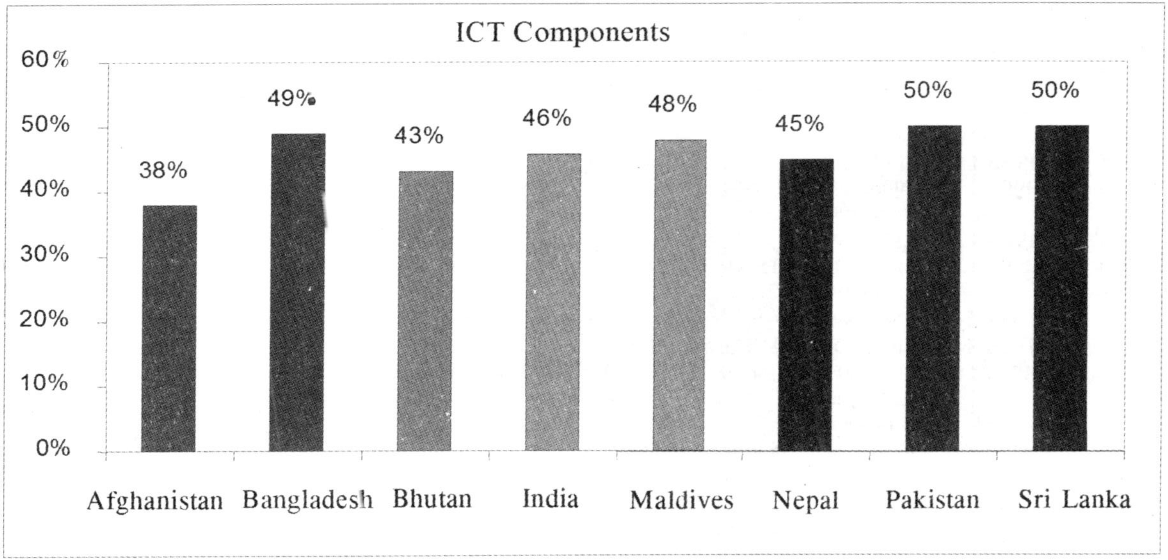

Source: ESAR The South Asia Region ICT Task Force (March 2005).

Table 3.1- ESAR: Strategy Programmes in South Asia

	Afghanistan	*Bangladesh*	*Bhutan*	*India*	*Maldives*	*Nepal*	*Pakistan*	*Sri Lanka*
IT literacy and skilled labour	Draft ICT policy	National strategy. ICT policy.	ICT Master plan	10th plan	6th NDP	ICT policy	IT policy I-PRSP 2000	telecom policy
Information and communication Infrastructure	SAF, draft ICT policy	ICT policy	ICT master plan	New telecom Policy 10th plan	Telecom Policy	10th plan ICT policy telecom policy	IT policy I-PRSP 2000	Telecom policy
Legal and Regulatory framework	SAF,draft ICT policy telecom and internet policy	ICT policy	ICT master plan	New telecom policy	6th NDP Telecom policy	10th plan ICT policy telecom policy	IT policy I-PRSP 2000	Telecom policy
E-government	Draft ICT policy	National Strategy ICT policy	ICT master plan	10th plan	6th NDP	ICT policy telecom policy	IT policy I-PRSP 2000	Telecom policy
ICT sector Development	Not mentioned	National Strategy ICT policy	ICT master plan	New telecom policy 10th plan	6th NDP	10th plan ICT policy telecom policy	IT policy I-PRSP 2000	Telecom policy
Sector Specific Applications	Draft ICT policy, telecom Internet Policy	National Strategy ICT policy	Not Mentioned	10th plan	6th NDP Telecom policy	10th plan ICT policy telecom policy	IT policy	Telecom policy
Knowledge Economy development	ICT policy for Afghanistan Final report	ICT policy	Not mentioned	World bank involve ment	6th NDP	Telecom policy	Not mentioned	Not mentioned

Source: ESAR the South Asia Region ICT Task Force (March 2005).

conditions of the CTBT, which was projected as a universal and comprehensive treaty, it seems that this treaty was only a camouflage, in reality it was designed to curb nuclear proliferation or non–dispensing of nuclear technology among the nuclear threshold states with India as its main target. This deduction is drawn from the fact that most of the Non-Nuclear Weapons States (NNWS) have already committed themselves not to acquire such technologies through the ratification of the indefinite extension of the NPT in 1995.

Both the South - Asian states, India and Pakistan, have refused to bow down to all pressures for signing the NPT, with India adopting a rigid stand and Pakistan tagging its acceptance to India's signature. Thus, it can be rightly stated that in the contemporary world South Asia in general and India in particular will have to bear the brunt of the new non-proliferation regimes, 'CTBT'.[7]

The barriers to counter-terrorism cooperation that exist at regional, national and local levels in each and every state of South Asia, except the Maldives are substantial and cannot be quickly surmounted and no nation in South Asia can of its own accord devise a mechanism to overcome the problems of collective action that needs to be solved to move towards a viable regional counter-terrorism strategy. In this context SAARC may be able to play a useful role.[8]

If South Asia is to play a leadership role in the new world that is taking shape, then it must undertake specific initiatives within a new policy paradigm for pursuing peace, overcoming poverty and protecting the life support systems of the world. However, this requires that governments should move out of a mindset that regards an adversarial relationship with a neighbouring country as the emblems of patriotism, affluence of the few at the expense of the many, as the hallmark of development, individual greed's as the basis of public action, and mistrust as the basis of interstate relations. The people of South Asia should affirm that their security and well-being lies not in interstate conflict but peace and cooperation.[9]

The Historical Background of South Asia

The term 'South Asia' refers to the political entities of the Indian subcontinent and associated island. These are the states of India, Pakistan, Bangladesh, Nepal, Bhutan and the island nations of Sri Lanka and the Maldives.

The Asian continent is the cynosure of all eyes. The countries of Asia - except a few that emerged in the middle of the Twentieth Century from long periods of colonial rule. South Asia is home to 1470 million people living in eight countries.

The area was usually referred to as Britain's Indian Empire prior to 1947. South Asia's location bordering the Indian Ocean opened it to maritime trade over 3000 years ago. It was first the European traders such as the French, the Dutch, and the Portuguese and later it was the British traders who took the great advantage of such maritime linkages.

Every major world religion is to be found in the subcontinent. Hinduism with its ancient roots, modern transformations and multiple interrelations plays a vital part in the culture and politics of the subcontinent. The majority of the population of India is, Hindus but they are distinguished along the lines of languages and caste. While the Buddhism may have dwindled in the land of its birth, it continues to flourish in Sri Lanka and Himalayas. Some of the greatest cultural and political achievements of Islam have taken place in the subcontinent, where more than 400 million of the world's 1.3 billion Muslim live today in India, Bangladesh and Pakistan. South Asia also has significant Jain, Zoroastrian, Christian and Sikh minorities.

Political History of South Asian Countries

At the federal level, India is the most populous democracy in the world. For most of the years since independence; the federal government has been led by the Indian National Congress (INC). Politics in the states have been dominated by several national parties including the INC, the Bharatiya Janta Party; the Communist Party of India (Marxist) and so on, from 1950 to 1990, barring two brief periods, between 1977 and 1980 where the INC enjoyed a parliamentary majority. In 1991, INC formed a minority government for a five year term. The years 1996-1998 were period of turmoil in the federal government with several short-lived alliances holding sway. In 1998, the Bharatiya Janta Party formed the National Democratic Alliance (NDA). In 2004, Indian elections, the INC won the largest number of Lok Sabha seats and formed a coalition government with the United Progressive Alliance (UPA).

Since independence, India has faced challenges from religious violence, casteism, naxalism, terrorism and regional separatist insurgencies, especially in Jammu and Kashmir and the North-East India. Since the 1990s, terrorist attacks have affected many Indian cities. India has unresolved territorial dispute with China, which in 1962 escalated into the Sino-Indian war and with Pakistan, which resulted in wars in 1947, 1965, 1971 and 1991. India is a founding member of the United Nations and the Non-Aligned Movement. In 1974, India conducted an underground nuclear test and five more tests in 1998, making India a nuclear state. Beginning in 1991, significant economic reforms have transformed India into one of the fastest growing economies in the world, increasing its global clout.

The history of Pakistan as a modern nation began with its independence from British - India on 14 August 1947. The political history of the eventual birth of the country began in the aftermath of the India rebellion of 1857, which culminated in 90 years of direct rule by the British crown, and subsequently spawned a successful freedom struggle led by the Indian National Congress and the All India Muslim League. In 1930, Muhammad Ali Jinnah espoused the Two Nation Theory and led the Muslim League to adopt the Lahore Resolution of 1940, demanding the formation of an independent Pakistan. Independence resulted in communal riots across India and Pakistan. Disputes arose over several princely states including Jammu and Kashmir whose ruler had acceded to India following an invasion by tribesman from Pakistan. Economic grievances and political dissent in East Pakistan led to violent political tensions and army repression, escalating into civil war followed by the India-Pakistani war of 1971 and ultimately the secession East Pakistan as the independent state of Bangladesh.

Military tensions in the Kargil conflict with India were followed by a Pakistani military coup in 1999 in which General Pervez Musharraf assumed executive powers. The assassination of Benazir Bhutto resulted in a series of important political developments, a coalition government came into power under the Presidency of Asif Ali Zardari since 18 February 2008. At present Mamnoon Hussain was elected President on July 30, 2013 and assumed office in September succeeding Asif Ali Zardari. On June 19, 2012, Pakistan's Supreme Court disqualified Prime Minister Yousuf Raza Gilani on charges of not obeying court orders, then on June 22, 2012. The National Assembly elected Raja Pervez Ashraf as the country's 17th Prime Minister of Pakistan.

On 15th January 2013, Pakistan Supreme Court ordered the arrest of Prime Minister Raja Pervez Ashraf over corruption allegations. At present Nawaz Sharif is acting as a Prime Minister of Pakistan since 5 June 2013.

Bangladesh became one of the last major nation states following its secession in 1971 from the nation of Pakistan, which achieved its independence from the British Empire along with India in 1947. The territory was part of the Mughal Empire for more than five centuries and then the Bengal Presidency and finally the British Empire. Since independence in 1971, successive government have had to define Bangladesh's democracy to this day.

The history of the Nepal is characterised by its isolated position in the Himalayas and its two dominant neighbours, India and China. Nepal was split in to three kingdoms from the 15th to 18th Centuries, when it was unified under a monarchy. Nepal experienced a failed struggle for democracy in the 20th century. During the 1990s and until 2008, the country was in civil strife. A peace treaty was signed in 2008 and elections were held in the same year. Many of ills of the Nepal have been blamed on the royal family of Nepal. In a historical vote for the election of the constituent assembly, the Nepalis voted to oust the monarchy in Nepal. In June 2008, the Nepalis ousted the royal house hold. Nepal was formally known as the Federal Democratic Republic of Nepal when it later became a federal republic.

The country's political history is intimately tied to its religious history and the relations among the various monastic schools and monasteries.

The consolidation of Bhutan occurred in 1616 when Ngawanang Namgyal, a lama from Tibet, defeated three Tibetan invasions, subjugated to rival religious schools, codified an intricate and comprehensive system of law, and established himself as ruler over a system of civil administrators. After his death infighting and civil war eroded the power of the last ruler for the next 200 years when in 1885, Ugyen Wangchuck was able to consolidate power and cultivated closer ties with the British in India. In 1910, King Ugyen and the British signed the Treaty of Punakha which provided that British India would not interfere in the internal affairs of Bhutan if the country accepted external advise in its external relations. Jigme Wangchuck became the next ruler in 1926, and when India gained independence in 1947, the new Indian government recognised Bhutan as an independent country. In 1949, India and Bhutan signed the treaty of Peace and Friendship which provided that India would not interfere in Bhutan's internal affairs but would be guided by India in its foreign policy. Succeeded in 1952, by his son Jigme Dorgi Wangchuck, Bhutan began to slowly emerge from its isolation and began a programme of planned development. Bhutan became a member of the United Nations in 1971.

In 1972, Jigme Singye Wanchuck ascended the throne at age of 16. He emphasised modern education, decentralisation of government, the development of hydroelectricity and tourism and improvements in rural developments. He was perhaps best known internationally for his over - arching development philosophy of "Gross National Happiness". It recognises that there are many dimensions to development and that economic goals alone are not sufficient. His son, Jigme Khesar Namgvel Wangchuck, became king upon his abdication.

In the Sri Lankan history, it was ruled by the local kingdoms for more than 2000 years and were colonised by Portugal and the Netherlands in the beginning of sixteenth century, before the control of the entire country by British empire in 1815. During the Second World War, Sri Lanka served as an important base for Allied Forces in the fight against the Japanese empire. A nationalist political movement arose in the country in the early twentieth century with the aim of obtaining political independence, which was eventually granted by the British after peaceful negotiations in 1948.

Sri Lanka has enjoyed democracy with universal suffrage since 1931. Politics in Sri Lanka are controlled by rival coalitions led by the left wing Srilankan freedom party, headed by President Rajapaksa, the comparatively right-wing United National Party led by former Prime Minister Ranil Wickremesinghe and Marxist Nationalist JVP. There are also many smaller Buddhist, Socialist and Tamil nationalist political parties that oppose the separatism of the LTTE but demand regional autonomy and increased civil rights. Sri Lanka has been a member of the commonwealth nations and the United Nations. It is also a member of the Non–Aligned Movement, the Colombo Plan, Asia Pacific Economic Cooperation and the South Asian Association for Regional Cooperation. Through the Cold War-Era, Sri Lanka followed a foreign policy of non-alignment but has reminded closer to the United States and Western Europe. Since the 1980s, the army has led the government response against the Marxist militants of the JVP and now the LTTE militant forces. Sri Lanka receives considerable military assistance from Pakistan and China. It has also been declared as "a stable democracy" amidst a ceasefire period of the long running civil war.

Maldives, among one of the nation of South Asian countries approved its constitution through referendum in 1968. On Nov. 1988, Sri Lankan Tamil mercenaries tried to overthrow the Maldivian government. At President Gayoom's request, the Indian military suppressed the coup attempt within 24 hours. Since 2003, the country has experienced occasional anti-government demonstrations calling for political reforms. Political parties were allowed in June 2005.

Violent protests broke out in Male on September 20, 2003 and on August 13, 2004 which led to state of emergency and to prevent independent reporting of events, the government shut off the internet access and some mobile telephony services to Maldives. A new constitution was ratified in August 2008, paving the way for the country's first multi-party Presidential election two months later.[10]

Hence, in South Asia, the conflicts are partly historic, dating back to colonial periods. But there are problems which have exacerbated old rivalries in recent times. There is also great capacity for extremism and high passion in these conflicts. Nationalism and strong religious loyalties have created a dangerous cocktail. The memory of the feelings of the two regional protagonists (India and Pakistan). Most of the South Asian conflicts have erupted because of the issues that have arisen in the post-1947 period. The regional conflicts which revolve around the touchy issues of nationalism and foreign interferences have also blinkered our world view and influenced the direction of South Asian politics.[11]

However, South Asian Association for Regional Cooperation (SAARC) has provided a concerted shape to regionalism and regional integration in South Asia. The journey of SAARC for the last two decades has been rather chequered and its functioning has generated several doubts and complexities. How to consolidate regional integration in South Asia has become a vital issue. It is therefore important to look into three major basic issues about the functioning of SAARC as to what has failed and what needs to be done to make a meaningful regional entity in the coming decades? These issues are important and need in-depth analysis so that it can become possible for SAARC to establish its worth.[12]

Profile of SAARC Member States

South Asian Association for Regional Cooperation consists of eight nations - Bhutan, Bangladesh, Nepal, India, Maldives, Pakistan, Sri Lanka and Afghanistan.

1. **Bangladesh**

Bangladesh emerged as an independent country on 16 December 1971. Its official name is the 'People's Republic of Bangladesh'. Dhaka is the capital of the Republic and Bangla is the State language. The population of the country stands at 123.15 million. About 80 per cent of the people live in rural area, 60 per cent of the people depend on agriculture for their livelihood. The four major religions in the country are Islam, Hinduism, Buddhism and Christianity.

Bangladesh is a unitary, independent and sovereign republic. Bangladesh has primarily an agrarian economy. Agriculture is the single largest sector in the economy producing about 30 per cent of the country GDP and employing around 60 per cent of the total labour force. The country has a considerable number of large, medium and small sized industries in both the public and the private sector based on both indigenous and imported raw materials. Among them are jute, cotton, textiles, fertilizer, engineering, shipbuilding, cement and leather.

2. **Bhutan**

The Bhutanese calls their country Druk-yul, the land of Drukpas (the people) and of the Druk (Thunder Dragon as in the national flag of Bhutan). Dzongkha is the official language. The ancient history of the kingdom remains shrouded in mystery. Since the Eighth Century A.D. Buddhism has played a large part in shaping the course of Bhutan's history. Bhutan has remained an independent country throughout its history and it was unified under a central authority in the seventeenth century.

Bhutan's population currently stands at 638,000 people. The people of Bhutan may be divided into two main groups, the Drukpas who are Buddhists and the Lhotsampas, or the southerners who are mainly Hindus of Nepali origin.

Bhutan is a monarchy ruled by the Wangchuck dynasty, which was founded in 1907 by King Ugyen Wangchuck and he devolved full executive power to a new council of ministers elected by the national assembly.

With over 80 per cent of the people dependent on subsistence farming, the Bhutanese economy is predominantly rural. The share of the agricultural sector in the GDP has dropped to less than 50 per cent with the increase in the contribution of hydroelectric power generation and sale which now accounts for over 30 per cent. The country has the potential to generate 30,000 MW of power from its river. Besides electricity, Bhutan exports calcium carbide, wood products and cement. Bhutan has followed a unique development philosophy called Gross National Happiness (GNH) which is receiving worldwide attention. It lays emphasis on good governance, culture promotion, environmental preservation and economic development.

3. India

Lying in the Northern hemisphere the mainland India measures 3214 km from the North to South and 2933 km from the East to West. India can be divided into three main topographic regions; the Himalayan mountain system on the north, the northern plains drained by the Indus. Ganges and Brahmaputra rivers in north-central India and peninsular India in the South. India is on ancient civilisation whose roots stretch back to over 5000 years in the course of which a composite culture emerged making it a land of unity in diversity. India today is the seventh largest and the second most populous country in the world. The constitution of 1950 provides for a federal system with a parliamentary form of government. Sovereignty is shared between the central government and the states, but the national government is given for greater power. India is the birthplace of Hinduism, Buddhism, Jainism and Sikhism. It is a secular states and its constitution guarantees religious tolerance to all groups.

More than 200 languages are spoken in India, and linguistic diversity provides an important key to understanding Indian civilisation. Hindi is the official language of India. Most of Indians live in more than 500,000 villages where the major source of livelihood is agriculture. Since independence the Indian government attempted to pursue a mixed economic policy with features of both a free market and socialist planning. Today, India ranks among the top ten industrial nations of the world. Major exports include textiles, tea, marine products, engineering goods, and computer software. There is immense potential for growth in technology and knowledge based products and services. The agriculture sector continues to be an important sector of the economy as it contributes 27 per cent of the GDP, provides employment to 65 per cent of the workforce and accounts for 18 per cent share of the total value of exports. India spends about one per cent of its GNP on scientific and technological developments.

4. The Maldives

The civilisations of the Maldives as far as can be estimated, date back more than 2000 years. The archipelago of the republic of Maldives is made up of a chain of 1190 small and low-lying island, stretching over 800 km from North to South. Out of them, only 198 islands are inhabited.

The population of the Maldives is 270,101. Maldivian comprises a mixed race, unified through sharing a common history, language and religion. Dhivehi is the official language. Islam is the strength and backbone of the country, permeating the entire fabric of the Maldivian culture, polity and civil society. A new constitution, that is more comprehensive and in tune with country's democratic principles was adopted by the country on 1 January, 1998.

The mainstay of the Maldives economy today comprises of fisheries and tourism. Nearly 19 per cent of the labour force is engaged in the fisheries sector which account for over six per cent of the GDP. Tourism, which has become a major industry since the mid-eighties, accounts for 33 per cent of the GDP. Industrial activity consists of a traditional and a modern sector. The traditional sector consists of boat building, mat-weaving, handicrafts and other cottage industries. The activities in the modern sector include fish canning, manufacture of garments, construction of fiberglass, boats and bottling of aerated water.

5. Nepal

Nepal has a population of about 23.9 million made up of over 61 ethnic group's living in different regions speaking 70 languages and dialects. Nepali is the national language. Hinduism is the official religion of Nepal and Hindus constitute over 85 per cent of the population. Buddhists account for 7.8 per cent of the population. A small minority of Nepalese adheres to Islam and Christianity. Nepal is a democratic country since 2008.

The mainstay of Nepalese economy is agriculture, which account for 41 per cent of GDP with more than 80 per cent of the people dependent on it. Manufacturing, trade and tourism follow farming as the main economic activities of the country.

6. Pakistan

Pakistan lies in the north-west of Indian subcontinent. Pakistan is divided into four provinces: Sindh, Baluchistan, Punjab and the North-West Frontier Province. Islamabad is the capital of the country. The total area of Pakistan is 796.095 sq. km and the population is around

145.96 million. The national language is Urdu while the official language is English. The leading religion of Pakistan is Islam having 95 per cent Muslim population. Other important religions are Hinduism, Christianity; smaller religious groups of Sikh, Parsi and Buddhist also exist. Pakistan has a federal structure. Agriculture and related activities engage 46.1 per cent of the workforce and provide 25 per cent of GDP. The current growth rate of GDP is 3.6 per cent. The main import includes machinery, electrical equipment and petroleum products. The major exports are cotton textiles, rice, carpets, leather, handicraft, fish and fruit.

7. Sri Lanka

Sri Lanka means 'resplendent' (from the Pali "alankara"). The population of Sri Lanka is 18.77 million. The country is multi ethnic nation. The Singhalese of Indo-Aryan origin, comprise 74 per cent of the population and the others are Sri Lankan Tamil, Indian Tamils, and the Moors, Buddhists, Hindus, Christians and Muslims. 90 per cent of the economy of the country at independence depended on the export of the three plantation crops of tea, rubber and coconut. Since the late 1970s, the economy has been progressively liberalised. Industrial policy has shifted from import substitution to export oriented production. The service centre now account for 52 per cent in the sectoral composition of the GDP; the manufacturing sector for 16.5 per cent, agriculture for 21.1 per cent, constructions for 7.6 per cent and mining for 1.9 per cent. Colombo is the largest Tea Auction centre in the world.

Other exports include textiles and garments, coconut products, petroleum byproducts. Major imports include rice, wheat, sugar, fertiliser, crude oil equipment and machinery.[13]

8. Afghanistan

Afghanistan is a mountainous land-locked country located in Central Asia. The exact population of Afghanistan is unknown; however it is estimated to be somewhere close to 32 million. There are four major ethnic groups, Pashtoons, Tajiks, Hazaras and Uzbeks. While the majority of Afghans about 99 per cent belongs to the Islamic faith, there are also small pockets of Sikhs, Hindus and even some Jews. The capital of Afghanistan is Kabul and official languages of the country are Pashto and Dari.

Today Afghanistan is on a road to recovery, after decades of war the economy is still in ruins and its environment is in a state of crisis. Hamid Karzai is the present interim president of Afghanistan.[14]

On the other hand, the United States of America and South Korea made formal requests to be granted observer status. The European Union has also indicated interest in being given observer status in July, 2006 on

Table 3.2. Comparative Data of South Asia, (2007-08), with Other Regions

Regions	*GDP(percapita current international 1)*	*Literacy 1*	*Life expectancy 1*	*(Millions) 2 Population*	*(Per 100 people) 2 Internet users*
East Asia and Pacific	4657	89.7	71.2	1,522	6.6
High income OECD	35843	99.3	78.9	1,912	14.6
South Asia	2411	52.1	63.4	1007	48.3
Sub Saharan Africa	1923	53.8	50.8	800	4.4

Source : *(i)* http://data world bank.org/data-catalog, accessed on March 12, 2010.

(ii) World Development indicators database, World Bank, April 20, 2009.

Agreement for establishment of SAARC Arbitration Council -:

Countries	*GDP I Per Capita*	*Poverty ii*	*HDI ii Rank*	*GDI I Rank*	*Life ii expectancy*	*Literacy ii Rank (out of 180)*	*Internet i users*	*Import i*	*Export i*	*Population iv*
Afghanistan	1,054	53.0	181	154	43.58	28.00	176	1.9		33,609,937
Bangladesh	1,241	49.6	146	123	65.67	53.48	147	0.3	23.0	162,221000
Bhutan	4,837	26.2	132	113	65.67	52.81		5.9	55.0	697,000
India	2,753	41.6	134	114	63.35	66.02	85	7.2	24.0	1,210,193,422
Maldives	5,196	1.0	95	77	71.07	97.05		16.3	110.0	396,334
Nepal	1,049	55.1	144	119	66.31	56.50	121	1.4	33.0	29,331,000
Pakistan	2,496	22.6	141	124	66.20	54.15	134	10.8	20.0	170,608,00
Sri Lanka	4,243	14.0	102	83	73.97	90.81	92	3.9	46.0	20,238,000

Source :

(i) *Human Development Report (2007-09).*

(ii) *Gray, George and mark purser, 2010. Human Development trends since 1970.*

(iii) *Corruption perception index. 2008. Transparency International.*

(iv) *Wikipedia-South Asian Association for regional Cooperation).*

2 August 2006, the foreign ministers of the SAARC countries agreed in principle to grant observer status to US, South Korea and European Union. In 2008, Iran had also requested observer status followed by Mauritius.

The People's Republic of China and Japan has shown its interest in joining SAARC. Indonesia also intends to become an observer as well, and is supported by Sri Lanka. Russia is also supported by India to become an observer. Myanmar has expressed an interest in joining as a full member, even though it is already a member of the ASEAN. South Africa has also participated in its meetings as well.[15]

In order to analyse the present condition of South Asia, the comparative data's given below are revealing the socio-economic condition of South Asia with other regions and among themselves.

Agreements Convention and Declaration of SAARC Summits

SAARC member countries motivated by the commitment to promote regional cooperation for the benefit of their people, in a spirit of mutual accommodation, with full respect for the principles of sovereign equality, independence and territorial integrity of all states have signed various agreements and conventions and have issued declaration during its summits.

SAARC AGREEMENTS

This agreement was signed on 13 November, 2005 at Dhaka. According to agreements there shall be a body known as SAARC Arbitration council whose objective will be to provide a legal framework within the region for fair and efficient settlement through conciliation and arbitration of commercial, investment and such other disputes, to promote the growth and effective functioning of national arbitration institution within the region, to provide facilities, fair, inexpensive and expeditions arbitration in the region, to promote international conciliation and arbitration in the region, to render assistance in the conduct of *adhoc* arbitration proceedings and to maintain registers/panels of expert witnesses and suitably qualified persons to act as arbitrators as and when required.

Agreement on South Asian Free Trade Area (SAFTA)

An agreement SAARC preferential trading agreement (SAPTA) was signed in Dhaka on the 11th of April, 1973 provides for the adoption of various instruments of trade liberalisation on a preferential basis.

Another agreement South Asian Free Trade Area (SAFTA) was also signed on 1 January 2006. This agreement supercedes the agreement on SAARC preferential trading agreement (SAPTA).

The main objective of this agreement are to promote and enhance mutual trade and economic barriers to trade in and facilitating the cross-border movement of goods between the territories of the contracting states; by promoting conditions of fair competition in the free trade area and ensuring equitable benefits to all contracting states taking into account their respective levels and pattern of economic development; by creating effective mechanism for the implement action and application of this agreement, for its joint administration and for the resolution of disputes and for establishing a framework for further regional cooperation to expand and enhance the mutual benefits of this agreement.

SAFTA shall be governed in accordance with the following principles :

(a) SAFTA will be governed by the provisions of this agreement and also by the rules, regulations, decisions, understandings and protocols to be agreed upon within its framework by the contracting states.

(b) The Contracting States affirm their existing rights and obligations with respect to each other under World Trade Organisation and other Treaties/Agreements to which such Contracting States are signatories.

(c) It shall be based on the principles of reciprocity and mutuality of advantages in such a way as to benefit equitably all Contracting States, taking into account their respective levels of economic and industrial development, the pattern of their external trade and tariff policies and systems.

(d) It shall involve the free movement of goods, between countries through the elimination of tariffs and non-tariff restrictions on the movement of goods.

(e) SAFTA shall entail adoption of trade facilitation and other measures and the progressive harmonisation of legislations by the contracting states in the relevant areas.

(f) The special needs of the least developed contracting states shall be clearly recognised by adopting concrete preferential measures in their favour on a non-reciprocal basis.

SAARC LIMITED MULTILATERAL AGREEMENT ON AVOIDANCE OF DOUBLE TAXATION AND MUTUAL ADMINISTRATIVE ASSISTANCE IN TAX MATTERS

An Agreement on Avoidance of Double Taxation and Mutual Administrative Assistance in tax matters with a view to promoting economic cooperation amongst the SAARC member states was signed on 12 November 2005 at Dhaka, Bangladesh.

SAARC Agreement on Mutual Administrative Assistance in Custom Matters

The South Asian Free Trade Area (SAFTA) came into effect on 1 January 2006 and it convinced that closer cooperation amongst their customs administrations will facilitate intra-regional trade. There is the need for regional cooperation in matters related to the application and enforcement of their customs, laws and the importance of accurate assessment of customs duties and other taxes for proper enforcement by customs administrations of prohibitions, restrictions and measures of control in respect of specific goods shall by consider.

To serve this purpose an agreement on mutual administrative assistance in customs matters was signed by SAARC member nation on 13 November, 2005 at Dhaka, Bangladesh.

The main objectives of the agreement are

1. "Custom administration" means the customs authority and any other authority of a contracting state authorised under national law and designated by that contracting state to apply any provision of this agreement.
2. "Customs law" shall mean any legal administrative provisions applicable or enforceable by the customs administration of a contracting state in connection with the importation, exportations, trans-shipment, transit and storage and movement of goods, including legal and administrative provisions relating to measures of prohibition, restriction and control.
3. "Custom" offence shall mean any breach or attempted breach of customs law.
4. "Person" shall mean both natural and legal persons.
5. "Personal data" shall mean any data concerning an identified or identifiable natural person.
6. "Information" shall mean any data, whether or not processed or analysed and documents, reports and other communication in any format, including electronic or certified or authenticated copies.
7. "Intelligence" shall mean information which has been processed or analysed to provide an indication relevant to a customs offence.
8. "Requesting Administration" shall mean the custom's administration which requests assistance.
9. "Requested Administration" shall mean the customs administration from which assistance is requested.
10. "Official" shall mean any customs officer or other government functionary designated by a custom administration.

Under Article (19) of this agreement it shall be applicable to the customs territories of the contracting states as defined in their national legal and administrative provisions.

Agreement on the Establishment of South Asian Regional Standards Organisation, (SARSO)

With the aim to develop harmonised standards for the region to facilitate intra-regional trade and to have access in the global market an agreement on the establishment of South Asian Regional Standards

Organisation (SARSO) was signed on 3rd August, 2008 at Colombo, Sri Lanka.

SAARC Standard

Standard that is developed or adopted by SARSO and made available to the SAARC member states.

Objectives and Functions of this Agreement

1. To promote and undertake harmonisation of national standards of the SAARC member states with a view to removing the technical barriers to trade and facilitate flow of goods and services in the region.
2. To develop SAARC standards on the products of regional/sub-regional interest.
3. To encourage the use of international standards published by international organisation such as ISO, IEC, etc.; by way of adoption.
4. To encourage exchange of information and expertise among the National Standards bodies of the member states in the fields of standardisation and Conformity Assessment.
5. To facilitate capacity building among the member state by way of training, workshops, seminars etc.
6. To act as source of information for the member states on standards, regulation and conformity assessment.
7. To present the common interests of the member states in the various international standardisation organisations.
8. To establish mutually beneficial corporation with the relevant international and regional organisations as per relevant SAARC guidelines.
9. To promote Mutual Recognition Arrangement (MRA) on conformity assessment procedures among the member states.
10. To encourage the sharing of facilities relating to conformity assessment procedures.
11. To explore the possibility of having a common mark of conformity.
12. The organisation shall have the powers necessary to enable it to carry out its objectives and functions.

Charter of the SAARC Development Fund (SDF)

With the need for promoting the welfare of the people of the region, the need for creating a sound, adequate and predictable finding mechanism for SAARC to facilitate undertaking sub-regional and regional programmers and projects and to resolve the economic, social and technical collaboration for promoting and strengthening collective self-reliance, the establishment of a SAARC development fund was felt, that would help serve these ends and would constitute a new and unique South Asian character.

An agreement on SAARC development fund was signed on 3rd August 2008, at Colombo, Sri Lanka.

To implement its objectives the fund shall have the following functions: (Article II)

(i) To identify, study prospect and approve projects.
(ii) Finance approved projects eight SAARC member states.
(iii) To leverage funding, arrange and mobilise financing and/or co-financing projects.
(iv) To provide grants for projects of strategic importance to SAARC
(v) To provide financial and technical assistance.
(vi) The management of the fund.

Under Article (IV) of an agreement the utilisations of the fund monies shall be for projects emanating from the following windows

(i) Social Windows.
(ii) Economic Window.
(iii) Infrastructure Window

The social window shall primarily fund projects on poverty alleviation, social development focusing on education; health, human resources development support to vulnerable /disadvantaged segments of the society; funding needs of communities micro enterprises, rural infrastructure development.

The economic window shall primarily extend funding to non–infrastructural projects related to trade and industrial development, agriculture, service sector, science and technology and in other non-infrastructural areas.

The infrastructure window shall primarily be utilised to fund projects in areas such as energy, power, transportations, telecommunications, environment, tourism and other infrastructure areas.

The economic windows should be utilised for supporting any other projects which are not covered explicitly under the social and the infrastructure window.

Agreement on Establishing the SAARC Food Bank

The importance of regional and sub-regional collective self-reliance with respect to food security as a means of combating the adverse effect of natural and man-made calamities was recognised by SAARC member countries and for this purpose an agreement for the establishment of a regional food reserve by member countries based on the principle of collective self-reliance that would improve their food security was signed on 3 April, 2007 at New Delhi, India.

The objectives of an agreement shall be

(a) To act as a regional food security reserve for the SAARC member countries during normal time, food shortages and emergencies.

(b) To provide regional support to national food security efforts; to foster inter-country partnerships and regional integration, and solve regional food shortages through collective action.[16]

CONVENTIONS

1. SAARC Regional Convention on Suppression of Terrorism and its Additional Protocol

SAARC member states being aware of the danger posed by the spread of terrorism and its harmful effect on peace, cooperation, friendship and good neighbourly relations and which could also jeopardise the sovereignty and territorial integrity of states it became necessary to take effective measures to ensure that perpetrators of terrorist acts do not escape prosecution and punishment by providing their extradition and prosecution.

For this purpose a declaration was recalled at Bangalore summit on 17 November 1986 in which the heads of state or government of SAARC agreed that cooperation among SAARC states was vital if terrorism should be prevented and eliminated from the region; unequivocally condemned all acts, methods and practices of terrorism as criminal and deplored their impact on life and property, socio-economic development, political stability and regional and international peace and cooperation.

This convention was signed on 4 November 1987 at Kathmandu, Nepal known as SAARC regional convention on suppression of terrorism.

During the twelfth SAARC Summit in Islamabad on 4-6 January 2004 the council of ministers signed the additional protocol to the SAARC Regional Convention on Suppression of Terrorism. The purpose of this additional protocol was to strengthen the SAARC Regional Convention on Suppression of Terrorism, particularly by criminalising the provision, collection or acquisition of funds for the purpose of committing terrorist acts and taking further measures to prevent and suppress financing of such acts.

Additional protocol to the SAARC Regional Convention on suppression of terrorism came into force on 12 January 2006. The Progress in the implementation of the SAARC Regional Conventional on Suppression of Terrorism and the Additional Protocol was taken up for discussion and member status informed the meeting on measures/actions taken by them to implement the convention and the additional protocol including enactment of enabling legislation at the national level to give effect to the provisions of this instrument.

2. SAARC Convention on Mutual Assistance in Criminal Matters

With the desire of extending to each other the widest measures of cooperation in combating crime by strengthening cooperation in the prevention, investigation and prosecution of crimes the SAARC member states recognised the importance of a convention on mutual assistance in criminal matters as an effective way of dealing with the complex aspects and serious consequences of crime in its new forms and dimensions, the SAARC Convention on Mutual assistance in criminal matters was signed on 3rd August 2008, at Colombo, Sri Lanka.

Objectives of Convention

(1) The states parties to this convention shall provide to each other the widest possible measures of mutual legal assistance in criminal matters, namely, investigations, prosecution and resulting proceedings.

(2) Mutual assistance shall be provided by the requested state party to the requesting state party in respect of offences the punishment of which at the time of the request for assistance, falls within the jurisdiction of the judicial authorities of the requesting state.

(3) Assistance may be provided without regard to whether the conduct would constitute an offence under the laws of the requested state party.

(4) Mutual assistance to be rendered by the requested state party in accordance with the present convention shall include locating and identifying persons and objects; service of judicial documents; providing information, documents and records; providing objects including lending exhibits; search and seizure; taking evidence and obtaining statements; making detained persons avoidance and obtaining statements; making detained persons available to give evidence or assist investigations; facilitating the appearance of witnesses or the assistance of persons in investigations; taking measures to locate, restrain or forfeit the proceeds and instruments of crime; taking measures to freeze and confiscate only funds or finances meant for the financing of all criminal acts in the territory of either state party; any other assistance consistent with the objectives of this convention and the laws of the requested state party.

3. SAARC Convention on Preventing and Combating Trafficking of Women and Children for Prostitution

SAARC member nations laid emphasis on the evil of trafficking in women and children for the purpose of prostitution is incompatible with the dignity and honour of human beings and is a violation of basic human rights and there's the need to strengthen cooperation in providing assistance, rehabilitation and repatriation to victims of trafficking for prostitution and for this purpose the importance was felt for establishing effective regional cooperation for investigation, detection, interdiction, prosecution and punishment of those responsible for trafficking for prostitution. Therefore, in this regard SAARC convention on preventing and combating trafficking in women and children for prostitution was signed on 5 January 2002, at Kathmandu, Nepal.

Objective of the Convention

The purpose of this convention is to promote cooperation amongst member states so that they may effectively deal with the various aspects of prevention, interdiction and suppression of trafficking in women and children; the repatriation and rehabilitation of victims of trafficking and prevent the use of women and children in international prostitution networks, particularly when the countries of the SAARC region are the countries of origin, transit and destination.

4. SAARC Convention on Regional Arrangements for the Promotion of Child Welfare in South Asia

A quarter of the world's children live in South Asia and many of them require assistance and protection to secure and fully enjoy their rights, and to develop to their full potential and lead a responsible life in a family and society. With recognising the efforts of SAARC towards building a regional consensus on priorities, strategies and approaches to meet the changing needs of children and bearing in the mind that the development of the full potential of the South Asian child is a critical concomitant to the region's collective march towards solidarity, justice, peace and human progress. SAARC convention on regional arrangements for the promotion of child welfare in South Asia was signed on 5 January 2002 at Kathmandu, Nepal.

Objectives of the Convention

1. To unite the state parties in their determination of redeeming the promises made by them to the South Asian Child at the world summit for children and at various other national and international conferences and successive SAARC summits.
2. To work together with commitment and diligence to facilitate and help in the development and protection of the full potential of South Asian child, with understanding of the rights, duties and responsibilities.
3. To setup appropriate regional arrangements to assist the member states in facilitating, fulfilling and protecting the rights of the child, taking into account the changing needs of the child.

(5) SAARC Convention on Narcotic Drugs and Psychotropic Substances

SAARC convention on narcotic drugs and psychotropic substances was signed on 23rd November 1990 came into force on 15th November 1993 at Male, Maldives. Matters related to awareness generation and counselling interventions, identification, treatment and rehabilitation of drug abuse victims and training capacity building for service providers were discussed at its meetings.

Objectives of the Convention

1. The purpose of this convention is to promote cooperation among member states, so that they may address more effectively the various aspects of prevention and control of drug abuse and the suppression of illicit traffic in narcotic drugs and psychotropic substances, which are specific to the SAARC region.
2. Member states in carrying out their obligations under this convention shall take necessary measures, including legislative and administrative measures, in conformity with the fundamental provision of their respective domestic legislative system.
3. Member states shall carry out their obligations under this convention in a manner consistent with the principles of sovereign equality and territorial integrity of states and that of non-intervention in the domestic affairs of other states.
4. A member state shall not undertake in the territory of another member state, the exercise of jurisdiction and performance of functions, which are exclusively, reserved for the authorities of that other state by its domestic law.[17]

SAARC Summits Declarations

1. Declaration of the First SAARC Summit, Dhaka

The Dhaka Declaration of the first SAARC Summit of the heads of state or Government of the Member countries of South Asian Association for Regional Cooperation was issued on 8 December 1985.

The Heads of State or Government underscored the historic significance of their first ever South Asian summit meeting. They considered it to be a tangible manifestation of their determination to cooperate regionally to work together towards finding solutions towards their common problems in a spirit of friendship, trust and mutual understanding and to the creation of an order based on mutual understanding and to the creation of an order based on mutual respect, equity and shared benefits.

They reaffirmed that their fundamental goal was to accelerate the process of economic and social development in their respective countries through the optimum utilisation of their human and material resources, so as to promote welfare and prosperity of their people and to improve their quality of life.

They also reaffirmed their commitment to the UN charter of sovereign equality of states and peaceful settlement of disputes and their deep conviction in the continuing validity and relevance of the objectives of the Non-aligned movement.

They acknowledged that the countries of South Asia were faced with the formidable challenges posed by poverty, underdevelopment, low levels of production, unemployment, and pressure of population compounded by exploitation of the past and other adverse legacies. Their countries were by many common values rooted in their social, ethnic, cultural and historical traditions regional cooperation will provide a logical response to this problem.

They also laid great emphasis on the involvement of the peoples of South Asia in strengthening regional cooperation.

During first SAARC summit, the heads of state or government approved that the standing committee should setup a study group to examine the problem of terrorism and its effects on security and stability of member states of SAARC and also approved a similar exercise to be carried out with regard to the problem of drug trafficking, improvement of world trading system through GATT taking particularly into account the interest of the least developed among the developing countries.[18]

Declaration of the Second SAARC Summit, Bangalore

The Second SAARC summit was held on 17th November, 1986 at Bangalore, India.

During Second SAARC summit the heads of state or government welcomed the signing of the Memorandum of Understanding on the establishment of the SAARC secretariat by the council of ministers and their decision to locate the Secretariat in Kathmandu and appoint Ambassador Abul Ahsan of Bangladesh as the first Secretary General of SAARC. During the second SAARC summit the Heads of States or Government underlined the importance of enhancing public consciousness and building a national political consensus on the rights of the right of the children. They directed the standing committee to undertake annual reviews of the situation of children in the SAARC countries.

They identified international economic issues including enlarged concessional assistance, the doubling in three years of the financial flow for the development of developing countries, amelioration of official debts, trade liberalisation, price stabilisation, transfer of technology and special treatment for least developed SAARC countries.

They considered several new ideas for expanding and strengthening the co-operative programmes under SAARC, including :

(a) A South Asian Broadcasting Programme covering both radio and television should be launched.
(b) They laid stress on people to people contacts and concrete steps should be taken to facilitate tourism in the region, including facilities for limited convertibility of national currencies for tourists from SAARC countries.
(c) They emphasised on the importance they attach to students, scholars and researchers in their countries having ready access to reliable and up-to-date information on technical, scientific and developmental matters. They, therefore, directed that a concerted programme of exchange of scholar be formulated and action taken for an early institution of SAARC scholarship, SAARC fellowships and SAARC chairs.

They took note of the recommendations of the standing committee on the financing of the institutional costs of regional institutions.[19]

3. Declaration of the Third SAARC Summit, Kathmandu

The declaration of the third SAARC summit was issued on 4 November, 1987 at Kathmandu, Nepal. At this summit, the SAARC Regional convention on suppression of terrorism was signed and the Agreement establishing South Asian Food Reserve by the foreign ministers of the SAARC member states was also signed.

They also declared their intention to initiate the process of dealing with the causes and consequences of natural disasters and decided to setup a commission to study on natural disasters and the protection and preservation of the environment in a well-planned and comprehensive framework.

They laid great emphasis on the greater participation of the Non-Governmental Organisations (NGOs) in the process of promoting socio-economic and cultural development of South Asia. They also examine the question of the admission of new members and the grant of observer/ guest status in the association, the standing committee should also include the aspects of the establishment of relations with similar organisations.[20]

4. Declaration of the Fourth SAARC Summit, Islamabad

The declaration of the fourth SAARC summit was issued on 31 December 1988, at Islamabad, Pakistan.

During this SAARC summit the heads of state or governments were deeply shocked at the armed attack on the republic of Maldives on 3rd November 1988 aimed at destabilising the government. They strongly condemned these acts of violence which disrupted the peace and security of member state.

(1) They decided to declare 1989 as the "SAARC year against Drug Abuse" in order to focus attention on always related problems facing the region.

(2) They also launch "SAARC-2000-A Basic Needs Perspective" which calls for a perspective regional plan with specific targets was to be met with care, interest such as food, clothing, shelters, education, primary health care, population planning etc.

(3) They directed the standing committee to examine the desirability of establishing a regional body to promote culture links among member states.

(4) They expressed their satisfaction at the progress achieved in the implementation of the Integrated Programme of Action (IPA).

(5) They welcomed the establishment of the SAARC Agriculture Information Centre (SAIC) at Dhaka and expressed satisfaction at the concrete steps being taken for the implementation of the SAARC Audio-Visual Exchange (SAVE) programme, enhancing people to people contact and concrete steps taken by including regional NGOs in SAARC activities.[21]

5. Declaration of the Fifth SAARC Summit, Male

The declaration of the fifth SAARC summit was issued on 23 November, 1990, at Male, Maldives.

During this SAARC Summit the heads of state and government welcomed the signing of the SAARC Convention on Narcotic Drugs and Psychotropic Substances. They decided to launch the special SAARC Travel Document within the region.

1. They noted the proposal for the establishment of a SAARC regional fund and directed the standing committee to submit its recommendations on the proposal for consideration at the next session of the council of ministers.
2. They expressed satisfaction that the work was well under way for the setting up of a nucleus centre for human resource development in Pakistan. They directed that the theme of "**poverty alleviation**" strategies should be discussed in depth by planners for formulating suitable recommendations, in order to maintain focus on the problems of the **girl child** the year 1991-2000 AD would be observed as the "**SAARC Decade of the Girl Child**".
3. They decided that the "SAARC **tuberculosis centre"** and the "**SAARC documentation centre"** would be setup in Nepal and India respectively.[22]

6. Declaration of the Sixth SAARC Summit, Colombo

The declaration of the Sixth SAARC Summit was issued on 21st December 1991, at Colombo, Sri Lanka.

The main emphasis of the sixth SAARC summit was on the need for vigorously promoting south-south economic cooperation to offset the negative consequences of the international economic developments.

The heads of state or government reemphasised that regional self-reliance should be resolutely promoted through closer cooperation among countries of the association.

They noted the progress made by the Integrated Programme of Action (IPA) in expanding to cover a member of sectors crucial for the economic and social progress of the peoples of South Asia. They were of the view that the challenge facing the IPA was to achieve its identified targets within specific time periods. They accorded the highest priority to the alleviation of poverty in all South Asian countries.

During the sixth SAARC Summit the heads of state or government approved that the Inter Governmental Group (IGG) setup the recommendation of the committee on economic cooperation should formulate and seek agreement on an institutional framework under which specific measures for trade liberalisation among SAARC member state could be furthered.

They expressed their satisfaction at the completion of regional study on the causes and consequences of natural disasters and the protection and preservation of environment.

They also welcomed the recommendation on the establishment of a shelter information network to be called "SHELTERNET".

7. Declaration of the Seventh SAARC Summit, Dhaka

SAARC issued its declaration of the seventh summit on 11 April 1993 at Dhaka, Bangladesh.

During this summit the heads of state welcomed the recent specific steps taken to consolidate and further streamline IPA-related SAARC activities. They also stressed the need for a progressive movement towards undertaking more well-defined target oriented and time bound projects and programmes to ensure tangible benefits for the people of South Asia.

They welcomed the finalisation of the framework agreement on SAARC preferential trading agreement (SAPTA). They expressed their deep satisfaction over the signing of the framework agreement and they also welcomed the offer of the Maldives to host a ministerial conference on youth in South Asia in 1994 to address the problems of the youth and focus broad theme of youth and development. They also agreed to designate 1994 as the "SAARC year of the youth".

They recalled their decision at the Male summit to observe 1993 as the "SARRC year of disabled persons", adopted the regional plan of action for the disabled persons they urged member states to take concrete steps to implement the plan. They also recalled that in pursuance of their collective will expressed in the Male summit to observe the 1990s as the "SAARC Decade of the girl child", member states had undertaken to formulate national plans of action for the condition of the girl child giving priority to her survival, protection and development they expressed satisfaction that some member states had already completed this task and others were expected to do so soon.

They decided that an expert group of the member states will examine the various requests for observer status at SAARC/SAARC meeting in all its aspects.

At the end of this summit the heads of state or government expressed their deep satisfaction over the positive outcome of this summit and expressed their conviction that this summit would greatly contribute towards strengthening the policies and cooperative actions of the member states in response to the challenges of the 1990s and beyond in areas where SAARC has a distinct contribution to make.

8. Declaration of the Eighth SAARC Summit, New Delhi

The SAARC declaration of the eight summits was issued on 4 May 1995 at New Delhi.

The heads of state or government expressed their satisfaction on the achievements of the first decade of the SAARC and resolved to celebrate its completion of the first decade both in the individual member states and collectively. They endorsed the proposal of the council of ministers to convene a commemorative session of the council on the theme "**SAARC-vision for the second decade**" to identify the areas on which SAARC should focus in its second decade.

They also decided to declare 1995 as the "SAARC year of poverty eradication" Recognising that poverty is a complex multidimensional problem with origins in both national and international domains, country-specific programme to tackle poverty and international efforts supporting national efforts and the parallel process of creating a supportive international environment conducive to economic growth and social development of developing countries are crucial for a solution of this problem.

They noted with satisfaction that subsequent to the signing of the framework agreement on SAARC preferential trading arrangement (SAPTA) during their seventh summit in Dhaka in April 1993, the first round of trade negotiations to exchange trade concession among member states has been completed. The leaders reiterated their firm belief that the operationalisation of SAPTA will herald the beginning of a new and significant process of Regional Cooperation and would lend strength to SAARC as an institution for promoting the welfare of the people of South Asia.

The Leaders also welcomed the establishment of the SAARC documentation centre (SDC) at New Delhi in May 1994 and the SAARC meteorological research centre (SMRC) at Dhaka in January this year. They decided to observe 1996 as the "SAARC year of literacy".

The leaders noted that SAARC law had been accorded recognition by SAARC. They also noted with satisfaction that the SAARC chamber of commerce and industry (SCCI) has been functioning satisfactorily.

They expressed satisfaction that the SAARC visa exemption scheme is being implemented smoothly and has enhanced the scope of people contacts.

At last they endorsed the establishment of a three window South Asian development fund with the merger of SAARC fund for regional projects and the SAARC regional fund and a third window for social development and infrastructure development.

9. Declaration of the Ninth SAARC Summit, Male

The ninth declaration of SAARC summit was issued on 14 May 1997, at Male.

During the summit the head of state or government welcomed the holding of the commemorative session of the council of ministers in New Delhi in December 1995 to mark the first decade, on the theme "SAARC-vision for the second decade". They observed that over the past decade SAARC has matured as an institution and scope and volume of cooperative activities have expanded.

They expressed satisfaction at the conclusion of the two rounds of trade negotiations under SAPTA, and welcome the decision launch the third round of trade negotiations.

They also welcome the decision of the council of minister to establish a Human Resource Development Centre in Pakistan.

The leaders decided that the feasibility of establishing a Regional Convention on Combating the crime of trafficking in women and children for prostitution be examined by the relevant technical committee.

The heads of state or government welcomed the decision to designate seventh December, 1997 and Eighteenth January, 1998 as "SAARC polio immunisation Days". They expressed the need to formulate a convention on Regional Arrangements on the promotion of child welfare in South Asia in launching the SAARC Decade of the rights of the child from the year 2001 AD to 2010 AD.

They fully endorsed the New Delhi Declaration issued at the end of the SAARC Ministerial conference on Environment held from 2-3 April 1997. Recognising that terrorism and drug trafficking pose a serious threat to security and stability of member states they emphasised the urgent need to complete enabling legislation in order to implement the SAARC

Regional Convention on Suppression of Terrorism and on Narcotic Drugs and Psychotropic Substances. While expressing satisfaction that the South Asian Development Fund (SADF) had been established in June 1996, they recognised the need to make the fund operational at the earliest.

10. Declaration of the Tenth SAARC Summit Colombo

SAARC issued declaration of the tenth summit on 31 July 1998, at Colombo, Sri Lanka.

In tenth SAARC summit the heads of state or government continued their review of the nature, extent and effectiveness of the cooperative activities of SAARC. They considered the report and recommendations of the group of eminent persons mandated by the Ninth Summit in Male to undertake a comprehensive appraisal of SAARC and to develop an agenda for 2000 and beyond.

They noted that a document entitled "Road Map to SAFTA" was presented by the President of the SAARC Chamber of Commerce and Industry (SCCI) to the chairperson of the twentieth session of the council of ministers.

They welcomed the results of the first conference of SAARC Communication Ministers held in Colombo in May, 1998. They noted that technological advances were making telecommunications an important medium for socio-economic development and developing commercial and business relations as well as promotion of people to people contact.

They also condemned the exploitation of children by terrorist groups in hostilities and called for special measures for the psychological, physical and social rehabilitation of child victims. They noted the initiatives taken by Maldives in pursuance of their directive at the ninth SAARC summit in drafting the convention on Regional Arrangements for the promotion of the child welfare in South Asia.[23]

11. Declaration of the Eleventh SAARC Summit, Kathmandu

The heads of state and government of SAARC countries met at the eleventh summit meeting of the South Asian Association for Regional Cooperation in Kathmandu, Nepal from 4 to 6 January, 2002.

At the eleventh summit they laid stress on the equitable sharing of the benefits of regional cooperation is essential to achieve and maintain a minimum acceptable level of economic and social development in each member state.

They recognised the importance of achieving a free trade area and reaffirmed that the treaty regime for creating a free trade area must incorporate binding timeframes for freeing trade, measure to facilitate trade and provisions to ensure and equitable distribution of benefits of trade to all states, especially for small and least developed countries, including mechanisms for compensation of revenue loss.

Recognising the need to move quickly towards a South Asian free trade area the heads of states or Government directed the council of ministers to finalise the text of the draft treaty framework by the end of 2002. They also directed that in moving toward the goal of SAFTA, the member states expedite action to remove tariff and non-tariff barriers and structural impediments to free trade.

They expressed their firm resolve to combat the problem of poverty with a new sense of urgency by actively promoting the synergetic partnership among national governments, international agencies, the private sector and the civil society.

In order to ensure social stability and to protect the vulnerable section of population from the adverse impact of globalisation and liberalisations they stressed the need to enhanced cooperation to create and maintain appropriate safety nets.

They decided to the mandate the meeting of minister of cultural affairs in Sri Lanka to finalise the details relating to the establishment of the SAARC Cultural Centre including its financing and to submit its report to the next session of the council of ministers.

Reaffirming their commitment to the Colombo Plan of Action and the Rawalpindi Declaration and recalling the declaration of 2002 to 2010 as the SAARC Decade of the Right of the child, they reaffirmed their conviction that the children in South Asia deserve urgent and focused attention to enhance the long-term and overall progress of the countries of the region.

For an early realisation of a rule-based and non-discrimination world trade region, they appreciated the positive element of the fourth WTO ministerial conference held in Doha and called upon the development countries to fulfill their commitment to address the particular concerns and needs of the development and the least development countries.

They also emphasized the need for the urgent conclusion of a comprehensive convention on combating International Terrorism. They endorsed the report of the council of ministers on the implementation of the recommendations of the group of eminent persons report, and directed the Council of Ministers to undertake a review of progress in their regard.

They also directed the council of ministers to explore the possibility of establishing a SAARC Seed Security Reserve to strengthen cooperation in the field of agriculture and to protect intellectual property right of the seed of the reserve.[24]

12. Declaration of the Twelfth SAARC Summit, Islamabad

All the SAARC member states met at the Twelfth Summit meeting of the South Asian Association for Regional Corporation in Islamabad, Pakistan, on 4-6 January 2004.

At the twelfth SAARC Summit the heads of state or government prioritise that attention should also be given to the need for harmonisation of standards simplification of custom procedures as well as cooperation among the central banks.

They reconstituted Independent South Asian Commission for Poverty Alleviation (ISACPA) and advocated it the role to prepare and submit to the next SAARC summit a comprehensive and realistic blueprint setting out SAARC development goals for the next five years in the areas of poverty alleviation, education, health and environment giving due regard among others to the suggestions made in the ISACPA report.

They expressed the need for easy and affordable health care prevention and treatment of HIV/AIDS tuberculosis and other serious communicable diseases. The year 2004 was declared as the "SAARC Awareness Year".

They welcome the early establishment of the coastal zone management centre in the Maldives. They reaffirmed the need to undertake and reinforce regional cooperation in the conservation of our water resources, environment pollutions prevention and control as well as preparedness to deal with natural calamities.[25]

13. Declaration of Thirteenth SAARC Summit, Dhaka

The heads of state or government issued a declaration of thirteenth SAARC Summit on 12-13 November 2005, in Dhaka, Bangladesh.

During the thirteenth SAARC summit they decided to declare the decade of 2006-2015 as the SARRC Decade of poverty alleviation. During the decade they endeavour both at the national and regional level which will continue to be made with a sense of commitment and urgency to free South Asia from poverty. Underlining the need for an exclusive forum for focused and comprehensive examination of poverty related issues they decided to replace the tier their mechanism on poverty alleviation by a two tier one, comprising the ministers and the secretaries dealing with poverty alleviation at the national level.

They decided to establish a SAARC Poverty Alleviation Fund (SPAF). They agreed that the SPAF shall function within the SADF to be reconstituted as SAARC development fund (SDF) to serve as the umbrella financial institution for all SAARC projects and programmes and comprise three windows namely, social window, infrastructure window and economic window with a permanent secretariat.

They stressed the importance of the entry into force SAFTA agreement on the scheduled date on 1st January 2006. The launching of SAFTA would mark an important milestone on the road to a South Asian Economic Union.

They recognised the need to take the process of regional economic integration further by expanding the scope of SAFTA to include trade in services, enhanced investment and harmonised standards.

They welcomed the signing of the following agreements during thirteen SAARC summit :

(a) The agreement on Mutual Administrative Assistance in Customs Matters.

(b) The Agreement on the establishment of SAARC Arbitration Council.

(c) The limited Agreement on Avoidance of Double Taxation and Mutual Administrative assistance in tax matters. They emphasised the need for parallel initiatives for dismantling of non-tariff and para-tariff barriers. They stressed on the need for closer regional cooperation in the field of Information and Communication Technologies (ICT), including telecommunications.

They welcomed the joint statement of the first SAARC energy ministers meeting in October 2005 in Islamabad. They agreed to the recommendation to establish the SAARC Energy Centre in Islamabad, to promote development of energy resource.

They called upon the member state to expeditiously complete the process of preparing their national strategy and plan of action. They also emphasised that national implementation efforts should be completed by regional projects and programmes. In this context, they directed that regional projects, particularly in health and poverty alleviation should be initiated.

They directed that a SAARC plan of action for science ICT and Technology be elaborated for consideration during a meeting of SAARC Science, ICT and Technology Ministers to be convened as soon as possible. They noted the offer of India to establish a South Asian University and agreed to examine this matter further.

While expressing satisfaction at the progress in implementation of the SAARC Environment Action Plan, the leaders welcomed the decision of the council of minister to establish a SAARC Forestry Centre in Bhutan. They also welcomed the declaration of the special session of the SAARC environment minister in Male in June 2005 convened in the wake of the tsunami catastrophe. They endorsed the recommendation for elaboration of regional programmes and project for early warning, preparedness and management of tsunami and other natural disasters.

The heads of state or government underlined the need for collaborative action in the area of environment, including water conservation to promote sustainable development. They decided to proclaim the year 2007 as the "Year of Green South Asia" devoted to a region - wide afforestation campaign. They decided their ministers for tourism to meet at an early date and elaborate a plan of activities to be undertaken during the year 2006.

They also emphasised the importance of pursuing effectively the global objectives of universal disarmament and preventing the proliferation of weapons of mass destruction.

During this SAARC summit it was also marked by the welcoming the request by the Islamic Republic of Afghanistan for membership and invited Afghanistan as a member; subject to the completion of formalities. They also welcomed and agreed in principle with the desire of the People's Republic of China and Japan to be associated as observers.

They agreed that as SAARC completed its twenty year of its existence, it was an opportune occasion to draw a roadmap for regional cooperation in South Asia for next decade.

They directed the Standing Committee to formulate its recommendations at its next special session on a vision for SAARC's Third Decade and the course of action for its realisation, to be elaborated by a high–level committee of Seniors Officials.

14. Declaration of the Fourteenth SAARC Summit

The head of state or government met at the fourteenth summit meeting of the South Asian Association for Regional Cooperation (SAARC) held in New Delhi, India on April 3-4, 2007 to issue its declaration.

During this summit they welcome the entry of the Islamic Republic of Afghanistan into SAARC. This was a historic moment as Afghanistan assumed its rightful place as a valued member of the SAARC fraternity.

They recognised the full benefit of an integrated multimodal transport system in the region, for this purpose they called for an extension of the SAARC Regional Multimodal Transport Study (SRMTS) to include Afghanistan as well and to identify and develop sub-regional and regional project. They noted the offer of India to hold the meeting of SAARC Ministers of Transport in New Delhi in 2007. They also directed that pilot project for improving connectivity be identified and implemented through mutual consulting among the member states.

They emphasised that in its third decade of existence, there was an urgent need to move SAARC from declaratory to implementation phase. They directed that the focus of SAARC should be on implementing collaborative project that are concrete and effective. They directed that the SDF should be made operational at the earliest. They agreed that the resources for SDF would be mobilised both from within and outside the region.

They also acknowledged the need of expediting development of conventional sources of energy in a sustainable manner and for strengthening renewable energy development such as in hydropower, bio-fuel, and solar wind.

They expressed satisfaction at the launching of 2007 as the "Year of Green South Asia". They reiterated that collaboration in addressing the problem of arsenic contamination of ground water; desertification and melting of glaciers and assistance to affected people should be deepened.

They also noted with satisfaction timely ratification of SAFTA Agreement by all member countries. They stressed the need for ensuring effective market access thorough smooth implementation of trade liberalisation programme and directed the SAFTA bodies to review the progress on a regular basis.

They appreciated the establishment of the SAARC standard Coordination Board that would function as a precursor to the SAARC Regional Standards Body.

They decided to establish the South Asian University in India and welcomed the signing of the Intergovernmental Agreement establishing the university.

Acknowledging that countries of South Asia face challenges of food insecurity and malnutrition. In order to manage emergencies caused by natural and man-made calamities and food shortages, they welcomed the signing of the intergovernmental agreement establishing the SAARC food bank with the participation of all the SAARC countries.

They welcomed the People's Republic of China, Japan, European-Union, Republic of Korea, United States of America, and Islamic Republic of Iran to be associated as observers to SAARC.

15. Declaration of Fifteenth SAARC Summit, Colombo

The declaration of fifteenth SARRC Summit was issued on 2-3 August 2008, at Colombo, Sri Lanka. The main objective of this Summit was the **"partnership for growth for our people".**

The heads of state or government recognised the importance of connectivity for realising the objectives of SAARC. They accordingly directed the SAARC mechanisms to continue to embody in their programmes and project a strong focus on better connectivity not only within South Asia but also between the region and the rest of the world.

The leaders expressed satisfaction at the adoption of SAARC action plan and Dhaka declaration on climate change by the SAARC Environment ministers at SAARC ministerial meeting on climate change held at Dhaka on 3 July 2008. They also expressed satisfaction at the adoption at a SAARC declaration on climate change for the United Nations framework convention on climate change (UNFCCC) by the twenty-ninth session of the council of ministers.

They expressed satisfaction at the signing of the charter of the SAARC Development Fund (SDF) and finalisation of its bye-laws and called for an early ratification of the SDF charter. They also welcomed early operationalisation of the Fund from the available funds. They accepted with appreciation the offer of the kingdom of Bhutan to host the SAARC Development Fund Secretariat in Thimpu.

They also welcomed the signing of the text of the Agreement on the Establishment of the South Asia Regional Standards Organisation. At this summit Afghanistan signed the Protocol for Accession to SAFTA.

The Heads of state or Government welcomed the substantial progress made in the establishment of the South Asian University in New Delhi and directed that the University should begin its session from 2010.

At the end of this summit they welcomed Australia and Myanmar to be associated as Observer to SAARC.

16. Declaration of the Sixteenth SAARC Summit, Thimpu

The declaration of 16th SAARC summit was issued on 28-29 April 2010 at Thimpu, Bhutan. The main objective of this summit was "Towards a Green and Happy South Asia". It was a **'silver jubilee year' of SAARC**.

In this summit the leaders expressed satisfaction that SAARC had achieved a number of important milestones with the completion of twenty five years of its establishment. The leaders underscored the relevance and importance of the association in providing a platform for regional cooperation to accomplish the charter objectives. They resolved that the silver jubilee year should be commemorated by making SAARC truly action oriented by fulfilling commitments implementing declarations and decision and operationalising instruments and living up to the hopes and aspirations of one-fifth of humanity. The leaders, while appreciating that all the member states had evolved into multiparty democracies underlined the challenges faced by them in ensuring effective, efficient, transparent and accountable government. They welcomed the announcement by the government of Maldives to nominate a Woman Secretary General as the tenth Secretary General of SAARC.

They emphasised the need to realise the full potential through reduction of the size of the sensitive lists acceleration of trade facilitation measures and removal of non-tariff, para-tariff and other barriers. They directed the SAFTA ministerial council to work in earnest in these areas in a time bound manner.

The leaders emphasised the need to strengthen the role of private sector in regional initiatives through appropriate mechanisms including through public-private partnership as well as the need for greater intra SAARC investment promotion efforts.

They called for collaborative efforts to achieve greater intra-regional connectivity and endorsed the recommendations to declare 2010-2020 as the "decade of the Intra regional connectivity in SAARC".

They also agreed that an action plan on energy conservation would be prepared by SAARC Energy Centre (SEC) Islamabad with inputs from the member states and submit to the inter-governmental mechanism for consideration.

They noted the proposal from India for preparing a roadmap for developing a SAARC market for electricity (SAME) on a regional basis as SAARC is considering electricity trading supported by enabling markets in the member states.[26]

The leaders welcomed the offer of the government of Maldives to host the seventeenth summit of the heads of the states or government of the South Asian Association for Regional Cooperation (SAARC) in 2011, 10-11 November.

Maldives has declared "building bridges" will be the theme of this summit.

"Building bridges" will be the both in terms of physical connectivity and figurative political dialogue.

The subjects as possible themes for the seventeenth summit maybe :

1. Women as catalysts for change.
2. Women as agents of development.
3. Women as partners for development.

The five sub-themes would be

1. Maternal health
2. Violence against women
3. Economic and political empowerment
4. HIV/AIDS/HPV and other STDs.
5. Cervical cancer for consideration of the esteemed government.

Conclusion

The heads of state or government of South Asian countries recognised the importance of connectivity in fulfilling the objectives. It was vital to first have better connectively with in South Asia and then with the rest of the world. They agreed to improve intra-regional connectivity. They agreed to the vision of a South Asian community, where there will be smooth flow of goods, services, people, technologies, knowledge, capital, culture and ideas in the region.

It has been noted that SAARC has evolved in a positive direction during the first two decades of its existence and that its agenda encompassed concert and areas vital for the fulfillment of the charter objectives of promoting the welfare of the peoples of the South Asia, accelerating economic growth, social progress, cultural development and strengthening collective self-reliance among the countries of the South Asia. The leaders have reiterated their commitment to make the SAARC an effective instrument for cooperation, which will visibly improve the quality of life of millions in South Asia.

References

1. Muni S.D., South Asian Journal, South Asia as a region. Vol.1, Aug–Sep. 2003.
2. Singh Gopal- South Asia: Democracy, Discontent Societal Conflicts, Published by Anamika Publishers and Distributors -1998, Delhi.
3. Sareen T.R. – Socio-Economics and Political Development in South Asia, Vol. 1, Social Development in South Asia, Isha Books-2004, p. 56.
4. Sareen T.R. – Socio-Economics and Political Development in South Asia, Vol. 2, Social South Asia, Isha Books, 2004, p. 76.
5. Hettiarachchi Chaminda – Role of information and communication technologies in Human in South Asia, University of Moratuwa, Sri Lanka, p. 8, April, 2011.
6. Dr. Prasad Kiran – the Digital divides : Implications of ICT's for development in South Asia, papers in international and global communication. p. 12, (2008)
7. Singh Gopal - South Asia: Democracy – Discontent and Societal conflicts, contemporary Non-proliferation Regime and South Asia: A study of India's response to CTBT, Anamika Publication, Delhi-1998, p. 111.
8. Ganguly Sumeet, Counterterrorism cooperation in South Asia-history and prospects, National Bureau of Asian Research, 2009, p. 9, http://www.nbr.org
9. Hussain Akmal – A vision for South Asia, Indian Journal of Politics and International Relation, Editor- K.M. Sethi, Jan-June 2008, Vol. 1, p. 75.
10. Dr. Malhotra Nitasha, South Asia- Political and Economic Region. The Association of Geographical Studies, p. 12. (1999)
11. Mohanty, K. Sanjeev, South Asian Conflicts- the Indian Journal of Political Science –Vol. 4, The Quarterly Review, pp. 1201—1211, Oct-Dec. 09, 12-3-2011.
12. Upreti B.C.- SAARC : Contemporary concerns and the Road Ahead, South Asian Studies –Bi-annual journal- Sep. 2008, Vol. 41, 12.3.2011.
13. Goel O.P.- India and SAARC Engagements –Vol. 2, Profile of SAARC member states, Isha Books, Delhi, pp. 602—616.
14. Qazi-Abdullah-General information about Afghanistan – http://www.afghan-web.com//.
15. Wikipedia - South Asian Association for Regional Cooperation- http://www.en.wikipedia.org/wiki/south_Asian_ Associate_for_ Regional_ cooperation//
16. SAARC Report, http://www.saarc.sec.org/agreement/.
17. Report- South Asian Association for regional cooperation, http://www.saarc.sec.org/converntion /
18. Goel O.P.- India SAARC Engagements, Vol. 1, Declaration of the First SAARC Summit, Isha Books, p. 123.

19. *Ibid.*, p. 140.
20. *Ibid.*, p. 154.
21. *Ibid.*, p. 169.
22. *Ibid.*, p. 184.
23. Goel O.P., India SAARC Engagements, Vol. 3, Isha Books, Delhi, p. 273.
24. Goel O.P., India SAARC Engagements, Vol. 2, p. 303, Isha Books, Delhi.
25. *Ibid*, p. 325.
26. SAARC Summits Report- South Asian Association for Regional Cooperation – http://www.saarc.sec.org/summit/

4

Political Dimensions of SAARC

The world today is at a turning point. The change that we are undergoing is global in scope, revolutionary, fundamental and structural in content. As we have entered the twenty-first century a sense of optimism prevails for attaining peace and prosperity through effective role play of regional as well as global organisations.

Many view Asia as having a variety of characteristics in common with Europe of the nineteenth century: under developed international institutions, mixed domestic orders, rising nationalism, high but differential growth rates and bitter emotional rivalries between insecure neighbours.

The formation of the South Asian Association for Regional Cooperation (SAARC) in December 1985 was hailed as a major diplomatic breakthrough in South Asia. But during its initial phase SAARC's slow progress and modest achievements have evoked different reactions among different people. To some, SAARC is merely than a lip service to the various issues of peace and development in the region. To others, SAARC may not be a panacea to the region's problems, but its existence has certainly provide an opportunity for the policy makers, administrators and experts to meet regularly and hold informal dialogues an important bilateral and regional issues[1].

At present SAARC is in its twenty third year of formal institutional existence. This is a long period in the history of any international organisation for it to show its results. SAARC has prepared a robust intellectual base for regional cooperation and spread awareness amongst more than a billion people of South Asia about the value of regional cooperation.

The report of the Eminent Persons Group and the SAARC social charter clearly reflect the priorities and needs of SAARC. SAARC can claim considerable success in conceptual evolution and in laying down theoretical ground work, where a number of creative ideas have been formulated, articulated and endorsed.

In recent years there have been important developments both around and within the region, these include-identifying South Asia's challenges and ways to address them through cooperative regionalism be this in the field of trade and investment, in relation to poverty alleviation and food security, or even with regard to fighting terrorism that raises hope of a faster and effective role of SAARC[2] Muni S.D. and Jaithley Rajshree-SAARC: The changing dimensions, UNU-CRIS working papers-w-2008/8, Institute of South Asian Studies, Singapore, United Nations University, and CRIS.

With the dawn of the twenty first century South Asian region has undergone radical transformation. It has witnessed a strong democratisation in its nations. Most of the South Asian economies have registered impressive growth. Some of its countries have also emerged as the hub of global terrorism. The international Community has also become far more involved in South Asian affairs due to the nuclearisation of the region. SAARC has moved ahead on its economic agenda and expanded its reach not only by adding new members (Afghanistan) but also by opening itself to the participation of many other countries, including China, Iran and the US, as observers.

The Organisation has not only come to stay, but the mood among member countries is distinctly optimistic. There is a growing conviction among these countries that the benefits of weaving a closer economic community can be bolstered by the possibility of opening a second track of harmonious regional relationship, which in turn would help overcome enormous political and security problems in the region.

But there is a need to revamp SAARC and create a structure within the framework of the organisation, enabling to address political issues, which have direct bearing on the socio-economic progress of the entire region. Although SAARC has made modest achievements its expected progress has been stalled due to the absence of provisions in its character to address bilateral contentious issues, as well as the lack of political will on the part of its members to resolve such contentious issues. Although SAARC, during its summit and ministerial level meetings, provides on the sidelines the opportunities to discuss bilateral issues, there is a need to institutionalise the mechanism for discussing contentious issues in an expanded SAARC framework.

Political Conflicts and Relationship Among SAARC Nations

In several parts of the world there have been efforts to solve the developmental problems through regional organisations. In South Asia also there is now the SAARC which aims at cooperation at the levels of research and flow of information to ameliorate some of the material problem faced by the region.

The positive aspects of SAARC as reflected in its activities notwithstanding, there are nagging doubts about its viability as an effective vehicle for intraregional cooperation. These doubts emanate primarily from the fact that old suspicions and animosities among the constituent units of South Asia have shown no significant signs of abating.

On the contrary, in some respects they seem to have been exacerbated. India and Pakistan have been trading charges exacerbated. India and Pakistan have been trading charges over the question of regional security, or Sikh terrorism or Hindu-Muslim riots, India and Bangladesh have accused each other over the question of insurgencies along the borders; India and Nepal face problems over trade and transit right and cross national migrations and India and Sri Lanka have perceptional gap with regard to the Tamil ethnic question which the recent accord has probably only temporarily bridged.

SAARC suffer from a few inherent contradictions. The contradictions impede the organisation's success. Essentially there is a deep seated political conflict in South Asia. The broad diversities of the region to which these conflicts are directly and indirectly attributable should be kept in mind while analysing nature, source and expressions of this political conflict[3].

Relationship and Conflicts among SAARC Nations

The political relation among South Asian nations are interested and often convoluted. The most important feature of the several nation states that now exist in South Asia is that they are mostly new as sovereign nations but contain some of the richest histories in the world. Regardless of their shared history, the relationship between Pakistan and India is forever plagued since the 1947 partition. Political issues have not subsided in recent years as military build-ups near their shared border have become a common event.

However in regard to political relationship among South Asian nations, South Asia is a conflict prone region subject to continuous political tensions. India, by far the largest country and geographically centrally located has developed differences with most of its smaller neighbours. Tensions have tended to recur periodically and have not allowed an atmosphere of mutual trust to prevail.

In the post SAARC period when South Asian countries were making effort to enhance regional trading arrangements, all the bilateral conflicts during this period have been Indo-centric reflecting to a large extent India's hegemonic aspirations, backed by its military supremacy in the region.

1. India and Pakistan

Except for the Maldives and Bhutan, India has bilateral disputes with all her neighbours.

The most crucial and serious problem that divides South Asia is the Indo-Pakistan conflict. Since independence, the relationship between India and Pakistan has shown a unique pattern of dualism: while the official relations are based on a zero-sum mentality and the classic **"security dilemma"**, ordinary people across the border continue to recall past contacts with nostalgia and are eager to maintain a close relationship with each other.

Since independence, the two countries have fought four wars, two of which were about Kashmir in 1948 and 1965, one on the Bangladesh liberation issue in 1971 and one in 1999 when Pakistan and India were embroiled in an armed confrontation in the Kargil region of Kashmir.

The security concerns between Pakistan and India peaked in 1998, when both sides tested nuclear weapons, introducing highly unstable dimension to the security paradigm.

Tension reached a new height in 2002 when India blamed Pakistan for having engineered terrorist attack on Indian Parliament.

Amidst continuing tensions, Pakistan and India have made several attempts to initiate a peace process geared towards setting their disputes. Major initiatives were undertaken preceding the Kargil war in 1999, when the two sides signed the **"Lahore Declaration"** and in 2001 when the Pakistani President Parvez Musharaff made an unsuccessful attempt at initiating a peace bid. The peace process is the latest attempt by the two sides to seek re-approachment. While the current effort has lasted longer than preceding initiatives, by and large, Indo-Pakistan tensions still remain high. The deep rooted suspicion between the two sides is unaltered and major outstanding issues remain unresolved. Even if the current peace bid were to stay on track, it would take decades before India and Pakistan begin to trust each other.

2. India and Sri Lanka

Sri Lanka shared the initial enthusiasm with Bangladesh and Nepal for the establishment of SAARC. Sri Lanka's enthusiasm for SAARC reflected the anxiety that usually exists in the small state-large state relationship.

While other countries in South Asia have contiguous neighbours besides India, Sri Lanka has only India as its neighbour to the north and on all other sides there in the Indian Ocean. Such a geographic reality coupled with India's overwhelmingly superior size, population, natural resources and military, economic and technological power, generate a great deal of anxiety in Sri Lanka. Not surprisingly, Sri Lanka's attitude towards SAARC has always been and will likely continue to be, determined by the degree of cordiality in the Indo-Sri Lankan bilateral relationship[4].

In the 1980s Sri Lanka slowly came under the grip of ethnic conflict between the majority Sinhalese and minority Tamil separatists seeking independence of Northern Sri Lanka. India had a natural interest in the issue, given the sizable Tamil population in Southern India. As in early 1983, India attempted to mediate Sri Lanka's conflict.

Ethnic violence in Sri Lanka led to serious Indo-Sri Lanka tensions as the Indian government openly began to sympathise with Sri Lankan Tamils. The Liberation Tiger of Tamil Elam (LTTE), was reportedly funded by the Indian state of Tamil Nadu, a fact tolerated by central government in New Delhi in 1995. Moreover, in 1987, when the Sri Lankan government attempted to regain control of its northern territory through an economic blockade, India came to the rescue of the Tamils. In July 1987, India decided to send the Indian Peace Keeping Force (IPKF) to Sri Lanka under an agreement that sought to disarm the Tamil and achieve peace. The agreement caused further resentment among Sri Lankan Sinhalese who saw this as an Indian attempt to establish its hegemony over Sri Lanka. India boycotted the 1991 SAARC summit in Colombo, causing its postponement. When the summit eventually took place, it was an abrupt one-day affair punctuated by the tensions between the hosts and India.

Since the early 1990s, whilst maintaining its interest in the Tamil movement, India has refrained from intervening directly. It has also started to officially support the Sri Lankan government's position. Moreover, the two sides have looked to enhanced cooperation in other sectors, leading to a significant improvement in their relationship.

However, with India showing support toward the Sri Lankan government's efforts to achieve peace in the island the Indo-Sri Lankan bilateral relationship has improved substantially in the post-1990 period. Since Sri Lanka has no major bilateral disputes with other states of South Asia, the improved Indo-Sri Lankan relationship has revived the latter's enthusiasm for SAARC.

3. India and Bangladesh

Bangladesh has an enormous interest in the growth of regional cooperation in South Asia. With a population of more than 115 million out of which 65 per cent live below the poverty line, limited natural resources, proneness to frequent floods and cyclones, absolute aid dependency, limited industrial, scientific and technological development, and more than 13 per cent of its export earning going to debts service, Bangladesh's capacity to cope with the nation-building process is severally limited. Despite the fact that India supported East Pakistani separatists, who eventually gained independence for what is now Bangladesh, relations between the two countries have been sawed. Although the two sides' penned economic agreements and an annually renewable treaty on the contentious issue of water sharing, a numbers of concerns remain unsettled. A general concern, which Bangladesh shares with other SAARC members, is its suspicion of India's quest for direct influence on its neighbours.

Among the issues which most adversely affect Bangladesh's cordial relationship with India in the post 1975 period, the conflicts over the sharing of the Ganges water, in late 1980s. India sought to build a fence on the Indo-Bangladesh international border Chittagong Hill Tracts to stop illegal immigrants from pouring into West Bengal, the river island of Muhurichar is also claimed by the two countries. However this issue has remained dormant since 1985, specifically in the early 1990s, India-Bangladesh relation deteriorated over a dispute concerning the Farakka Barrage, where India has built a feeder canal to divert water to its side of the river. Tensions surface intermittently as no permanent solution to major outstanding issues has been found and in 2001, India and Bangladesh found themselves in the midst of a minor border confrontation. The conflict centered on the disputed border territory near Pyrdiwah village but remained contained to the border force on both sides.

Lately, India has also accused Bangladesh of being sympathetic towards Pakistan and acting as a conduit for anti-India terrorist operations. Bangladesh, on the other hand, blames India for supporting anti-Dhaka Chakma insurgents.

Except with India, Bangladesh has no outstanding dispute with any SAARC country. Bangladesh's political and economic relations with Pakistan have improved after a brief disruption from 1971 to 1975.

4. India and Nepal

Nepal has no deep routed political conflicts with her neighbours. It is because of her cordial relationship that the South Asian countries unanimously agreed to set up SAARC's Permanent Secretariat in Kathmandu.

Two major considerations guide this interest of Nepal :

1. The desire to promote the country's security through multilateral diplomacy.

2. The desire to promote balanced interdependence as opposed to an absolute dependence on India. Land locked between India and China, Nepal has been dependent on India for its security and economic development since the signing of the Indo-Nepal Treaty of Peace and Friendship in July 1950. Nepal's thousands mile border with Tibet is critical to India's security interest therefore, India has always tried to maintain a close strategic relationship with Nepal.

As far as, the Indo-Nepal is concerned it has also been fraught with tension although the two sides have not allowed their overall relationship to be held hostage to their differences. The Indo-Nepal equation is a classic example of big-small power political maneuvering with the smaller power. Nepal is trying it's almost to retain an independent posture, despite being economically dependent on India. The bulk of the problems between the two sides are grounded in economic concerns.

Indo-Nepal relations were quite strained when SAARC was formed. India had denied Nepal's bid to be declared an international security zone. Nepal's acquisition of Chinese weaponry met with a strong official protest from the Indian government, worried about losing its accommodate Indian demands on the long standing transit treaty between the two countries. Nepal took a hard line approach and after the expiration of the treaty in 1989, faced on economic blockade from India, a development that led to further escalation in Indo-Nepal tensions.

More recently, a conciliatory strain in bilateral relations has emerged. Although India and Nepal also have an outstanding territorial dispute on a 75 sq km. area, the issue has not impacted Indo-Nepal relations to any significant degree. Since the early 1990s, Nepal's worsening economic and political situation has forced it to seek rapprochement with India. In 1990, the special security relationship between the two countries was restored and in the mid-1990s fresh trade and transit treaties were signed along with other economic agreements. India has also supported the Nepalese Government in the fight against the ongoing Maoist rebellion in the country, a fact that has further improved relations between the two countries.

Afghanistan as a New Member of SAARC and Its Relationship with South Asian Nations

Afghanistan was endorsed as a new member of the forum at the thirteenth SAARC summit in Dhaka. The country formally joined SAARC as its eighth member at the fourteenth SAARC summit[5]. It had been believed that the entry of a new member and that too Afghanistan will involve understand and integrate with the region and the forum. Afghanistan being a member of SAARC can act as a bridge to West Asian countries and can open up new trade avenues for SAARC.

In terms of its relationship with South Asia, it has historically had a marked impact on the Indian Subcontinent. South Asia is deeply impacted by Afghanistan as a result of the long Pak-Afghan borders (The Durand Line which is disputed by Afghans of all political hues including Pakistan's protégé). Pakistan in its game of the **"pretender power"** in South Asia, had used Afghanistan along with Kashmir in its South Asian power games.

India and Afghanistan

But due to Afghanistan, India's security problems had enhanced. The immediate security impact on India would be to face heightened levels of Islamic Jehadis operations in Jammu and Kashmir and the North Eastern States. It had been noticed that India and Afghanistan were never in direct conflict with each other.

At present, Afghanistan and India shares cordial relations with each other. India continued to send humanitarian assistance to Afghanistan both bilaterally and through the UN.

Pakistan and Afghanistan

The exit of the Taliban from Afghanistan imposes heavy losses on Pakistan in virtually every conceivable field Afghanistan along with Kashmir was the strategic centre-piece of Pakistan's Foreign, military and state sponsored terrorism politics for over a decade.

Politically, in South Asia also, Pakistan's image gets affected considerably. South Asian states which would cozy up with Pakistan to discomfort India would now have to think twice of Pakistan's reliability to stand by them. The strategic losses of Pakistan resulting from the Afghanistan events impact heavily on Pakistan's pretension to emerge as the **'second pole'** in South Asian Politics[6].

Except India and Pakistan, Afghanistan never had any problems with other SAARC nations.

Relations between Other SAARC Members

Apart from tensions between Indian and its neighbours, other SAARC members have by and large, maintained free relations. Since SAARC was initiated, there have been no noticeable conflicts between any member states except India. In fact, India has often been wary of designs of smaller state to **'gang up'** in order to neutralise its influence. This has added to mutual suspicious between smaller members and India. Indeed countries like Sri Lanka have turned to Pakistan to offset setbacks in relations with India. In 1999, Sri Lanka acquired military assistance from Pakistan to defend against possible aggression from the Tamil rebels at a time when New Delhi refused to come forward with such assistance. India has also blamed Bangladesh for allowing Pakistani intelligence to function on its territory and for acting as a base for terrorist attacks inside India, an allegation it levies against Pakistan as well. Nepal-Bangladesh relations have also been cordial, as Kathmandu has attempted to neutralise some of New Delhi's influences by entering into various agreements with Dhaka[7].

Role of India in SAARC : (Political Dimension)

After India adopted the policy of NSR (National Self Reliance) in order to remove dependence on foreign aid, India took the step of forming SAARC along with the 6 neighbouring countries. This step has helped India develop good and cordial relationship with its neighbouring countries in all aspects (socially, politically and economically). After SAARC being formed by India along with six of its neighbouring countries, India has been able to develop trade relations with all the SAARC members.

India had the chairmanship of SAARC during the year 1996-97. India hosted the 17th Session of the SAARC council of ministers at New Delhi in 1996. Recently the 14th SAARC summit was held in New Delhi.

India has also cooperated actively in SAARC activities and vigorously promoted trade and other forms of economic, social and technical cooperation within SAARC. India also actively supports people-to-people initiatives aimed at fostering greater mutual understanding and goodwill in the region. India is the only SAARC members that shares land borders with four members and sea borders with two. No other SAARC country shares a common border with each other.

In the terms of trade, commerce, investments India is a source of potential investments and technology and a major market for product form all other SAARC members.

One of the foremost challenges facing South Asia is the issue of poverty eradication. At the twelfth summit held in Islamabad in January 2004. India offered to contribute US $100 million for poverty alleviation projects in SAARC countries. India has additionally offered to finance feasibility projects in SAARC countries to finance in this regard. India has also granted the highest members of tariff concessions to all SAARC members.

Effects on Indo-Pak Relations

SAARC has failed to resolve dispute between India and Pakistan especially the Kashmir issue. The progress of SAARC was limited for some years due to the absence of cordial relationship between India and Pakistan.

SAARC's inability to play a crucial role in integrating South Asia is often credited to the political and military rivalry between India and Pakistan.

However during Prime Minister Atal Bihari Vajpayee's visit to Islamabad for the 12th SAARC summit Pakistan persuaded India to resume talks about maintenance of peace and the stalled composite dialogue, while India received assurances the Pakistan would not allow its territory to be a hub for terrorist activities. The composite dialogue had then started.

At present India's export to Pakistan are limited. For example, in the year 2001-2002 India's total export were $ 44 billion out of which a mere $ 204 million went to Pakistan. On the other hand India's exports to Bangladesh stood at $930 million and exports to Sri Lanka at $ 662 million.

Pakistan has to pay heavy price for importing goods from other countries except India. India's exports suffer due to non-availability of neighbouring markets.

In relation to conflict resolution between India and Pakistan SAARC had failed until now. There is still discontent between both the countries.

SAARC has yet to become an effective regional organisation largely because of mutual distrust between India and its neighbours.

The reluctance of India and other South Asian countries to turn SAARC into a forum for resolving major regional disputes hampers SAARC's ability to deal with many of South Asia's economic and political problems.

Cooperation Trouble between India and SAARC Members

SAARC is structured in a way that often makes regional cooperation difficult. In a regional organisation it is difficult for countries to establish balanced relations when one has a significant advantage in power over the other state. In the case of SAARC India is the most powerful country in terms of its economic might, military power and international influence. Thus, India's potential as a regional hegemony gives SAARC a unique dynamic compared to an organisation such as ASEAN. Pakistan was initially reluctant to join SAARC due to fears of SAARC succumbing to Indian hegemony. Indeed, if India does take a prominent role in SAARC, it could further fears that India will use SAARC for hegemonic purposes. While the smaller states in South Asia recognise that they will need India's help to facilitate faster economic growth, they are reluctant to work with India, fearing that such cooperation will admit Indian dominance in SAARC.

Aside from a few overtures to its neighbours; India has done little to allay the fears of other South Asian states. The core of these fears is likely derived from the displays of India's power by New Delhi in the past. Bangladesh is afraid of India exploiting its geographical position to redirect water flows vital to Bangladeshi agricultural production.

Nepal and Bhutan are still worried about India's control over their world trade and transit links as their geographical position will always make them dependent on India. These dispute between India and its neighbour have directly affected SAARC.

Disputes between South Asian States have undermined SAARC efforts to promote regional trade. As in the case of Pakistan and Sri Lanka how conflicts have proven detrimental to SAARC. When Indian intervention in Sri Lanka from 1986-1990. The Indian military intervention put down an insurgency by the Liberation Tigers of Tamil Elam (LTTE) made Indo-Sri Lankan relations tense during these four years. Subsequently, the apprehension between India and Sri Lanka was considered a primary reason behind Sri Lanka's **"Lukewarm"** support for SAARC into economic and social spheres of its member states until relations improved with India.

A second, more prominent example of conflict derailing SAARC progress is the Indo-Pakistani conflict. Pakistan has demanded a resolution to its dispute with India over the Kashmir Valley before discussing trade relations with New Delhi. Pakistan has enforced this Policy by Violating WTO regulation for failing to confer Most Favored Nation (MFN) status on India.

India has attempted to improve its relationship with the rest of South Asia. Under the Gujral Doctrine established by former India Prime Minister I.K. Gujral, India signed a 30-year water sharing treaty with Bangladesh and a trade and transit treaty with Nepal. India also joined a sub-regional group within SAARC compromising of Bangladesh, Bhutan, Nepal and India. Moreover, if India and Pakistan arguably the largest powers in SAARC, pushed for economic cooperation, it is likely that other state will follow their lead. Therefore, it is not surprising that the Indo-Pakistani dispute over Kashmir is considered a primary cause of SAARC's impotence. Due to these conflicts, the desire for South Asian state to trade with one another has been limited.

In SAARC, India needs to play a major role in SAARC. India being an important member of the group should initiate steps to ensure that the nations should go beyond the rhetoric and make the summit meaningful in the future.

India should also maintain peace and take proper and appropriate steps to resolve disputes and solve issues amongst the SAARC members especially with Pakistan.

According to Former Prime Minister Atal Bihari Vajpayee "Countries in the SAARC region have to make a bold transition from mistrust to trust, from discord to concord and from tension to peace"[8].

Indian leaders know well that the smooth operation of SAARC will provide them the opportunity to convince the world about their ability to pull the South Asian countries together. By demonstrating such leadership in SAARC, they can hope to recapture some of India's lost prestige in the international arena. Moreover, to the extent that Indian political perceives that the existence of SAARC can ensure the status quo in South Asia, leading to political stability in the region and future improvements of

Table 4.1. Political System in SAARC Nations

	Bangladesh	*Bhutan*	*India*	*Maldives*	*Nepal*	*Pakistan*	*Sri Lanka*	*Afghanistan*
Political system	Parliamentary Democracy	Monarchy until 2007	Parliamentary Democracy	One Party Presidential democracy	Constitutional monarchy / parliamentary democracy 1990	1999-2008 Military rule under Mushrraf	1978 All Powerful executive presidency	Taliban (1996-2001)
	Interim Caretaker Govt. (Jan 2007-08)	2007 Parliamentary democracy	1975-77 (emergency aberration)	Pressures for changes since 2003	King-led rule from 2002-05	2008 elections, Parliamentary democracy	Rising demands for reversal to Parliamentary democracy	Interim Govt. (2001-04)
	Parliamentary elections expected December 2008	2008 elected government in office		New constitution (2008)	King assumes direct rule 2005	Replacement of military rule by civilian President		New Constitution (2004)

(Contd.)

(Contd. Table)

	Bangladesh	*Bhutan*	*India*	*Maldives*	*Nepal*	*Pakistan*	*Sri Lanka*	*Afghanistan*
				Presidential elections scheduled for Oct-10, 2008.	Jan Andolan 2006			Presidential Republic
					April 2008 Elections			Parliamentary provincial Elections 2005
					August 2008 Elected Representative government			
Party System	Multiparty	Multiparty	Multiparty	One Party Democracy turned into multiparty democracy	Multiparty	Multiparty	Multiparty	

India's bilateral relations with its neighbours, one would expect a validation[9].

India's Renewed Commitment

India has remained a reluctant and hesitant participant in SAARC from the beginning. Due to the apprehension of the neighbours **"ganging up"** against it, and the neighbours' fear that a closer engagement with India could result in the latter's domination. India's enthusiasm with SAARC has been kept at a low profile. In India's assessment, the economic potential of the region also did not appear to be very attractive. Indian policy makers have been convinced for a long time that SAARC could not offer the economic opportunities it had been looking for. Frustrated by Pakistan's position on the Kashmir issue and Bangladesh's strong inclination to politicise any bilateral and regional cooperation issue, India at one time, during the late nineties, had even started drifting away from SAARC. The creation of BIMSTEC, although the initiative came from Thailand, was one such manifestation of India's drift. It persuaded even Nepal and Bhutan subsequently to join BIMSTEC, making it almost a parallel organisation to SAARC without Pakistan.

This phase of drift in India's approach to SAARC seems to have come to an end over the past three to four years, as India is gradually realising that its credibility and acceptance as a rising Asian power will remain under cloud if it fails to carry its immediate neighbour along. SAARC was reassessed as a political and strategic necessity, if not so much an economic promise. Without all boats rising in South Asia at the same time, India can neither prosper nor be secure.

SAARC, as the only regional instrument available to carry its neighbour along cannot be neglected or undermined. Instead, it has to be endowed with greater vigour and a sense of purpose. The change in India's stance towards SAARC also emanates from its growing economic self-confidence and political resilience.[10]

Political Challenges Facing SAARC

Since its foundation in 1985, SAARC was meant to pursue and unite the subcontinent under the noblest aims of social and economic development, mutual understanding and crucially the creation of an order based on mutual respect, equality and shared benefits but South Asia as we know it a region sadly famous for being ridden at all levels of the most volatile and bitter political challenges. It is the fact that SAARC was born with a strictly a political vocation and mission. But had SAARC been able to bridge its institutional endowment-deficit with the complex reality of the region to political issue in the region?

Political Challenges

Political Challenges is one which is concerned with matter of legitimacy, democracy, governance, civil society, insurgency, conflict and empowerment.

The political challenges of SAARC are interesting and often convoluted. The most important feature of the several nation-States that now exist in SAARC is that they are mostly new as sovereign nations but contain some of the rich histories in the world. The nature of political challenges of SAARC are unique because they have linked histories followed by a clean and subtle break Some of the important political challenges facing by SAARC which are impediments to the growth and development of South Asian region. SAARC already faces difficult social and economic challenges which are made more acute by the presence of violence, lack of good governance and a weak civil society which is not empowered.

Political Challenges

South Asia is turning out to be a **"most dangerous place"** in the world especially in the context of a breeding ground of bloody terror and radical extremism as exemplified by the December 2007 assassination of Pakistan's former Prime Minister Benazir Bhutto.

Undoubtedly, the intra-regional problems in South Asia is of such a vast magnitude that they demand not only a comprehensive understanding of region specifies and particularities but also have short and long term modalities and mechanisms to manage the manifold nature of security threat perceptions and conflicts from a pragmatic perspective.

Ruling leaders in South Asia have failed to address the mounting internal problem virtually on all fronts facing each other country of the region. People are fed up with political slogans. They have garnered enough to demonstrate their disenchantment with ruling leader's mis-governance by resorting to street politics. The mass upsurge against policies of their ruling elites is an overt and covert manifestation, as demonstrated in Nepal, Pakistan and Bangladesh of their deep-rooted anguish and frustration over the mismatch of promise and performance. Only Bhutan and Maldives are identified as the only two countries in the region, which were comparatively free from ethno-religious conflicts and political violence[11].

1. Kashmir Issue

One problem that has continued to plague South Asia causing an array of a political challenge for SAARC is the Kashmir conflict. Kashmir, the northwestern most area of South Asia, is controlled by Pakistan, China and India. In the past few years, many serious negotiations have been undertaken to contrive a plan to settle the Kashmir conflict between India and Pakistan, but it remains unclear whether anything will solve these political issues.

There have been four wars fought between the two countries on this issue. It has wasted precious lives and good money[12].

Much of the Indo-Pakistan conflicts can be attributed to the following factors:

1. Structural imbalances between the two countries.
2. India's desire to maintain a hierarchical regional order and Pakistan's opposition to this design.
3. Divergent political systems (Now democracy prevails in both).
4. Pakistan's emphasis on Islam as the basis of the state as opposed to India's secularism.
5. Scapegoating by the ruling elites of India and Pakistan in order to ensure their political survival.

Pakistan's regional policy has always revolved around an objective to prove the validity of the Two Nation Theory through the liberation of Kashmir. After 1971, Pakistan became increasingly dependent on the Gulf States, China and the United States for military and Shimla Agreement of 1972 created an opportunity for both India and Pakistan to resolve their disputes on Kashmir, Pakistan subsequently violated the stipulation of the agreement by raising the Kashmir issue in various international forums. Kashmir remains the major bone of contention between India and Pakistan and unless it is resolved Pakistan and India's participation in the growth of regional cooperation in South Asia (SAARC) likely to remain limited[13].

2. Bilateral Issues

The principle of '**No Discussion**' on bilateral issues has influenced negatively the dynamics of regional cooperation, thus reading the effectiveness of SAARC as available vehicle for economic progress and regional integration.

The roller coaster nature of the relations between India and Pakistan swinging from euphoria over what seemed to be the beginning of a new era of peace and cooperation, to being on the verge of military conflicts reflects the general trend, particularly since the nuclearisation of the subcontinent in 1998. Bilateral relations swerved between the euphoric Lahore summits in February 1999, the Kargil conflict of May-July 1999, the Agra summit in July 2001, the massive troop deployment following the terrorist attack on the Indian Parliament in December 2001, the return to peace process in 2003, the fallout of the Mumbai train blasts in 2006 and the Manmohan Singh-Parvez Musharraf meet on the sidelines of the summit of the Non Aligned Movement a few month later.[14]

Major unresolved bilateral problem may undermine the evolution of effective regional cooperation. For a cooperative venture like SAARC to succeed, the member countries need to have a high degree of trust in one another. But it will be difficult for any two partners with outstanding

Table 4.2. Chronology of Major Conflict in South Asia

Year	*India-Bangladesh*	*India-Sri Lanka*	*India-Nepal*	*India-Pakistan*
1985	Muhurichar Island conflict			
1987		Indian Peace Keeping Force (IPKF) sent to Tamil Nadu to disarm the Tamils		
1988			Tension over disagreement on transit treaty	
1989		Withdrawal of IPKF demanded by Sri Lankan Government.		
1991		India boycotts SAARC Colombo summit		

(Contd.)

(Contd. Table)

Year	*India-Bangladesh*	*India-Sri Lanka*	*India-Nepal*	*India-Pakistan*
1998				Both countries test nuclear weapons
1999				Kargil conflict in India- held Kashmir
2001	Pydiwah Village border Conflict			Terrorist attack on Indian parliament blame on Pakistan.
2006				Mumbai Train Blast Pakistan was accused by Indian government.
2008				26/11, Hotel Taj terrorist intrusion and Pakistan was blamed for it.

Source: SDPI in - House Compilation, August 2006.

major bilateral problem to have adequate trust in each other when working on a regional basis.

The Charter categorically excludes bilateral and contentious issues from the scope of SAARC, thus side tracking major obstacles to effective cooperation. It is conceded that major bilateral issue may be excluded from the concern of SAARC at the initial stage to give the association a chance to find its feet but unless the issue are faced and resolved within the framework of SAARC or outside, there may not only be a dampening of the wind for the sail of the SAARC ship but there may in fact be very turbulent patches tossing it about[15].

Currently, the pressure to include bilateral, contentious political issues in SAARC deliberations is increasing with the passage of time, which has never allowed SAARC to take off.

India quiet diplomatic maneuverings to keep away the political issues from the SAARC forum have always been is stark contrast to Pakistan's obsession to raise such issue. Over the years, Pakistan has been able to galvanise and garner some sustained support in this regard from at least some of the member countries. Unlike the argument that once political issues are brought to the SAARC forum, it may totally be mesmerised by and submerged into petty political scoring, there are fresh and newer arguments emerging against such thinking.

There is the urgent need and usefulness of raising political issues in the SAARC forum. The main contention has been that by constantly evading political issues, SAARC has pushed itself to farcical corner and rendered itself as an unrealistic and disoriented forum. In this context, the 11th summit would have been a watershed. The ball has been set rolling by the Sri Lankan President Chandrika Kumartunga who spoke at length about the inevitability of gradually inserting political issues in the SAARC.

There is a consensus among all members of SAARC, except India, to include bilateral Contentious Issues on the SAARC agenda, at least at the level of summit and foreign minister meeting. Only India is averse to this idea and seeks the resolution of such issues on a bilateral basis. Also India is adamant against a third party for mediation in complex and contentious issues like Kashmir, which cannot be solved bilaterally, given the historical experiences and inflexible positions of the countries involved. This approach towards resolution of bilateral problem has adversely affected creation of an environment conducive for regional cooperation.

3. War on Terror

The war against terror has its epicentre in Afghanistan and Pakistan. The SAARC nations will become more brittle and human development and growth is likely to suffer. The war is likely to lead to more radicalisation and destabilisation. There are going to be more social problem for the inhabitants of these two nations. War will also lead to breakdown of institutions. This is already visible in Pakistan; Afghanistan is in the process of nation building from scratch and it will take many years for the region to stabilise. Governance and capacity building is therefore an area for continuous assistance.

US had also begun to fight the Taliban and Al-Qaeda in Afghanistan, Pakistan and elsewhere, the nature of the war changed. It now became a universal war. Though the US homeland is now comparatively better protected but matters have deteriorated for Pakistan and Afghanistan where the war has now shifted.

Pakistan also used Afghan Jihadi in Kashmir. It is today paying a very heavy price for such policies. These Jihadis introduced sectarianism and helped in the Talibanisation of many areas in Pakistan.

A robust economic and a democratic response is needed to battle this menace. The war against terror cannot be fought by the military alone. It requires the whole hearted support of all classes. Benazir showed her commitment by sacrificing her life for such a cause.

In Sri Lankan the fight between the government and the Tamil LTTE was harming the country's potential for growth. According to a report the cost of this war was the loss of 2.3 per cent points of growth a year.

In Nepal the withdrawal of the monarchy from active politics has been a major reason for creating conditions for a settlement with the Maoists. It depends on time whether the understanding reached in Nepal is long lasting or not[16].

4. Size of Member Countries and Built in Contradiction

SAARC suffer from a built in contradiction. The unequal size of the member countries is truly monumental. India with a population of 765.1 million and an area of 3.3 million sq. km. In fact compared to India's size, all the other look like pigmies. In these circumstances, there may be questions relating to the nature and meaning of cooperation between India on the one hand and other individual SAARC members on the other. Much depends on India's understanding of the sensitivities of its smaller partners without an air of big-brotherliness and Indo-centric attitude and the other countries approaching their relations with India on the basis of goodwill and a positive attitude. It would be necessary for all the countries to correctly perceive their own individual country interests and the interest of the region as whole that can be promoted through regional cooperation. It is commendable that there has been an agreement that decisions at all levels would be made on the basis of unanimity thereby giving the same voting and vetoing powers to each member country irrespective of its physical size and economic or military strength. This provision no doubt will act as a stabilising factor for SAARC.

5. Historical Burden

Serious misgivings about SAARC developing into a vehicle of purposeful and effective cooperation among the member countries are also caused by the history of the region which is replete with conflicts and discords. India and Pakistan both countries have remained locked in conflicts syndrome since independence. A contradiction developed between India and Sri Lanka the ongoing LTTE ethnic conflict in Sri Lanka causing death and destruction. A historically rooted uneasiness also pervades the relationship between Nepal and India. Nepal, a land locked country with India providing the main overland need to be approached with understanding, keeping in new the needs may override the historical burdens, removing their obstacles to cooperation.

At the same time cultural, social and historical traditions which are part of the common heritage of the people of this region may be researched, documented emphasized and disseminated to strengthen the cooperative environment in the region. The historical burdens need to be thus tackled, and not ignored or brushed aside.

6. Extra-regional Linkage

The development strategy pursued by the SAARC member countries meant the establishment by them of strong linkages with their respective major donor countries. As long as the dependent development strategy continues to hold sway in the SAARC member countries the prospect for growth based on the inter-country trade appears to be limited.

It has adverse consequences for SAARC because the member countries may continue to remain externally oriented to the detriment of their contribution and commitment to the growth of cooperation in the region and even giving rise to mistrust or fanning any existing mistrust[17]. Lack of movement at the multilateral level, member states are more inclined to take a bilateral course of creating bilateral free-trade areas.

There are also trilateral (India-Bhutan-Nepal), multi-lateral (Bangladesh, India, Myanmar, Thailand, Sri Lanka) BIMSTEC and quadrilateral (Bangladesh-India-Nepal-Bhutan) arrangements. There is multiplicity of contracts that hinders the growth at the SAARC level.

7. India's Look East Policy

The one of the major challenges that SAARC is facing today is the **'India's Look East Policy'** which is directly or indirectly affecting the progress of SAARC. India's role in the BIMSTEC evolution and very close association with ASEAN do make up for the ineffectiveness of SAARC. India's frustration with SAARC is more than made up by growing India-ASEAN cooperation.

It was hoped that BIMSTEC could fill the gap caused in SAARC by Pakistan's attitude. BIMSTEC had chosen members both from SAARC and ASEAN. There was no possibility of Pakistan being associated for that would lead this grouping also the way SAARC has been going[18].

India being an important member of SAARC should initiate steps to ensure that the nations should go beyond rhetoric and make the SAARC a meaningful organisation. It can't just remain a member of SAARC; rather it should look for avenues to ensure that it creates greater opportunities for its export-import community to carry out trade.

8. Conflict over Water Resources

The SAARC region is being one of the most populous and poverty stricken regions of the world, needs more of those cooperative efforts to address its problems; including those related to allocation and development of water resources for the benefit of more than one-fifth of world population to inhabit this subcontinent. In this context, the role of SAARC can also be noted. Because of the institutional framework it provides, SAARC can also facilitate the process of negotiations on several political issues, whether water related or not. Indeed although the charter of SAARC does not include a specific reference to cooperation over shared water resources, it does stress the need for joint action and enhanced cooperation among the respective political and economic systems of its members. Such statements of intent certainly are beneficial for countries in the subcontinent to generally promote an environment that systematically augurs discussions and decision-making at a higher level. Disputes between India and Bangladesh over the sharing of Ganga water and the dispute between India and Pakistan over Indus, Jhelum and Chenab, Ravi, Sutlej and Beas which were bilaterally solved. India and Bangladesh have addressed major problems on water sharing dispute in 2011 with which the Testa river that crosses between India, Bangladesh, Bhutan and Nepal can be turned from a river of discard to common water security. Although, treaties and other legal instruments over international rivers will not, by themselves solve all the problems in such rivers, it is equally true that there can be a no resolution of water disputes and conflicts without them. Such instruments like SAARC are indeed the only means for translating cooperative political will into applicable and enforceable action[19].

9. South Asia and Nuclear Conflicts

The joint statement by US and India issued on July 18, 2005 indicated the existence of a future road map for strategic partnership between the two nations based on cooperation in the use of nuclear energy as well as in the military domain. The US is thus looking at India as a strategically.

Pakistan feels that once the nuclear agreement is implemented between the two countries, it will affect the South Asian balance of power. Pakistan fears that new technology will permit India to make qualitative and quantitative improvement to its nuclear arsenal. Since Pakistan holds an Indo-specific threat perception, the implementation of the agreement is likely to create a new arms race.

Instead of focusing on larger issues beneficial for the economic well-being of South Asia, acrimony on this matter stifle initiatives in other fields.

It is apparent that India also wants a peaceful settlement with Pakistan. Prime Minister Vajpayee extended a hand of friendship to Pakistan in 2003. It was a reciprocal realisation in the mind of the Pakistani leadership when the Islamabad Declaration was signed in Jan. 2004, to begin a composite dialogue for solving all outstanding disputes including Kashmir[20].

The positive aspect is that the SAARC states have shown the capacity to sustain democratic processes and preserve democratic institutions while coping with violence. As the levels of violence have increased so also has there been a simultaneous strengthening of the coercive state apparatus.

The negative trend and probably of much more serious concern has been the ability of most of the South Asian states to make use of intangible, unformalised, extra-constitutional and extra-legal agencies of state violence in their counter violence strategies so that the questions of legality and accountability can be side-stepped.

There is mutuality in the interaction between the politics of development and the politics of violence.

The uneven developmental process it is a major factor in distracting the state from the developmental agenda. Scarce resources are consumed and lost in the containment of violence. There is a little doubt that tremendous amount of developmental potential is lost in violence ridden societies of South Asia. Resources lost in meeting the costs of violence can be saved and invested in the growing costs of modernisation. Peace and stability are preconditions to bring what is known as peace dividends in violence ridden societies of South Asia[21]

10. Problem of Diverse Political Culture

The Diverse Political Culture of the region is also not conducive to cooperation. On the question of state-religion relationships, India, notwithstanding its being predominantly Hindu and of late witnessing in an unprecedented Hindu Militancy, stands for secularism, while all the remaining seven avoid declaring themselves as such. Bangladesh, the Maldives and Pakistan have an Islamic thrust; Bhutan and Sri Lanka Buddhist; and Nepal Hindu. With respect to structural linkages with the global system, there were two categories, broadly speaking. The first in which India was included, had a fairly powerful capitalist class which had over the decades developed stakes in both the world capitalist and socialist systems, though remaining independent of both. The other had deep structural linkages with the world capitalist system and the bourgeoisie there was largely comprador. Bangladesh, Maldives, Pakistan and Sri Lanka belonged to this category. Bhutan's and Nepal's economy is largely Indo-centric.

These systematic diversities led to divergent nation-building strategies which tend to thrive at each other's expense rather than contribute to each other. In terms of interethnic relationships, India bears the brunt in more than one way. Situated at the core of the region, its boundary launches that of almost all the countries of SAARC while no two other members have common borders. As a multi-ethnic, multilingual and multireligious society, it offers all the countries in the region some connection to their ethnic, linguistic or religious brotherhoods while no two other countries have cross national ethnic populations visible enough to be of any consequences barring the notable exception of Bhutan and Sri Lanka. The **'Indo-centricity'** of the problem often drags India into the region's ethnic strife.

11. Resource Development Issue

Another area in which progress is negligible is resource development. The Indian subcontinent's river system is such that if properly tapped, with the entire region in mind, it would do wonders in terms of development, affording irrigation, power generation and drinking water. Here, regional consciousness gives way to national susceptibilities[22].

12. Crisis of Trust at SAARC

A major issue is the trust deficit between South Asian countries. This is based on competitive nationalism which originated during state formation in post colonial South Asia and continues as a tool in domestic and regional politics and nation building approaches of the South Asian elites.

Topmost in this competitive nationalism and distrust is the unresolved conflict and strategic competition between India ana Pakistan. India is able to use its economic, cultural and political power to leverage its influence in the neighbourhood, while Pakistan uses primarily its influence over illegal non-state actors and military muscle. Even though SAARC charter prohibits any bilateral issue from discussion, this animosity stalls SAARC from moving ahead on key economic and political decisions.

China's territorial dispute and competition with India, their close linkages with Pakistan and their attempts to influence Nepal and Sri Lanka at different periods have led mutual distrust between these countries.

Nepal and Bangladesh have tried to balance India with other neighbours. There is the no common search for security within the region which is necessary input into any regional body.

Other problems like unresolved territorial demarcations on land and sea; the issue of illegal migrations; the unofficial terror linkages; the harbouring of criminals/ terrorist of one state by another, allowing camps of insurgent groups and using these as bargaining chips; the treatments to each other's citizen and treatment to prisoners of wars all add up to the trust deficit and stall the progress of the SAARC as an effective body[23]. There remain a number of unresolved issues yet ranging from Sia Chin to Sir Creek, but there is little doubt that the overall political atmosphere between these countries is far more conducive that what it was five years earlier.

Thus, the problem identified cannot be exhaustive and yet they constitute a formidable agenda. They need to be earnestly addressed and carefully resolved so that the association can become an effective regional grouping that can make its contribution to development, peace and security in the region and beyond.

The ways and means of solving the problems faced by SAARC can be properly formulated only through intellectual process anchored on and necessitated by the dynamics and realities pertaining to this region. It is, therefore, essential that genuine intellectual foundations, wherever they are lacking are created for satisfactorily tackling the problems.

Finally, there may be lessons to be learnt from the experiences of other regional grouping such as COMCON, ASEAN and EU that how they have been tackling such of their problem as may have similarities to those faced by SAARC and how they have been planning and implementing action programmes.[24]

Ways to Overcome Impediments

SAARC cannot be denied as being only an **"empty forum"**. It bears in fact a large potential also in the political field, even though still almost unexploited.

The informal and quasi official political dimension of the organisation is in fact essential to its functioning. SAARC can contribute to the emergence of a twenty-first century by helping to establish a sustainable relationship between South Asian nations.

Following recommendations can be made to overcome impediments in its functioning and to strengthen the process of regional cooperation

1. The countries in the SAARC region will have to discard the weight of history and work together as a region rather than as individual countries pursuing their separate interests.
2. There is a consensus among all members of SAARC, except India, to include bilateral contentious issue on the SAARC agenda, at least at the level of summit and foreign minister meeting. That

would largely depend on India's willingness to allow such a development. India needs to be persuaded by friendly countries to allow the creation of South Asian institution/mechanism, which can facilitate a dialogue among the regional countries on political issues. Therefore, Charter of SAARC may be amended with a view to add bilateral contentious issues at the official fora.

3. Instead of sticking to their positions on core issues that resolution of bilateral disputes should precede regional cooperation, India and Pakistan should adopt an integrated approach move on both bilateral and regional tracks. Pakistan should raise the Kashmir issue but not at the cost of all other matters. An integrated approach through confidence building measures is adopted. This could happen if these two countries of this region would bring about a fundamental change in their thinking about each other and the region to which they belong. Pakistan also needs a significant reorientation in its approach towards India. It needs to recognise the importance of working within a regional economic framework to deal with some of the structural problems the country currently faces. Its policy towards India should be of collaborator rather than competitor.
4. There is hardly any justification for Pakistan not trading with India on political reasons. At present in Male summit in Maldives in 2011 Pakistan has agreed to grant MFN trade states (Most favoured Nation) to India, as already done to other WTO members.
5. Many of South Asia's security problems need a regional context to be successfully addressed. The threat terrorism poses to peace, stability and economic progress in the region, which emphasizes the need for close cooperation in combating all forms of terrorism and international crime. There is a need for effective comprehensive inclusive security architecture.

It is widely realised that the summit is mostly hijacked by security concern of the two nuclear powers. It is suggested to establish a SAARC peace forum which should have the authority and power to act as a mediator for intervening and resolving political tensions. There is urgent need to recognize that in order to attain regional nuclear stability they will have to have a SAARC component to any mutual stability regime. Instead of creating a balance of power barrier, it is proposed that Chinese collaboration in the security of South Asia should be bought by giving China more interest to protect in South Asia.

There is also a need to maintain balance in the promotion of nuclear energy technology which would take in to account the concerns of Pakistan.

SAARC countries may adopt ASEAN three step strategy:

- Each Country Should Build Up Its Own Resilience And Other Countries Should Help That Country To This End.

- The Low Key Approach of its Biggest Member (Indonesia).
- The habit of working together.[25]

6. To combat and root out terrorism there is a need for an early conclusion of the UN comprehensive convention on international terrorism conclusion of the ratification of the SAARC convention on mutual assistance in criminal matters. Countries of the region must cooperate to contain the impact of the war on terror by enlarging and empowering civil society.
7. The removal of poverty and hunger is the most important objective, since it will not only improve economic growth but will have a positive impact upon conflict reduction, counter terrorism, improving human rights and bring a positive gender change.
8. One of the most important regional disputes is Kashmir. A positive movement in pushing Kashmir away from the conflict agenda is a pre-requisite for reduction of poverty not only in India and Pakistan but also regionally. The resolution of this problem will contribute to the growth of trade under SAARC and also lead to energy cooperation.
9. All the SAARC nations need to invest heavily in their institutions through capacity building[26].
10. South Asia will only be able to take advantage of the opportunities that have been created by the change in the global economic system and the evolution of the international political order if the countries in the region act together rather than against one another.
11. There is the need for Indian leadership in SAARC. Only India, which along with being the region's largest country by far and its largest economy in South Asian states can play that role. The experience from other parts of the world shows that smaller countries benefit from regional associations centred on an anchor economy for South Asia, India is such an economy. In creating a working economic and political region, South Asia will have to find the leaders from within their own system[27].
12. If SAARC has to become a dynamic and functional regional vehicle cooperation, it must focus on specific area that can provide a palpable foundation to kick-start the becoming a union of energy, communication, information and tourism and to move onward to a free trade area. Of course, as the bilateral disputes could not be put aside and they are quite serious and range from bilateral trade to cross-border disputes and terrorism a forum on the lines of ASEAN's may be created to find solutions to bilateral problems.
13. In this age of globalisation and interdependence SAARC cannot afford to remain isolated. Most issues in the countries in South Asia face, be it in the realm of terrorism, maritime security, health,

environment or economic growth are transnational in nature and require a coordinated response. Cooperation between SAARC and its neighbours is therefore both desirable and necessary. Observer countries could in addition play a useful role in terms of toning down political differences between member countries in SAARC as well as reinvigorating the economic equations between them. Breaking out of the prison of an Indo-Pak deadlock might release new energies. Additionally, the presence of extend observers could enhance SAARC's external image and give it a voice in global institutions, including the United Nations[28].

14. This will perhaps be the most sensitive as well as the biggest change which can propel the SAARC agenda a long way forward. There will be resistance from all countries to allowing political issues, particularly outstanding bilateral issues, to be taken up in formal meeting. But in this decade, SAARC must foster a change in the schedule of meeting of heads of government as well as foreign ministers. Like EC and ASEAN, a greatly increased frequency of meeting allows leaders to build up trust and confidence, breaking down the barriers of formality. In these Informal sessions, bilateral issues could be discussed, without prejudice to their existing national position on issues.
15. There must be a gradual introduction of political issues into the SAARC agenda. In order to develop consensus amongst the member states, the SAARC charter could be strengthened with an optional protocol, which would allow for the setting up of Conflict Conciliation Groups (CCG). These CCGs could be activated when all parties to a particular dispute agree to seek SAARC help, either to investigate the particular problem, or conduct a fact finding study or adjudicate on the issue. The composition of the CCG would include a representative each from the parties seeking help of a group as well as one or more representatives from other member states to ensure impartiality. Such a group would initially be useful to settle problems such as those relating to water dispute that affect more than two countries or refugee problems. Such group could take up factual studies of problems relating to child labour, exploitation of women and children and other issues on which countries from within the region are signatories to international statutes.
16. The third innovation within the political sphere must be to allow for political discussions amongst the leaders on international issues, especially those relating to common problems of international peace and security, environment, trade and technology transfers, etc. Presently, the existing mechanism does not allow for such

discussions, with the summit statements being crafted by bureaucrats well before the summit meeting begins. Such a move doesn't allow for these leaders to exchange views on matters of international interest which affect the region as a whole. These meeting must provide for a basis on which SAARC countries could eventually coordinate their positions in international forums on these issues. In case of the Comprehensive Test Ban Treaty (CTBT) negotiations in Geneva. India and Pakistan, notwithstanding their own mistrust over nuclear matters, had similar concern about the proposed CTBT. Rather than work together, the two countries consciously fought shy of each other in Geneva, diluting collective strength that could have helped them.

17. Structural changes in the Secretariat are needed to make it more responsive to existing needs as well as to act as a catalyst for new ideas and quicker implementation. Among the structural changes, the size of the secretariat should be increased considerably from the present strength of 20 to over 200 to deal with the wide range of issue being undertaken by SAARC under the IPA.
    These areas should receive additional funding, greater staff attention and creation of a graduated but quick progress chart.
18. There are already suggestions that SAARC's objectives could be met through the creation of a SAARC Parliament. While this could be a laudable objective for a well - integrated economic community, the secretariat could undertake a concept paper for discussion in member countries in evolving such an institution. As an achievable goal, setting up of a SAARC Assembly could be envisaged. This assembly to begin with may only have deliberative and non-legislative functions.

Confidence-Building Measures

(a) Countries in the region should agree to work on several pilot projects that would seek to integrate the economies of the countries. These could be taken up in areas of socio-economic development :
    (i) Harnessing river water for irrigation. There are several rivers in the subcontinent that flow through three countries. The least contentious of these rivers could be taken up either for building dams, or for generating hydro-electric power, which could be shared by the countries in the region on an agreed basis. The effort should not merely be towards building the dams or hydroelectricity project, but in consciously trying to use manpower, material and technology available within the region. This conditionality might make the project slightly expensive, but in the long run would provide for useful enhancing of trust and confidence among the countries.

(ii) Creating anti-flooding structure to prevent deluges that are a regular occurrence on transnational river systems in the region. The Indus and Brahmaputra river systems inundate large tracts of land in Pakistan, India, Bangladesh, Nepal and Bhutan, causing considerable loss of life and damage to property. With all these countries relying on agriculture, the spiral effect on the economies is massive. Better information about flooding patterns, utilisation of technologies developed inside the SAARC region to prevent flooding could be shared in the region as well. All countries could be linked through emergency lines of communication to take coordinated measures in times of natural disasters[29].

Notwithstanding the snail peace progress of SAARC and the political realities it has been confronted with since its inception, it has emerged as the only forum in the South Asia, where the leaders of the member countries are brought together, despite their intense political inhibitions and insurmountable national reservations on certain political issues.

With the starting of the twenty-first century, South Asian region has undergone radical transformation. It has witnessed a strong democratic sweep. Most of the South Asian economies have registered impressive growth. The international community has become far more involved in South Asian affairs due to the nuclearisation of the region. SAARC keep pace with the changing regional dynamics. It has more ahead on its economic agenda and expanded its reach not only by adding new members (Afghanistan) but also by opening itself to the participation of many other countries, including China, Iran and the US as observers.

Achievements of SAARC (Political Dimension)

In its third decade in existence, the organisation has not only come to stay, but the mood among member countries is distinctly optimistic. There is a growing conviction among these countries that the benefits of weaving a closer economic community can be bolstered by the possibility of opening a second track of a harmonious regional relationship, which in turn, would help overcome enormous political and security problems in the region.

SAARC has remarkably crossed major hurdles of misperception, suspicion and lack of trust in its first decade of existence. Its existence however has enabled South Asian political leaders to meet regularly and carry on informal discussions to address their mutual problems.

Informal talks among the leaders at regularly held SAARC meetings have led to inter-elite reconciliation on many sensitive issues, producing some noteworthy results in South Asia. The informal talks between the Indian and Pakistani Prime Minister at the second SAARC summit meeting at Bangalore in November 1986 led to the diffusion of tension between the two countries on the issue of India's military exercise, Operation Brass-tacks, on the Indo-Pakistan border, and the India-Sri Lanka talks at the 1987 SAARC foreign ministers' meeting led to their accord on the Tamil Problem. As a result of an informal meeting and discussion between Prime Minister of India and Pakistan, Mr. Narashimha Rao and Mr. Nawaz Sharif, at Davos (Switzerland), in 1992, The Pakistani government took action to prevent the move of the Jammu Kashmir Liberation Front (JKLF) to cross the ceasefire line in Kashmir later that year. The Davos meeting was possible because of an earlier informal agreement between the two leaders at the sixth SAARC summit meeting at Colombo in December 1991.

The Heads of State or Government during the Ninth SAARC summit agreed for the first time that a process of informal political consultations would prove useful in promoting peace, stability, amity and accelerated socio-economic cooperation in the region[30].

There is some hope that the countries in the region may have withdrawn from the move towards the accommodation of religion in politics and arrested the drift towards regionalism in the area's larger countries. These changes provide some hope that the South Asian countries may begin the work towards greater economic region.

The major achievement of the organisation since its formation was that it has contributed a lot in releasing tensions at the regional level. Although initially its progress was slow but later SAARC's role as a major regional organisation increased. It has developed understanding among the states, suppressed terrorist activities through taking common steps for the promotion and establishment of peace and security.

SAARC's SAVE programme is also a notable contribution by the organisation as it has enabled in the exchange of both cultural and technological skills relating to the mass media and communication.

A new member, Afghanistan, has been admitted into the seven-nation body and China's and Japan's request for observer status or as dialogue partners has been favourably viewed. That means the powerful states see a bright future for the SAARC if it moves in the right direction.

Notwithstanding the snail peace progress of SAARC and the political realities it has been confronted with since its inception, it has emerged as the only forum in the South Asian context, where the leaders of the members countries are brought together, despite their intense political inhibitions and insurmountable national reservations on creation political issues.

The Male summit can be viewed as a landmark in that the Heads of state/Govt. recognised that the promotion of peace, stability and amity and socio-economic cooperation may best be achieved by fostering good-neighbourly relations, relieving tensions and building confidence and agreed that 'a process of informal political consultation would prove useful in this regards'. There is no formal institutionalised process for discussion of bilateral political disputes among member states within the existing framework of SAARC. These discussions are not part of the agenda of SAARC meetings and collective discussions of these issues do not take place.

Thus, these sidelines meetings facilitate a deepening of the understanding of the contentious issues in an informal manner and at times have proved to be helpful in critical decision-making. As the understanding reached at the 10th SAARC summit in Colombo, between India and Pakistan, greatly reduced tension between the two countries, which had been heightened after the nuclear explosions by both the countries in May 1998, and facilitated the signing of Lahore Declaration in February 1999.

The other achievement of SAARC, worth mentioning and which has indirectly affected the political climate of South Asia, is that it has significantly contributed in bridging the gap among the non-state actors and civil-societies of the regional countries. While SAARC is a government-led organisation, in recent years, following summit directions, SAARC has helped facilitate greater involvement and interaction among representatives of civil society throughout the region. SAARC has been successful in putting in place scheme designed for the promotions of people to people contact such as the SAARC Audio-Visual Exchange Programme (SAVE), the SAARC chairs, fellowships and scholarships, SAARC Volunteer Exchange Programme etc. It has also helped to bring the private sector of South Asia together, by linking the national chamber of commerce and industries into an apex SAARC Chamber of Commerce and Industries, which provides pertinent practical inputs to the association's economic agenda. SAARC has encouraged and recognised a number of professional groups and specialists in different fields. Efforts to reconvene the 11th SAARC summit have been initiated by the Citizen's Commission for South Asia (CCSA).

The first meeting of the Commission was held in December 2000, in Kathmandu, where former Prime Minister of India I.K.Gujral had also taken part. The activism on the part of the non-governmental actors and members of the civil society is reflective of the fact that these groups can contribute positively towards regional cooperation by influencing their respective governments. This is an encouraging trend growing under the umbrella of SAARC.

Since the May 1998 nuclear tests by India and Pakistan, a new dimension has been added to the South Asian security, which need immediate attention of all the regional states. With their nuclear and missiles capabilities, both India and Pakistan must consider the security requirements of the whole region. Both India and Pakistan have recognised that in order to attain regional nuclear stability, they will have to have a SAARC component to any mutual stability regime.

In recent years there have been important developments both around and within the region that raises hope of faster and effective role of SAARC.

SAARC has also succeeded in stirring up regional consciousness throughout South Asia about cooperation and collective action on various economic and social fronts. This has been achieved by a number of professional SAARC groups of lawyers and doctors, journalists and academics, businessman and entrepreneurs and politician, all engaging and interacting with each other beyond national boundaries under the SAARC flag, which is raised outside the official meetings.

The one of the major achievement of SAARC was started with SAARC summit in Islamabad in January 2004 between India and Pakistan when a peace process was launched between the two countries, under the aegis of the composite dialogue to bring about the 'peaceful settlement' of all bilateral issues including Jammu and Kashmir, to the satisfaction of both sides. This dialogue was sustained by both countries and it has continued till date.

SAARC is the regional instrument available to carry its neighbours along cannot be neglected or undermined. Instead, it has to be endowed with greater vigour and a sense of purpose. The change in India's stance also emanates from its growing economic self-confidence and political resilience.

Although SAARC has made modest achievements, its expected progress has been stalled due to the absence of provisions in its charter to address bilateral contentious issues, as well as the lack of political will on the part of its members to resolve such contentious issues. Although SAARC, during its summit and ministerial level meetings, provides on the sidelines the opportunities to discuss bilateral issues, there is a need to institutionalise the mechanism for discussing contentious issues in an expanded SAARC framework.

Factors Leading to Development of SAARC

A number of significant changes are also taking place with in South Asia that directly affects the texture and pace of progress in SAARC. These intra-regional developments cover five significant areas :

- Within the region almost all the South Asian countries are experiencing satisfactory growth trajectories, notwithstanding international economic pressures and turbulent domestic politics.
- In terms of politics, domestic turbulence is driving the South Asian countries in the direction of greater democratisation, opening political space and encouraging greater grassroots participation in it.
- One of the banes of SAARC's stultified growth, the India-Pakistan hostility and Pakistan's insistence on not moving in the direction of cooperation until the Kashmir issue is resolved seems to be softening.

- From a structural point of view, SAARC has expanded not only by including Afghanistan as a new member, but also by opening its space to new members from outside the region.
- The fact that India, the biggest and fastest growing member, has been promising to transform its regional role from being a reluctant participant to a dynamic leader, by indicating greater commitment to SAARC in recent years.

1. Upsurge of Democracy in South Asia

The factor that may infuse greater development of SAARC in the growing upsurge of democracy in South Asia. The most powerful and decisive manifestation of this upsurge has been in Nepal in the form of Jan Andolan II, which brought nearly 10-12 million people onto the streets of the former kingdom's various cities and towns or 19 days from April 6 to 24, 2006. As a result of this upsurge a 240-year-old feudal order under the dominance of traditional monarchy has been thrown out and a full-fledged secular inclusive democracy ushered in within a republican framework.

Another important manifestation of democratic upsurge has taken place in Pakistan, where within a short period of less than two years, the 10 year old military regime has been forced to withdraw and make room for elected representatives. This change has also been principally orderly and peaceful except the assassination of Benazir Bhutto, who was in the forefront of the struggle for democracy.

People's march towards democracy is also loud and clear in other smaller South Asian countries like Bhutan and Maldives. In Bhutan, the monarchical farsightedness deserves wholesome tribute for initiating the process of democratic transition from the top. It is the king of Bhutan who himself reached out to his simple and innocent people to persuade them to get ready for governing themselves.

The democratic processes initiated are still guarded, gradual and cautious, but the direction is clear. An elected government has assumed office and the monarchy seems commits to accept a constitutional role.

In the Maldives, the one party dominance system is gone and President Gayoom has been pressured to open the polity to greater participation and transparency.

In the SAARC region, these changes constitute significant redefinition of its political texture. Two countries where democratic movements appear to confront uncertainties are Bangladesh and Afghanistan. Bangladesh's military-packed interim regime that assume office in 2006 promises to streamline a constructive and enduring democratic governance by look it out of the pathological personal rivalries of the two principal political parties and their leaders. The signals emanating from the interim government's efforts in this respect sometimes look confusing and contradictory, particularly when the army chief indulges in political sermons.

In Afghanistan, there is a democratic regime functioning under president Karzai who was elected as President in 2004, but its writ does not run effectively even within the capital city of Kabul. Nowhere does the raging internal conflict precipitated by the **"Global War on Terror"** appear to be nearing its resolution.

The international forces fighting terror in Afghanistan are nowhere near achieving their objective, while extremism and violence seem to be in ascendance. Under such circumstances, the fragile democratic experiment is in a real danger of collapse. There is need for terrorism to be controlled and democratic institutions to be reinforced through greater support from the Afghan people.

There are two ways in which the democratic drive will add to the SAARC momentum. One is that spread and consolidation of democracy in South Asia will dent all such intra-regional and bilateral political tensions and contradictions that arise from the democratic divide in the region. Reducing of such tensions will naturally stimulate better regional understanding and cooperation giving a positive push to the SAARC process.

The democratisation of all the SAARC countries will facilitate a broader political understanding amongst the regimes, create a better atmosphere for negotiated and mutually advantageous resolution of dispute and drive them towards enhanced economic and social cooperation.

Secondly, democratic regimes may find it politically rewarding to pursue the issue like economic development, question of social well being and harmony in the region through implantation in nursing their respective constituencies. Greater cooperation will also energise business constituencies in support of the respective democratic regimes in South Asia.

2. Improved India-Pakistan Relations

The third notable change in South Asia is about India Pakistan relations. Even though India and Pakistan have been locked in an adversarial relationship for many decades, the desire for peace is palpable on both sides and relations are widely seen to be in positive mode today. There remain a number of unresolved issues yet, ranging from Siachin to Sir Creek, but there is little doubt that the overall political atmosphere between the two countries is far more conducive than what it was five year earlier.

There are also some positive strategic factors that are creating a conducive environment for Indo-Pak rapprochement. Given the present challenges facing Pakistan, it has little desire and capacity to divert attention to fuel hostilities with India. Pakistan is stretched in its military engagement with Al-Qaeda and Taliban-linked militant elements in the border areas as well as on ongoing insurgency in Baluchistan. In addition, India, through its economic reform and opening up to the world, has moved ahead at a dramatic pace in developing closer ties with major powers including the United States, Southeast Asia, Central Asia and the Middle East. This is forcing Pakistan to re-evaluate its own strategies and especially to look inward to determine whether its fundamental interests are best served by continuing the decades-old hostiles with India, or whether it should mend its relations with India and focus on developing its own basic infrastructure and economy. There is a growing realisation in Pakistan that it would be in Pakistan's interest to shift away from its India-centric foreign policy to one that improves relation between the countries and allows greater energy to be focused on the far more important issues of domestic stability, growth and development.

It is also in India's interest to improve relations with Pakistan as this will be the strongest way of contributing to the stability of the South Asian region. Such stability will benefit all South Asian countries and make the region attractive to foreign investment, international tourism and business opportunities. India's ongoing dialogue and readiness to remain engaged with Pakistan has resulted in many confidence building measures including the opening up of many transportation link between the two countries. In early 2006, a weekly train service (Thar Express) was started between Munabao (India) and Khokhrapar (Pakistan) to complement the already existing bus services between Delhi-Lahore. This Service which began in February 1999 was suspended briefly in the aftermath of the 2001 attack on the Indian Parliament but was resumed thereafter in July 2003. Both countries have also put in place confidence building measure relating to conventional and nuclear issues to alleviate their mutual security. The agreement of pre-notification of Flight Testing of Ballistic Missiles and a memorandum of understanding on communication links between the Pakistani Maritime Security Agency and the Indian Coast Guards was signed on 3 October, 2005 were significant steps in this regards. It is well known that India-Pakistan relation is the key to the pace of development in SAARC. It is the two largest members of the regional grouping gather their respective political wills to move SAARC; it will become a robust forum of regional cooperation in all walks of life.

3. Expansion of SAARC

SAARC has in recent years been expanding. This expansion has taken place in two ways; firstly through the addition of new members, followed by the opening up of SAARC to the **'Observers'** outside the region. The example of direct expansion of SAARC is the inclusion of a new member, namely Afghanistan. Afghanistan has been waiting in the wings for SAARC membership for a long time. Pragmatically, Afghanistan's presence in SAARC makes sense as it may bring about new realism in the regional grouping. By virtue of its geography, it can open up opportunities for India-Pakistan cooperation and play a vital role in facilitating energy cooperation between South and Central Asia. Pakistan, which has been keen to raise bilateral issues in SAARC ignoring the charter conditions not to do so, may be deterred in this respect as Afghanistan may also encouraged to raise its bilateral contentious issues with Pakistan in the regional forum.

Apart from adding a new member, SAARC has also borrowed from the ASEAN experience to invite observers.

A nuclear South Asia which also has the roots of global terrorism and is growing fast, cannot be neglected by the global players, hence the interest of the US, China, the European Union and Russia.

There could also be hope in the region that the inclusion of foreign powers as observers could stimulate competition among the outsiders for assistance and influence resulting in some dynamism in the South Asia.

4. India's Renewed Commitment

India has remained a reluctant and hesitant participant in SAARC from the beginning. Due to the apprehension of the neighbours **"ganging up"** against it, and the neighbours' fear that a closer engagement with India could result in the latter's domination, India's enthusiasm within SAARC has been kept at a low profile. In India's assessment, the economic potential of the region also did not appear to be very attractive. India policy makers have been convinced for a long time that SAARC could not offer the economic opportunities it had been looking for. Frustrated by Pakistan's position on the Kashmir issue and Bangladesh's strong inclination to politicise any bilateral and regional cooperation issue, India at one time, during the late nineties, had even started drifting away from SAARC.

This phase of drift in India's approach to SAARC seems to have come to an end over the past three to four years as India is gradually realising that its credibility and acceptance as a rising Asian power will remain under cloud if it fails to carry its immediate neighbours along. SAARC was reassessed as a political and strategic necessity, if not so much an economic promise.

There are clear indications that India is prepared to make huge investments for the SAARC enterprises to move and move fast. India has offered $100 mn for a SAARC development fund and agreed to allow duty free imports for all the least developed countries of the region, which would include Nepal, Bangladesh, Bhutan, Maldives and Afghanistan.

Its approval for the presence of observers in SAARC is also an indication of India's confidence to deal with the extra-regional powers and secure recognition as a major regional player. India has also taken the lead in establishing a South Asian University to extend regional integration to the intellectual and academic realm.

SAARC, as the only regional instrument available to carry its neighbours along cannot be neglected or undermined. Instead it has to be endowed with greater vigour and a sense of purpose. The change in India's stance also emanates from its growing economic self confidence and political resilience.

Hence, the changing regional dimensions promise to have comprehensive impact in strengthening SAARC, not only as a regional instrument for economic cooperation but also as a forum for building political and strategic understanding among all members.

Role of Observer Nations

The Indian foreign Secretary, Shyam Saran, remarked in 2005 **"if we really wish SAARC to move ahead, if we really want to achieve our dream of South Asian Economic Union, unless we move forward to interconnect from South Asia to the larger Asian capitals, then we cannot really move forward in any significant manner."**

The same sentiments were echoed by the Pakistani Prime Minister Gilani who stated at the recent 15th SAARC summit that **"In an independent, fast globalising world, no regional groupings can hope to function in isolation. SAARC should develop positive links with the adjoining region and beyond. We must adopt an inclusive approach. We should be open to mutually beneficial interactions, especially with our larger Asian neighbourhood. Such links and interdependence would create a win-win support system."**

SAARC has also borrowed from the ASEAN experience to invite observers. At the Delhi 2007 summit, seven countries joined SAARC as observers, namely China, US, Mauritius, the European Union, Japan, South Korea and Iran. At the next 15th Summit in Colombo, Australia and Myanmar was included as observers, bringing the total tally of observer states to nine. This explains the surge of interest amongst outside countries to be associated with SAARC.

As for the interest of the outside powers in South Asia which also has the roots of global terrorism and is growing fast, cannot be neglected by the global players, which resulted in the interest of US, China and The European Union. There could also be hope in the region that the inclusion of foreign powers as observers could stimulate competition among the outsiders for assistance and influence resulting in some dynamism in the South Asian growth story.

China enjoys good relations with Pakistan, Sri Lanka, Bangladesh and Nepal. These countries have always been interested in China's presence in SAARC to balance, in their perception, India in regional affairs. India was reluctant to share the strategic space its sensitive immediate neighbourhood with any extra-regional powers, least of all with China. However there seems to have been a mutual softening of attitudes between India and China with regard to letting each other engage with their neighbourhood regions. While China lowered its reservations on India's entry in East Asia Summit and in Shanghai Cooperation Organisation (as an observer) in 2005, India has also reciprocated by not resisting China's entry as a SAARC observer. This is also in harmony with the improving economic and strategic relations between India and China.

China is looking towards South Asia to tap into its enormous market for trade and investment and explore opportunities for cooperation in energy, natural resources, infrastructure and people to people relations. China's trade with South Asia was estimated to be USD40.89 billion in 2007. But more importantly, China's presence in SAARC could help consolidate its strategic interests in the region. Underlining China's interest in SAARC, foreign minister Li Zhaoxing remarked on the occasion of the 14th SAARC summit that **"Good political atmosphere, close geographical location and popular support will greatly boost China-SAARC cooperation, which serves our common interests and peace, stability and development of the region."**

Similarly Japan, the single largest donor to South Asian countries during the last two decades, and also the first country to express interest in joining SAARC, saw its inclusion in SAARC in line with its initiative of creating an "**Arc of freedom and prosperity**" of which South Asia remained a central pillar. Japan has shown a keen interest in promoting both political stability and a cooperative environment in South Asia and is the only country, which has been supportive of regional integration in South Asia through an institutional interaction with SAARC. Since 1993, it has been supporting activities of SAARC through a special SAARC-Japan Fund. At present, Japan is considered by all the states of the region as a friendly country, which has a more acceptable face for playing any meaningful role to help strengthen the SAARC framework, for security related cooperation through friendly persuasions. Japan wishes to establish a bilateral relationship with South Asian countries based on the broad understanding and participation of people from both sides, so as to foster the expansion of people to people contact at all levels.

Like China, Iran and Myanmar have actually gone as far as to show interest in becoming SAARC members and would have their own agenda for doing so. Iran is actively seeking strategic and economic engagements to strengthen its position in the world order. In order to reduce its isolation from Gulf Cooperation Council and garner some support for it to resist

US moves to marginalise it in Asia. Iran has been cultivating ties with countries in South and Central Asia, and China to counter US moves.

Iran can also be powerful factor in building a web of interdependencies between India, Pakistan and Afghanistan. It can become a source of addressing the region's energy challenge as is evident in the proposal for Iran-Pakistan-India gas pipeline.

Myanmar's interest in South Asia has been building in recent years. Its participation in BIMSTEC and keen desire to promote an India-Bangladesh-Myanmar gas pipeline were clear notifications in this respect. This proposal has not taken off the ground due to Bangladesh's reservations, but Myanmar's growing economic cooperation with India will continue to reinforce its interest in South Asia. Myanmar's increasing difficulties in ASEAN, particularly after the adoption of ASEAN Charter that lays emphasis on issues like democracy and human rights, appear to have hastened its search for wider regional engagements. Myanmar may find it politically useful to secure membership of other organisations. Myanmar's interest in SAARC could also spur interest of ASEAN or some of its members to join SAARC as observers.

US interest in SAARC as observers could be to develop a new strategic relationship with India based on commercial, scientific, technological and political-military interests; to deepen relationship with Pakistan besides counter terrorism cooperation; to stabilise and democratise Afghanistan; to become an influential players in South and Central Asia and to assist the region in issues related to climate change, globalisation, energy security, AIDS and other diseases, terrorism and weapons of mass destruction.

Between 1994 and 2004, the European Union concluded five cooperation agreements with SAARC. The basis of all the agreements is a respect for human rights and democratic principles. The objective of these cooperation agreements were to enhance and develop the various aspects of cooperation between the parties, and in particular develop two-way trade and promote investment, improve economic, technical and cultural links, support overall sustainable development and protect the environment. In light of the growing competence of the European Union and with SAARC moving into core areas of cooperation, there are good prospects in the immediate and long term of EU-SAARC cooperation.

Russia also intends to become an observer and is supported by India.

Having bought into the mantra of the Asian renaissance and globalisation, South Asia is on the whole, more open to foreign observers in SAARC than ever before. It may be recalled that India, which had been wary of external influence in the region and inducting external powers into SAARC, has now accepted that opening up is inevitable. The recently concluded 15th SAARC summit has also envisaged a greater role for observers and inter-governmental organisations such as the World Bank and the Asian Development Bank in the improvement of multi-modal transport and transit infrastructure to facilitate trade and business prospects in the region.

Smaller SAARC nations that look towards balancing India's predominant position in the region are also reassured by the presence of outside powers who could balance the asymmetry in the region. India, although initially reluctant to allow China to be an observer, agreed after the inclusion of Japan, US and EU, who could effectively thwart any moves by China to dominate SAARC at India's expense. Its relations with China have improved in recent years and India would not like to upset the present equilibrium in Sino-Indian ties.

In this age of globalisation and interdependence, SAARC cannot afford to remain isolated. Most issues that countries in South Asia face be it in realm of terrorism, maritime security, health environment or economic growth are transnational in nature and require a coordinated response.

Observer countries could, in addition, play a useful role in terms of toning down political differences between member countries in SAARC, as well as reinvigorating the economic equations between them.

Additionally, the presence of external observers could enhance SAARC's external image and give it a voice in global institutions, including the United Nations[31].

SAARC and the United States of America

South Asia has emerged as a region of strategic international interest. The emergence of India as a major power and one of the balance of power in near future.

Large countries like Pakistan and Bangladesh with their big populations can be significant players. Pakistan has an especial role since she is also a nuclear power and has the capacity to weigh in on any new strategic re-arrangement in South Asia.

Because of these configurations, the present US policy for the region is based on the following objectives:

- To develop a new strategic relationship with India based on commercial, scientific, technological and political-military interests.
- To deepen relationship with Pakistan besides counter-terrorism cooperation.
- To stabilise and democratise Afghanistan.
- To become an influential players in South and Central Asia.
- To assist the region in issues related to climate change, globalisation, energy security, AIDS and other diseases, terrorism and weapons of mass destruction.

- Balancing any new power that could disturb the existing power configuration in global politics.
- Diffusing regional weaknesses that could threaten US security and well being.
- To find regional partners who can assist in the reduction of such risks.

The US charge de affairs in Nepal called on the SAARC Secretary General on March 22, 2006 to convey the US keen interest to become at observer. The SAARC Secretary General asked US to approach Dhaka, as Bangladesh was the chair of the forum that year. Speaking at a meeting organised in New Delhi by the Confederation of Indian Industry (CII), Richard Boucher, the then US Assistant Secretary of State for South and Central Asia also confirmed that the US had approached SAARC's Secretary General requesting observer status.

Though the US is already a member of the Asia-Pacific Economic Cooperation (APEC) and attends the forum of Association of Southeast Asia Nations (ASEAN) it has not participated in the East Asia summit. It has also been successfully kept out of Shanghai Cooperation Organisation.

If America as a leading power wants to play important role in world affairs then it has to increase its interaction with such regional groupings. SAARC can be one of them.

The US is in the process of outsourcing its manufacturing industry and service to Asia and is concerned about how the economic scene develops in South Asia too[32].

In 2011, at Maldives the United States has further acknowledged the importance of SAARC by appointing US Ambassador to Nepal Scott Delisi as the US representative to the SAARC Secretariat.

The United States is committed to working with SAARC and all the governments of South Asia to expand cooperation, prosperity and opportunity in this vital region of the world[33].

Conclusion

It has elapsed two decades since the SAARC came into existence with the lofty goals of bringing about positive changes in the life of South Asian people through mutual cooperation and collaboration. But there are widespread frustrations that regional body has been unable to live up to the expectations of its people. It is not that the SAARC made no achievement. Its achievements are very modest compared to that of other regional organisations such as ASEAN and European Union.

SAARC has been hijacked and remained a political hostage to bilateral disputes between India and Pakistan, the low level of mutual trust, the spillover effects of the ethnic and religious conflicts in South Asia had a serious impact on summits held so far. The very fact that these summits could be held, despite political tensions and differences is a testimony to the SAARC leaders' willingness to continue regional cooperation.

Efforts should be made to make it work and serious thoughts should be given to making it a more effective body. Still, SAARC has a very long way to go before it catches up with other regional groups such as ASEAN and EU. The realisation of durable peace and the future of economic integration through SAARC depend upon the ability and interest of South Asian leaders to resolve domestic as well as long-standing differences through peaceful deliberations.

It may not be too much hope that SAARC is also now poised to launch itself onto a more dynamic pace of progress and evolution. The SAARC region is undergoing significant changes both internally and in the way of global dynamics impinges upon it.

References

1. Kishore C. Dash, "The Political Economy of regional cooperation in South Asia", Pacific Affairs, Vol. 69, No. 2 (Summer 1996).
2. Muni S.D. and Jaithley Rajshree-SAARC: The changing dimensions, UNU-CRIS working papers-w-2008/8, Institute of South Asian Studies, Singapore, United Nations University, and CRIS.
3. Ghosh-Parthsarathy-Cooperation and conflict in South Asia, Some Theoretical and General Issues, Manohar Publications, New Delhi, 1995, p. 13.
4. Kishore C. Dash, "The Political Economy of regional cooperation in South Asia", Pacific Affairs, Vol. 69, p. 2.
5. Online-International News Network – Afghanistan happy to be back in family as SAARC's 8th member-http://www.onlinenews.com/-2006.
6. Dr. Kapila Subash-South Asia Analysis Group-South Asia and the impact of Afghanistan events, p. 39, http://www.southasianadtheimpactof afghanistan events.htm/.2001.
7. Aska Tanveer, Yusuf Moeed, ShaHeen Faisal Haq, Khan Rafi Shaheen-Regional Integration, Trade and conflict,Mapping Regional Trade Agreements and Conflicts, International Institute for Sustainable Development Publication, Jan 2007, p. 14.
8. India and SAARC-PDF document, www.scribd.com/doc/38575394/India-and-SAARC.
9. Kishore C. Dash "The Political Economy of Regional Cooperation in South Asia", Pacific Affairs, Vol. 69, p. 16, 2011.
10. Muni. S.D. Jaithely Rajshree-SAARC- The Changing Dimension, UNU-CRIS Working Papers, United Nations University, p. 24.
11. Jain B.M. and Chatterji Manas- conflict and Peace in South Asia-retrospect and prospect, p. 338, Emerald Publishing Ltd UK 2008.
12. Aziz Khalid- Social and Political Issues in South Asia, p. 11.

13. Dash.C. Kishore, "The Political Economy of Regional Cooperation in South Asia", Pacific Affairs, Vol. 69, No. 2, 1996.
15. Hussain Akmal and Wigharya Poona- The Challenge in South Asia-SAARC: Evolution and Elements of a Future Agenda, Sage Publications, London, 1989, p. 359
16. Aziz Khalid- Social and Political Issues in South Asia, Political Issues facing South Asia, p. 9.
17. Hussian Akmal and Wigharaja Poona- The Challenge in South Asia- SAARC evolution and element of a future agenda, Sage Publication, London, 1989, p. 359.
18. Khanna V.N. - Foreign Policy of India,Vikas Publication, Delhi, 2005, -255.
19. Uprety Kishore and Salman M.A. Salman-Conflict and Cooperation on South Asia's International Rivers- A legal perspective, general conclusion, Kluwer law international, 2002, p. 202.
20. Aziz Khalid- Social and Political Issues in South Asia, India-U.S. Nuclear Cooperation, p. 8.
21. Pandey Aditya- South Asia: Conflicts of South Asia-Vol. 2, South Asia and Nuclear Conflict, Ch. 3, p. 252, Isha Publications, Delhi, 2005.
22. PDF. Acrobat-Unit 24, SAARC. http://www.egyankosh.ac.in/.
23. Central Chronicle-Crisis of trust at SAARC, http://www.centralchronicle.htm. 11-11-2011.
24. Hussain Akmal and Wigharaya Poona- The Challenges in South Asia SAARC: Evolution and Elements of a Future Agenda, Sage Publication, London, 1989, p. 359.
25. Ahmed Rashid- Should SAARC be wound up? NIPA- Karachi, Vol. 7, p. 82, Dec. 2002.
26. Aziz Khalid-Social and Political Issues in South Asia-Recommendations, p. 15.
27. Burki Javed Shahid-ISAS- working paper, South Asia; Overcoming the past, Meeting the Challenges of present and availing opportunities, of future, p. June-2009. www.isas-nus.edu.sg
28. Muni.S.D. and Jaithely Rajshree-UNU-CRIS Working Papers, SAARC: The Changing dimension, Institute of South Asian Studies, 2008, p. 23.
29. Dixit Aabha, SAARC: Toward Greater Cooperation, 2011, p. 15 Http://www.saarctowardsgreatercooperation.htm//
30. Iqbal Jamshed Muhammad-SAARC: Origin,growth,potential and achievements, Pakistan Journal of History and Culture, Vol. 27/2(2006), p. 138, http://www.nihcr.edu.pk.
31. Muni. S.D. and Jaithely Rajshree- SAARC: The changing dimensions, UNU-CRIS Working Papers, W-2008/8, Institute of South Asian Studies, Singapore, p. 23.
32. Kumar Anand, Making a beeline for Saarc, South Asia Analysis Group, 17.4.06, p. 1770, http://www.MAKING A BEELINE FOR SAARC.htm/

33. News.com,Blake at SAARC Summit,17-11-2011, http:// www.Blake at SAARC Summit Asia Editorial.htm/

5

Economic Dimensions of SAARC

The growth of regional economic cooperation arrangement is one of the major developments in the post - World War II period. The formation of regional integration has been greatly successful in bringing historically hostile countries together. The basic premise on which SAARC was founded was that by activating cooperative cultural identities and economic interests, political conflicts and tensions in South Asia could be moderated, if not completely eliminated.

This South Asian Association for Regional Cooperation was created to promote economic integrity and cooperation among South Asian nations. However, over the years it has been seen that SAARC mainly worked towards development of economic relationship among the SAARC nations. Attempts are also on to further trade relations with the member nations of ASEAN and the European Union (EU).

Despite of lying in the vicinity of one another, trading activities were restricted among the SAARC nations. Over the years, there has significant improvement in the trade relations among the eight SAARC members.

The focus has been shifted to get access to the markets of the other members. Methods have also been devised to attract foreign direct investments to strengthen economic infrastructures of the SAARC nations. All these initiatives points towards an improvement in the economic relationship among the South Asian countries.

South Asia is home to about one and half billion people or 23 per cent of the world population. Its share in world gross domestic product (GDP) is 2.3 per cent. The eight countries in the region—Afghanistan,

Bangladesh, Bhutan, India, Maldives, Nepal, Pakistan and Sri Lanka - have diverse economic features with India and Pakistan being the two largest economies in terms of the regional GDP and population. But India's dominance in nearly all respects is a central and special feature of the region that can be seen as both a positive and negative feature in the context of promoting greater economic cooperation.

India has nearly 77.8 per cent of the region's GDP, accounts for 40.3 per cent of its trade and 75.8 per cent of incoming foreign direct investment (FDI). It is the only country in South Asia that has common borders with all others. India is both literally and otherwise central to South Asia.

However, in terms of economic well-being, as measured by the human development index, Sri Lanka and Maldives are better off than the other six.

However, alleviating widespread poverty, sustaining employment generation, improving infrastructure and sustaining rapid and inclusive economic growth remain the common and pressing challenges in all the countries of the region. India's stance has also been changing in recent year. Presently, India recognises the advantage of an integrated South Asian economic space for all SAARC members, including itself, as equal partners in any regional cooperation initiative. This tendency needs to be further strengthened and can emerge as the major driver for regional cooperation in South Asia.

South Asia, stretching from Kabul to Chittagong and from Kashmir to Male has historically been an integrated economic, cultural and environment space. This is a necessary condition for the region and its member countries to fully exploit their potential and achieve their objective of achieving rapid, sustainable and inclusive economic growth[1].

Table 5.1

Country	*2005*	*2006*	*2007*	*2008*	*2009*	*2010*
Afghanistan	14.00	5.34	11.1	3.4	20.4	8.2
Bangladesh	5.96	6.63	6.4	6.2	5.7	6.1
Bhutan	7.02	8.47	17.9	4.7	6.7	7.4
India	9.23	9.20	9.8	4.9	9.1	8.8
Maldives	-5.09	23.53	12.1	12.0	-6.5	9.9
Nepal	3.12	2.80	3.4	6.1	4.4	4.6
Pakistan	7.67	6.92	5.7	1.6	3.6	4.1
Sri Lanka	6.03	7.35	6.8	6.0	3.5	8.0

Source: World Development Indicators Online, 2011, World Bank.

Growth Rates of SAARC Countries

With the failure of WTO talks, regional trade assumes greater importance for South Asian countries. Despite slow growth in North America and Europe, South Asian economies remain amongst the fastest growing in the world with 6-9 per cent GDP growth.

Economic Profile of SAARC Nations

(ECONOMIC GROWTH DURING 2005—2010)

Almost all of the South Asian economies are growing at a steady pace, though the rates of their respective growths are different and range from about 3 per cent to more than 23 per cent according to the available figures.

Fig. 5.1: Growth rate of Nepal

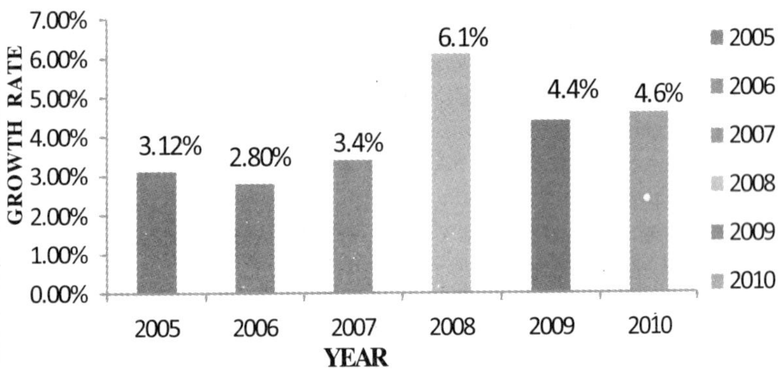

1. NEPAL

Nepal was at less than 3 per cent at 2.8 per cent, and even that was because of serious instability, arising from the Maoist insurgency in 2006 and the people's uprising against an autocratic monarchy in 2006. Nepal has now come out of the phase of violence and instability through its unique peace process. The latest IMF estimates suggest that Nepal may register a growth of 4 per cent for 2010. The Maoists, having succeeded in turning Nepal into a "Democratic Republic" from a Constitutional Monarchy, have declared the conclusion of their "political revolution" and have launched their "economic revolution" so as to raise the economic standards of common people in Nepal.

2. AFGHANISTAN

Afghanistan's growth has been 8.2 per cent in 2010 after an increasing and decreasing level since 2005 from 14 per cent to 5.3 per cent in 2006, it was 11.1 per cent in 2007 and became 3.4 per cent in

Fig. 5.2: Growth Rate of Afghanistan

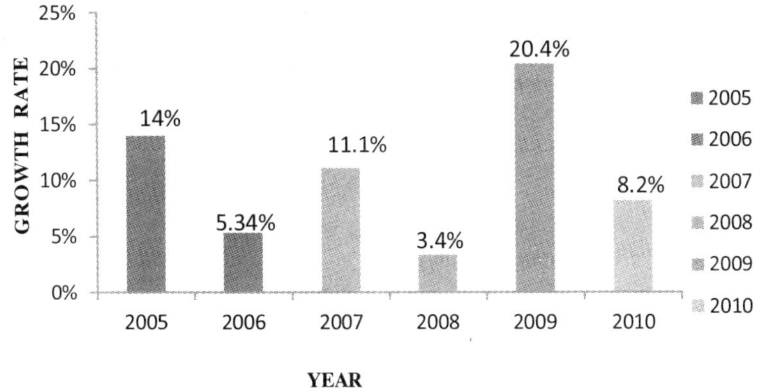

2008, from 20.4 per cent to 8.2 per cent in 2009-10 in growth rate. There also, the specter of violence and instability seems to be endless ever since the launching of the global war on terror in 2001. At present the political condition of Afghanistan is stable which is also leading to economic stability after the end of Taliban.

3. BANGLADESH

Bangladesh, the proverbial basket case of South Asia has been doing remarkably well in a sustained manner and the estimate shows that it may emerge as one of the most dynamic economy of the region. It is visible that since 2005 there is minute decease in growth rate from 5.96 per cent in 2005 to 6.1 per cent in 2010.

Fig. 5.3 : Growth rate of Bangladesh

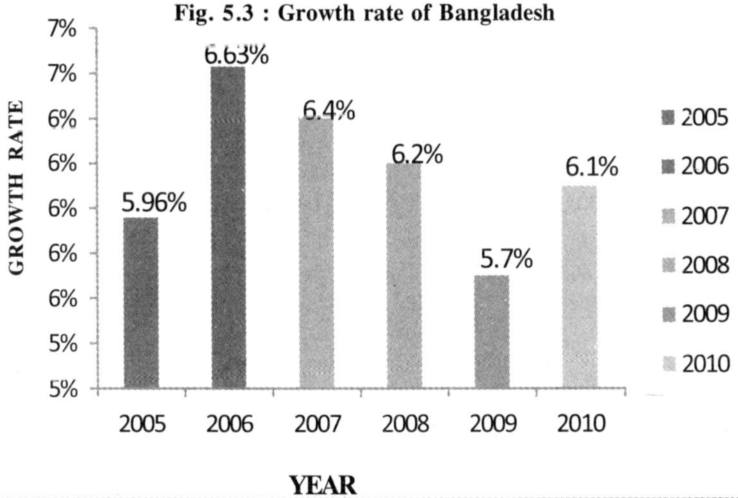

On the other hand, Bangladesh's export sector has also been sustained by growing trade with India, through trade with India is grossly one sided for Bangladesh, which suffers a heavy trade balance of more than $1bn. Bangladesh in also keen to explore bilateral FTAs with India, Pakistan and Sri Lanka.

4. MALDIVES

Maldives, one of the smallest nations of SAARC the growth rate of the Maldives in GDP percentage terms was 23.5 per cent, the highest in the region, at least for the year 2006.

Fig. 5.4: Growth rate of Maldives

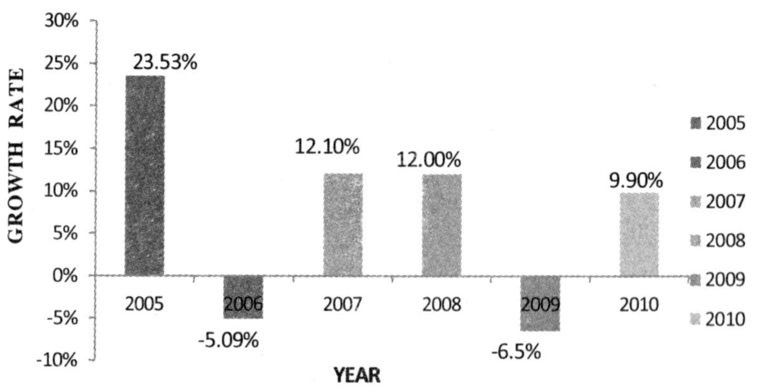

But it gradually fell down from 23.53 per cent to 6.5 per cent from 2006-2009, and there is growth of about 9.9 per cent in 2010. But the economic possibility in future of Maldives is very progressive.

5. PAKISTAN

As stated in the above indicator, there is decrease in the growth rate of Pakistan since last five years from 2005-2010 and the level of growth after 2008 was also very low. The main reason for low level of economic growth in the year 2008 was the political instability in Pakistan due to the shifting portals of power from the quasi-military rule of President Musharraf to the democratic parties. Despite having to deal with several political crises, both domestically and internationally, Pakistan has managed to keep a respectable growth rate from 1.6 per cent in 2008 to 4.1 per cent in 2010. Trade growth also stands out as an impressive development even between India and Pakistan, which has the potential of reaching $10bn mark with the required political support from the two sides. Pakistan is also facing growing competition and protection in its

Fig. 5.5: Growth rate of Pakistan

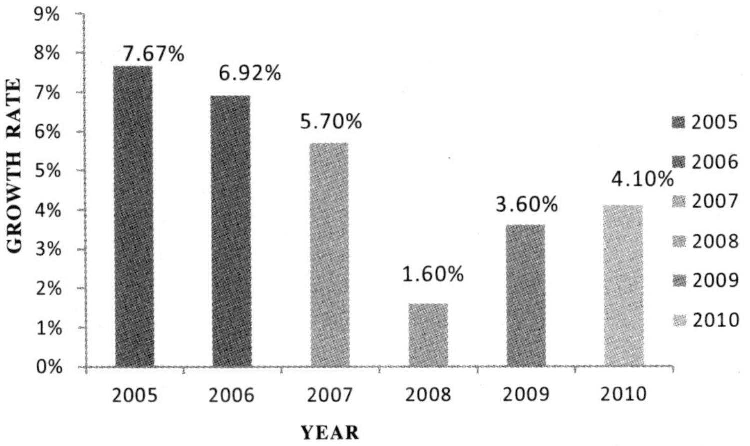

external markets in the developed world as well as in the Gulf and Central Asian regions. Consequently, it is also looking towards SAARC to see how it can leverage its relative advantage as the second largest economy in the region.

6. SRI LANKA

From the above indicator, we can see that Sri Lanka has witnessed an impressive growth during 2009-2010. The growth rates during the last

Fig. 5.6: Growth rate of Sri Lanka

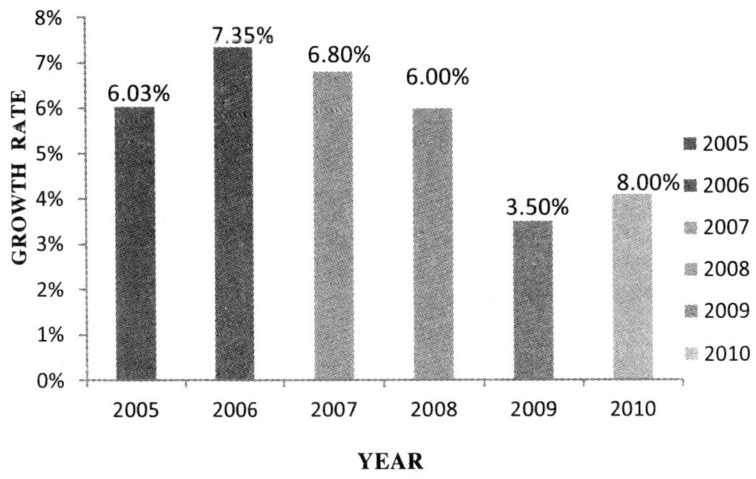

five years are also little varied. There is very less difference among these growth rates. This symbolises that among all the South Asian nations, Sri Lanka is also emerging as an economic power in South Asia.

Sri Lanka has also signed FTAs with both India and Pakistan. The Indo-Sri Lanka Free Trade Agreement (FTA) contributed to Sri Lanka's economic performance and cushioned the impact of ethnic conflict raging there incessantly. The Sri Lankan economy, being based on Special Economic Zones, tourism and the estate sector is, in a significant way, insulated from the ethnic conflict in the north east. But enhancement of trade through re-exports with India has also contributed to Sri Lanka's economic health. The contribution of the FTA may be assessed from the fact that while the bilateral trade was around $500 million before the FTA, it reached $2.5 billion by 2008. The success of the FTA has encouraged both India and Sri Lanka to raise the level of FTA to Comprehensive Economic Partnership Agreement (CEPA).

Sri Lanka has seen its exports to developed countries suffer due to the growing protectionism and it is very keen to increase its trade with SAARC countries. It remains an ardent champion of trade liberalisation within the region.

7. BHUTAN

Bhutan being the smallest country of South Asia is witnessing impressive economic prosperity during the year 2005-2010. It reflects the wise investment made by the kingdom in the hydro-power sector, which reaps its rich earnings through the sale of power to India. India's trade with Bhutan operates more openly than even the FTA patterns.

Fig. 5.7: Growth rate of Bhutan

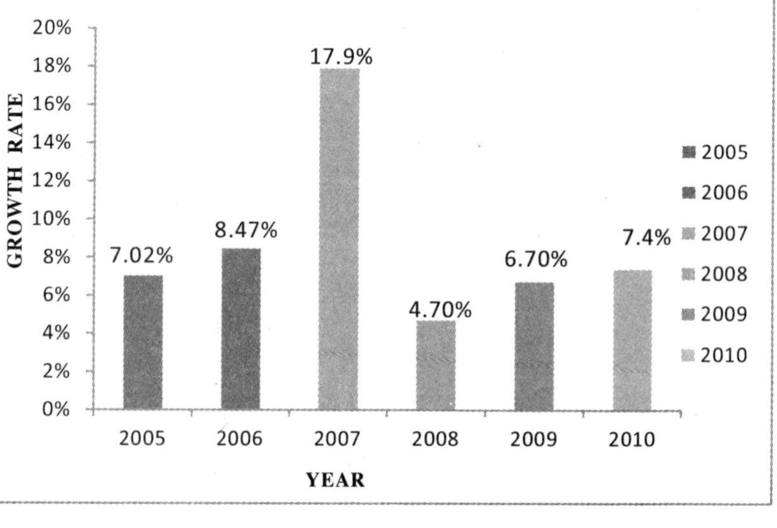

8. INDIA

The growth rate of India in GDP percentage was around nine per cent after Maldives in 2010 and the government has committed itself to raise this to at least 10 per cent and to maintain it there as the bottom line.

It is true that, as noted earlier, in the cases of Bangladesh and Sri Lanka, heavy trade reliance upon India has also precipitated the problem of trade deficit and many other South Asian countries fear that greater economic interaction in the region might lead to India's dominance over their respective economies.

The region seems ready to more consciously towards greater mutual engagement, as the smaller South Asian countries become conscious of the opportunities and advantages that India's growing, diversified and huge economy may offer. India, at the same time, realises that it needs to leverage the advantages it enjoys by virtue of its size and geography to engage with the other smaller countries in a spirit of trust, generosity and non-reciprocity. This policy could have a win-win impact in raising the cumulative profile of the region, not only in trade and economic matters but as a whole.

In pursuit of this objective, India has recently deleted 264 items from the existing sensitive list of 744 for the least developed countries (LDCs) in a move to enhance trade by removing the duty on these items. India, being the largest economic power in SAARC will have the greatest impact through its policies.

The energy crisis is a real challenge which is seriously affecting the Indian economy more than any other South Asian economy, but the impact will not be a serious and lasting one.

There are two unmistakable aspects of the South Asian growth story. One is that despite the tardy progress of SAARC, the South Asian growth pattern is somewhat rooted into regional economic engagement.

It is expected that this growth in bilateral trade may receive a further boost from SAFTA, which became operational in July 2006, opening up immense potential to increase intra-regional trade.

With the effective implementation of SAFTA, it is estimated that the current level of intra-regional trade could rise from \$ six billion to \$ 14 billion. SAFTA has not yielded optimum results thus for a number of reasons. The first reason concerns the fear experienced by smaller countries that India, by virtue of its sheer size, would flood their markets. Further reasons include the imposition of protectionist policies with high import tariffs on manufactured goods produced by South Asian countries, lack of adequate transport and information links, and competition between South Asian countries for outside markets. Finally the political issues, especially between India and Pakistan, have cast their shadow on the prospects for intra-regional trade in South Asia.

Despite these constraints, economies in the region are gradually opening up. Some South Asian countries are steadily improving the regulatory environment for doing business as the latest report on this issue shows. Imperatives of globalisation and compulsions of development and growth have gradually made these economies realise the importance of forging bilateral and multilateral engagements both within the region and outside for economic benefits. There is now greater acceptance that benefits can be multiplied many times over if South Asian countries can overcome their differences and harness their strengths to engage with the outside world as a cohesive entity. The gaps that previously existed in the information and awareness about each other's strengths and weaknesses, and needs and surpluses have over the years been gradually narrowed down.

The importance of reducing protectionist barriers was reiterated at the fifteenth SAARC summit, which urged all SAARC Heads of State to resolve the issue of Non-Tariff Measures (NTMs) and Para Tariff Measures (PTMs) to facilitate trade under SAFTA. With the exception of India and Pakistan, all other South Asian countries protect more than half of their total imports under the negative list.

The other countries can also contribute to intra-SAARC trade, especially if there is a competitive advantage to trading within SAARC as compared to trading with countries outside the bloc.

The second aspect of the growing South Asian economies is that they will maintain their growth momentum while facing the twin challenges of rising oil prices and the slowdown in the US/Western economies.

Fig. 5.9: SAARC Country Shares of Regional GDP

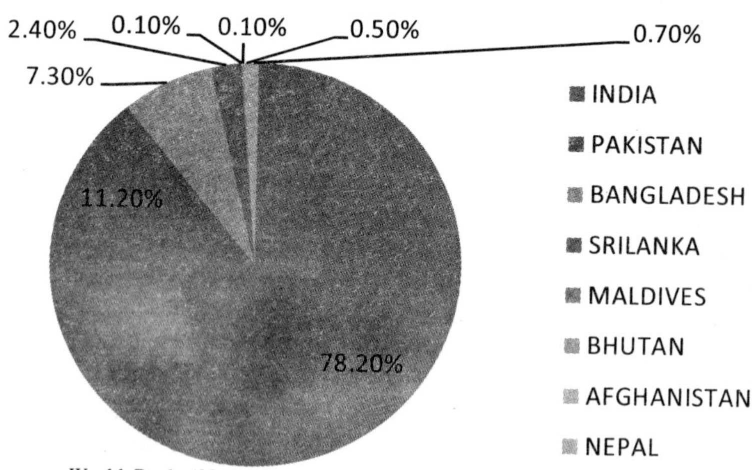

Source : World Bank (2011)

Table 5.2. Select Economic Indicators of SAARC Countries

Indicators	*Year*	*Afghanistan*	*Bangladesh*	*Bhutan*	*India*	*Maldives*	*Nepal*	*Pakistan*	*Sri Lanka*
GDP Growth (per cent)	2006	5.34	6.63	8.47	9.20	23.53	3.12	6.92	7.35
	2007	11.10	6.40	17.90	9.80	12.10	2.80	5.70	6.80
	2008	3.40	6.20	4.70	4.90	12.00	3.40	1.60	6.00
	2009	20.40	5.70	6.70	9.10	-6.50	6.10	3.60	3.50
	2010	8.20	6.10	7.40	8.80	9.90	4.60	4.10	8.00
Inflation (per cent)	2006	5.1	7.2	4.9	5.4	3.5	8.0	7.9	9.6
	2007	9.8	7.2	5.2	4.4	7.4	6.4	7.8	20.2
	2008	10.2	9.0	4.5	4.5	6.0	7.0	8.0	16.2
	2009	7.2	8.0	4.5	4.5	6.0	6.5	6.5	14.0
	2010	8.2	7.3	6.1	9.2	5.1	9.5	11.7	6.9
Export Growth rate (per cent)	2006	0.4	21.5	47.2	21.8	39.4	2.6	14.9	8.5
	2007	3.3	15.8	64.5	18.1	2.8	4.3	4.4	12.5
	2008	8.0	12.0	33.9	16.0	-	6.1	8.0	8.0
	2009	8.7	15.0	9.0	18.0	-	4.3	10.0	9.0
	2010	14.4	18.5	64.7	21.5	-	9.8	13.6	21.7
Import Growth rate (per cent)	2006	10.0	12.1	-5.6	21.8	24.4	17.8	33.3	15.7
	2007	15.0	16.6	15.1	28.5	14.8	11.3	8.0	10.2
	2008	13.2	20.0	19.5	22.0	-	14.0	13.0	9.5
	2009	-1.4	16.0	23.4	24.0	-	14.5	10.0	9.0
	2010	-	24.9	-	24.8	-	37.4	19.4	30.8

(Contd.)

(Contd. Table 5.2)

Indicators	*Year*	*Afghanistan*	*Bangladesh*	*Bhutan*	*India*	*Maldives*	*Nepal*	*Pakistan*	*Sri Lanka*
Trade Balance (per cent of GDP)	2006	-60.4	-4.7	75.2	-6.5	-46.0	-16.9	-.67	-10.3
	2007	-59.3	-5.6	5.1	-7.6	-48.8	-16.7	-6.8	-11.9
	2008	-65.2	-8.6	-5.9	-9.3	-49.7	-20.5	-10.3	-11.3
	2009	-58.2	-7.6	-7.9	-8.8	-39.7	-21.4	-8.1	-14.7
	2010	-	-8.3	-22.8	-5.9	-41.8	-25.4	-6.6	-10.5
Current A/c Balance (per cent of GDP)	2006	-4.6	1.3	-4.7	-1.0	-23.5	2.2	-3.9	-5.3
	2007	0.8	1.4	15.8	-1.3	-29.0	-0.1	-4.8	-4.3
	2008	-1.9	0.9	-2.2	-2.2	-36.2	3.1	-9.5	-9.5
	2009	-3.9	2.7	-1.7	-2.8	-24.0	4.2	-5.9	-0.5
	2010	-	3.7	-14.3	-2.3	-24.2	-2.4	-2.3	-2.9
External Debt (US$ mn)	2006	12,083	18603	677	169,629	574	3,249	35,655	12,235
	2007	1,883	19703	756	190,516	-	3,218	38,699	16,130
	2008	2089	2286	692	224713	716	3685	48471	15,611
	2009	2328	23820	762	237692	780	3683	53710	17,208
	2010	2328	-	-	-	-	3683	-	-
Exchange rate (US$1)	2006	49.9	67.1	44.70	45.30	12.8	71.90	59.90	104.0
	2007	50.1	69.0	44.20	40.20	12.8	70.60	60.60	110.6
	2008	50.25	68.60	43.51	43.51	12.8	69.76	36.57	108.33
	2009	50.23	69.04	48.41	48.41	12.8	77.55	42.90	114.95
	2010	46.45	69.65	45.73	45.73	12.8	73.15	45.96	113.07

(Contd.)

(Contd. Table 5.2)

Indicators	Year	Afghanistan	Bangladesh	Bhutan	India	Maldives	Nepal	Pakistan	Sri Lanka
Foreign	2006	2,064	3,484	479	199,179	232	1,834	10,760	2,515
Exchange	2007	2,335	5,077	599	306,488	309	2,401	13,345	3,100
reserves	2008	0	5789	765	254024	241	8	8903	2561
(US$ mn)	2009	201	10343	891	274668	261	100	13771	5358
	2010	193	11178	-	287051	350	94	17210	7197
Fiscal	2006	-3.1	-3.2	-0.8	-6.4	-6.7	-1.6	-4.3	-8.1
Balance of	2007	-2.9	-3.2	-3.4	-5.5	-7.9	-2.0	-5.8	-7.7
Central Govt.	2008	-4.2	-5.3	0.7	-6.0	-11.9	-2.1	-7.3	-7.0
(per cent of	2009	-13.[illegible]	-3.7	1.8	-6.4	-22.1	-3.2	-5.1	-9.9
GDP)	2010	-	-3.9	-4.7	-5.1	-15.8	-2.3	-5.9	-7.9

Source: Asian Development Outlook, 2008, Asian Development Bank.

Asian Development Outlook, 2011.

Asian Development Bank, key indicators for Asia and the Pacific – 2011.

The assessment has been reinforced by the Asian Development Bank. It is projected that notwithstanding the challenges facing South Asian economies, growth will remain in the range of seven per cent to eight per cent. In meeting the challenges, South Asia will do better through collective and cooperative action than individually. This creates a situation where SAARC may look forward to greater dynamism.[2]

The Economic Agenda of SAARC

SAARC was created to promote economic integrity and cooperation among South Asian nations. Its aim was to ensure social and economic development of the member countries. The South Asian countries in the recent years attached increasing importance to regional economic corporation for accelerating the pace of economic development and raising the standards of living of people in the member countries.

The Economic Agenda of SAARC is as follows

The main economic agenda of SAARC include :

(a) SAARC Preferential Trading Agreement (SAPTA)

The Agreement on SAPTA was signed on 11 April 1993 and entered into force on 7 December 1995. The Agreement reflected the desire of the member state to promote and sustain mutual trade and economic cooperation within the SAARC region through the exchange of concessions.

Principles of SAPTA

The basic principles of SAPTA are as follows :

- SAPTA shall be based and applied on the principles of overall reciprocity and mutuality of advantages in such a way as to benefit equitably all contracting states, taking into account their respective levels of economic and industrial development, the pattern of their external trade and their trade policies and systems.
- SAPTA shall be negotiated step by step, improved and extended in successive stages with periodic reviews.
- The special needs of the least developed contracting states shall be clearly recognised and concrete preferential measures in their favour should be agreed upon. The special treatment for the least developed contracting states include, duty-free access, exclusive tariff preferences of deeper tariff preferences in respect of special products, removal of non-tariff and para-tariff barriers. These preferential measures are not required to be multi-lateralised among other developing country contracting states.
- The concessions agreed to under SAPTA, except those made exclusively to the least developed contracting states, shall be extended unconditionally to all contracting states.

- The tariff, para-tariff and non-tariff concessions negotiated and exchanged amongst contracting states shall be incorporated in the national schedules of concessions.
- Products contained in the national schedules of concessions shall be eligible for preferential treatment if they satisfy the rule of origin established under SAPTA.
- The concession agreed upon shall not be diminished or mollified by the application of any measure restricting trade by the contracting states except under the provisions specified in the Agreement.
- Safeguard measures can be taken in the event of injury to domestic producers from import under SAPTA or in the event of deterioration of balance of payment position during the implementation of SAPTA.

One of the core principles of the SAPTA Agreement listed above is that there should be special treatment for least developed countries through the consideration of additional measures.

It was accordingly decided in 1999 to reduce the domestic content requirement further under the SAPTA Rules of Origin to enable the smaller

Table 5.3
SAPTA Rules of Origin

	Before Amendment		*After Amendment*	
	For non-LDCs	*For LDCs*	*For Non-LDCs*	*For LDCs*
Rule 3 (a): Not wholly produced or obtained.				
Domestic value addition in an exporting country	50%	40%	40%	30%
Maximum input permitted from non-contracting states. (outside SAARC region)	50%	60%	60%	70%

Rule 4: Cumulative Rules of Origin

	Before Amendment		*After Amendment*	
	For Non LDCs	*For LDCs*	*For Non-LDCs*	*For LDCs*
Aggregate Domestic Value Addition in an Exporting Country including inputs sourced from within the SAARC region.	60%	50%	50%	40%
Maximum Input permitted from outside the SAARC Region.	40%	50%	50%	60%

Source: Publications from SAARC Secretariat, Kathmandu.

and least developed countries to benefit equitably from economic liberalisation. This reduction would apply to all products covered so for in the trade negotiations.

The Table 5.3 below shows the reduction in the rules of origin criteria which has been approved by the member states:

Since 1995, four rounds of SAPTA negotiations have been completed. The SAPTA - IV is completed and the customs notifications are to be issued by individual countries for its implementation. The Table 5.4 shows the number of products on which preferential tariff concessions have been granted by the member states in the three rounds of trade negotiations and the depth of preferential tariff concessions.

Numbers of Products covered and the Depth of Preferential Tariff Concessions agreed to by SAARC Member States. In the first three rounds of trade negotiations under SAPTA:

Table – 5.4
Tariff Concession under SAPTA

Country	*No. of Products*	*Depth of Tariff Concessions*
Bangladesh	572	10% and 15%
Bhutan	266	10%, 13%, 15%, 18% and 20%
India	2402	10%, 15%, 20%, 25%, 30%, 40%, 50%, 90% and 100%
Maldives	390	5%, 7.5%, 10% and 15%
Nepal	425	10% and 15%
Pakistan	685	10%, 15%, 20% and 30%
Sri Lanka	211	10%, 15%, 20%, 30%, 50%, 60% and 75%
TOTAL	4951	

During the first and second round, trade negotiations were conducted on a product-by-product basis. In the third round, the negotiations were also conducted on product basis. In the fourth round, negotiations were conducted on product wise, sectoral and across the Board basis.

Since 1997, attempts have been made to clear the duck for the smooth transition of region from SAPTA to SAFTA. Owing to geo-political situation in the region, the ambitious target of SAFTA implementation had been deferred for 2003. At present SAFTA had been implemented since 2006.

(b) South Asian Free Trade Agreement (SAFTA)

The Agreement on South Asian Free Trade Area (SAFTA) was signed on 6 January 2004 during the Twelfth SAARC summit in Islamabad. The

Agreement came into force on 1 January 2006. Outstanding issues in key areas of the tariff liberalisation programme (TLP), rules of origin, sensitive lists and so on, were completed on schedule by January 2006. Under the proposed tariff liberalisation programme (TLP), SAFTA will become fully effective for non-least developed country (LDC) member countries of SAARC by 2013 and by 2016 for LDC members states.

As far as the TLP is concerned, the approach adopted makes a commitment toward a top-down reduction of tariffs in which non-LDC members states are required to reduce existing tariffs to 20 per cent within two years of implementation of the agreement, and thereafter to further reduce tariffs to a range of 0-5 per cent in the next five years. LDC member countries are required to reduce existing tariffs to 30 per cent in two years and further ensure a reduction to a range of 0-5 per cent in the next eight years.

Table 5.5
TLP across FTAs in South Asia

	SAFTA
Immediate 0 per cent	Not applicable.
TLP for others.	Non-LDCs : reduce tariffs to 20 per cent over 2 years. (LDCs 3 years). Non-LDCs : reduce to 0-5 per cent over next 5 years (LDCs 7 years).
Date of full implementation	2016.

Source: Respective Agreements.

Note: TLP – Tariff Liberalisation Programme

One criticism that may be made of this formula is that it may allow back-loading in the tariff-reduction process.

That is, those countries whose tariffs are well below 20 per cent may not have to commit to substantial reductions until the last minute. The agreement only requires a 10 per cent margin of preference reduction in each year in the second phase. However, the formula adopted is not without its benefits. It is likely to be more efficient if convergence is achieved initially by all countries lowering their tariff to a maximum rate and then proceeding further. An alternative of an annualised percentage reduction, on the other hand, would have meant that countries with high tariffs still continue to benefit in relation to the other regional partners. International experience of regional blocs generally finds clauses that favour convergence, as in SAFTA to be more successful in ensuring that benefits of tariff reduction are extended to all member countries.

Another key area is rules of origin (ROO), which is an important provision in any FTA. Within trade arrangements, ROO have a number of functions. The most important are to limit the benefit of preferences to countries within the agreement, and related to that, to encourage industrial development within the member countries. ROO can have positive as well as negative effects. Positive effects of properly constituted ROO requirements generally include prevention of trade deflection, facilitating value addition and augmenting the volume of intra-regional trade. On the negative side, it is often argued that ROO might inhibit intra-regional trade and favour high cost and inefficient production. Ideally ROO should be open, transparent, predictable and inconsistent in application as, simple as possible and leave little room for administrative discretion.

Three criteria are generally used to determine whether '**substantial transformation**' of goods, the final product should be distinct from its constituents has taken place. Each rule could be applied in isolation, in the alternative. The rules are:

- A percentage test according to which a minimum percentage of domestic value addition (DVA) should be achieved on the basis of domestic inputs.
- A change in tariff heading (CTH) test whereby the tariff heading of the final product is different from the tariff headings of its components.
- Specified process tests that require a product to undergo certain stipulated processes.

The SAFTA agreement requires domestic value addition (DVA) of 40 per cent for India and Pakistan (as non-LDC member countries), 35 per cent for Sri Lanka (as a small economy) and 30 per cent for LDCs, in

Table 5.6
Rules of Origin of FTA in South Asia

SAFTA	
Single Country ROO DVA India and Pakistan	- 40%
Sri Lanka	- 35%
LDCs	- 30%
CTH	- 4 – digit.
Cumulative ROO	
Minimum Aggregate Content	- 50%
Input from Exporting Country	- 20%
Derogation from General Rule	DVA : 25, 30, 40 or 60% CTH : at 4 or 6 digit. Process : PSR (Process Specified Rule)

Source: Respective agreements.

Note: CTH – Change of Tariff Headings.
DVA - Domestic Value Addition.
LDC – Least Developed Country.
ROO – Rules of Origin.
SAFTA - South Asian Free Trade Agreement.

combination with a change of tariff heading (CTH) at classified at the four digit Harmonised Commodity Description and Coding System (HS) code. However, derogation from the General Rule has been permitted under SAFTA because some products may undergo substantial transformation and allow the DVA criteria to be met without CTH at the four-digit code. Besides the single – country ROO, there is also provision for cumulative ROO with a minimum aggregate content of 50 per cent with the provision that the minimum input from the exporting country should be 20 per cent. The SAFTA ROO is more or less the same as those under the bilateral FTAs in the region.

One of the most critical provisions in SAFTA is the one that deals with sensitive sectors. It seems reasonable that each country has some sensitive industries that should not face increased competition, even from relatively less competitive neighbours. An improvement in the SAFTA treaty compared with the bilateral FTAs in the region was that it provided room for negotiations to ensure a maximum ceiling on items that can be placed under the negative list by each member country.

It appeared in the initial stages of negotiations that a fairly liberal approach would be adopted, perhaps limiting the negative list to 10 per cent of tariff lines, but the final decision was to retain a negative list of 20 per cent of tariff lines for non-LDC member states and a close approximation of that for the LDC member countries.

Table 5.7
Comparative Negative Lists across FTAs in South Asia

	SAFTA	*ISFTA*	*PSFTA*
Bangladesh	1,254		
Bhutan	137		
India	865	419	
Maldives	671		
Nepal	1,335		
Pakistan	1,183		540
Sri Lanka	1,065	1,180	697

Source: Respective Agreements.

Note: FTA = Free Trade Agreement.
ISFTA = India – Sri Lanka Free Trade Agreement.
PSFTA = Pakistan – Sri Lanka Free Trade Agreement.
SAFTA = South Asian Free Trade Agreement.

This means, in principle, that the actual trade coverage of the negative lists of each country could be quite high. Perhaps of more concern is that there is no formal and binding provision in the framework agreement requiring that negative lists are pruned down overtime. The only provision that the SAFTA treaty has made is for a "review" of the negative list at least every four year "with a view to reducing the number of items" [Agreement of South Asian Free Trade Area, Article 7 (3b), p. 5]. The underlying intention may be to prune it, but the provision is vague and has no authority to require any movement from the current position of member countries. Given that SAFTA has left the issue of negative lists fairly open ended even after four years is a fairly long time horizon to wait for any improvement in the agreement. There is always the danger that the agreement will fall short of free trade even in the long term. By comparison to SAFTA, the negative lists of existing bilateral FTAs in the region are more limited. Indeed, mapping the sensitive list of each country to their imports from the rest of South Asia reveals that nearly 53 per cent of total import trade among South Asian countries by value is excluded from the liberalisation of tariffs proposed under the SAFTA treaty (Table 5.8). The LDC member countries such as Bangladesh, Maldives and Nepal have sought to "protect" 65-75 per cent of their imports from South Asia by excluding them from being subject to tariff liberalisation. Sri Lanka (51.7 per cent) and India (38.4 per cent) also have restricted a fairly high share of imports from being subject to tariff cuts. It appears that Pakistan has been fairly generous in restricting only around 17 per cent of its current imports to the sensitive list, despite the fact that it has the largest member of items in the sensitive lists of non-LDC members. However, Pakistan maintains a positive list of items in regard to its trade with India. That, in theory, can limit the potential trade volumes to a great extent.

Table 5.8
Trade Restriction under SAFTA

	Value of imports from SAARC subject to SL (per cent)	*Value of exports to SAARC subject to SL (per cent)*
Bangladesh	65.0	22.0
India	38.4	56.5
Maldives	74.5	57.6
Nepal	64.0	46.4
Pakistan	17.2	34.0
Sri Lanka	51.7	47.0
Total	52.9	

Source: Weerakoon and Thennakoon 2008.
Note: SL = Sensitive List.

Another area of concern in the SAFTA treaty is the lack of an explicit commitment to deal with the issue of non-tariff barrier (NTBs). In identifying NTBs, a distinction can be made between those that have to be eliminated and those that have to be harmonised, such as measures relating to technical standards, plant and animal health, and environmental protection and safety. If any quantitative restrictions exist, there can more easily be converted to tariffs and subsequently reduced. Generally, the experience of FTAs has been that customs surcharges, technical measures and product characteristic requirements and monopolistic measures (particularly in relation to exclusive import rights of state controlled enterprises) are the most difficult to identify and eliminate. While South Asia has made significant progress in eliminating quantitative restrictions (QRs), non-tariff measures do exist that can act as a barriers to the free flow of goods between SAARC countries.

The SAFTA framework agreement has provisions to deal with para-tariffs and NTBs, but no explicit commitment is required of countries. In particular, there is no commitment in the SAFTA framework agreement to eliminate NTBs on items for which tariff reductions are to be made.

The SAFTA treaty has been confined to trade in goods, which is viewed as a limiting factor. Globally, the trends governing bilateral and regional trade initiatives are towards implementing broader economic partnership agreements that include trade in service and investment, and areas of economic cooperation. SAARC has taken some initial steps to incorporate services and investment into the SAFTA framework agreement by commissioning a joint study to examine the issues that need to be addressed.

Thus, it is clear that SAFTA as it stands contain certain limitations. Nonetheless, implementation is progressing as per the terms of the agreement, subject to the early dispute that arose with regard to the application of Pakistan's positive list of trade with India regarding the implementation of SAFTA. However, the required initial tariff liberalisation is quite minimal given that most South Asian economies have been unilaterally lowering Most Favored Nation (MFN) tariffs quite substantially over time. For instance, if liberalisation formula is applied to the Sri Lankan context, leaving aside those items in Sri Lanka's SAFTA sensitive list, it is clear that the only commitment required is to reduce tariffs from 28 per cent to 20 per cent on approximately 300 tariff lines (at HS six digit) in three installments over a two year period.

The other main area of progress is perhaps that of pruning sensitive lists. But, it is confined largely to a voluntary exercise, with India taking the initiative with an offer to unilaterally prune its sensitive list ahead of schedule by removing an additional 264 items applicable to LDCs. India has long been viewed as the key to enabling a successful regional economic integration effort in South Asia, given the significantly asymmetric nature of economic power it wields.

From SAPTA to SAFTA

It has long been recognised that the fact that South Asian countries share some basic similarities of low income, relatively abundant labour, comparative advantage in similar commodities such as tea and garments, reduces the potential for comparative advantage by trade. But it has been argued that increased economic integration would carry with it the ability not only to secure new and larger markets for traditional products, but also to enable the diversification of domestic economic structures. From pursuing economic integration in South Asia, benefits not only in trade in goods but also in services and investment can be achieved. The notion that deeper regional trade integration can create spillover effects that would strengthen economic and political ties between South Asian countries. SAPTA was intended as the initial step in the process to support regional economic integration. Three rounds of negotiations were completed under SAPTA where the consolidated list of concessions covered 3,857 tariff lines, including special concessions (2,762 tariff lines) offered to LDCs. The most limiting factor of SAPTA was the actual trade coverage of preferential access granted. In fact, it has been estimated that on an average only 8.4 per cent of tariff lines in the case of imports from non-LDCs and 6.2 per cent in the case of imports from the LDCs were covered. In reality, products imported under SAPTA concessions translated to only 15 per cent of total imports between SAARC member countries. Thus, SAPTA had little or no impact in changing the existing trade patterns in South Asia.[3]

SAARC had in principle agreed to create a free trade area (SAFTA) but there were number of problems it had to overcome. The problems include issue of trade imbalances and lifting of non-tariff barriers. Pakistan's grant of "most favoured nation" status to India, and demand by smaller economies for level playing fields are other issues to be tackled for effective change from SAPTA to SAFTA. But, business community led by trade union bodies and chambers of commerce and industry of SAARC countries were keen on an early introduction of free trading in the region.

The decision to convert preferential trading (SAPTA) into free trading by establishing a South Asian Free Trade Area (SAFTA) between 2000-2005 AD was given a concrete shape when Male summit in 1997 formally decided to establish SAFTA in the year 2001. This took four years to prepare. The decision on SAFTA was an important step reflecting the growing sentiment among the members countries to consolidate economic interaction at a fast pace.[4]

In contrast to SAPTA, SAFTA has a well-defined approach to trade liberalisation. It specifies time staggered tariff reductions for each member country. Regarding trade related dispute resolution, SAFTA goes a step further than SAPTA in stipulating that the anti-dumping and safeguard provision of SAFTA cannot be invoked against a product originating in a

LDC, provided its share in exports to the contracting country does not exceed five of its total imports.

A more comprehensive agreement than SAPTA, SAFTA addresses a broader range of trade related issues, such as the harmonisation of standard and certification, customs clearance procedure and classification, transit and transport facilitation, rules of fair competition and foreign exchange liberalisation. Both with respect to its fair trade provisions and the broadening of its economic agenda, SAFTA offers better prospects than SAPTA for improving relations between the member countries, through a similarly indirect route. In the intrastate context, countries are allowed to maintain higher tariffs for sensitive lists of commodities and pull back from the agreement due to the balance of payment difficulties. While in the face of liberalisation, it does underscore the fact that SAPTA is sensitive to national economic concerns and aware that these can affect a country's political stability.

SAFTA's dispute settlement mechanism is substantively similar to SAPTA if anything there is more tiers of consultations, involving a committee of experts (COE) and the SAFTA Ministerial Council (SMC). However, much as in the case of SAPTA, no institutional or legal mechanisms for dispute settlement exist and both the COE and the SMC will continue to devise procedure on a case by case basis.[5]

International experience of regional blocs generally finds clauses that favour convergence as in SAFTA to be more successful in ensuring that benefits of tariff reduction are extended to all member countries.

Challenges and Prospects for SAFTA

Two key issues that arise in this context are whether SAFTA has a meaningful role or whether it has already lost the opportunity to be the main dynamic force from within South Asia.

As previously mentioned, India is the key to South Asian economic integration. Bilateral market access is fast providing an environment that could reasonably approximate free trade in South Asia. Bhutan, Nepal and Sri Lanka have virtual free trade access to the Indian market for their exports despite having a significant share of their exports to India restricted under SAFTA. India has restricted only a limited share of import from Maldives (3.6 per cent) and Bangladesh (11.2 per cent) under SAFTA.

Alternative regional initiatives in the pipeline will grant Bangladesh opportunities to further its access to the Indian market. These include the proposed transition of the Bangkok Agreement to an FTA under the Asia Pacific Trade Agreement (APTA) and the implementation of on FTA under the Bay of Bengal Initiative for Multi Sectoral Technical and Economic Cooperation (BIMSTEC). In addition, Bangladesh has indicated interest

Table 5.9. Bilateral Trade Restriction under SAFTA

Per-centage of import under SL	*Bangladesh*	*India*	*Maldives*	*Nepal*	*Pakistan*	*Sri Lanka*
Bangladesh		11.2	0.0	29.7	31.3	45.2
Bhutan	69.4	36.8	0.0	15.0	50.4	0.0
India	66.0		65.2	64.2	14.5	53.5
Maldives	72.9	3.6		0.0	0.0	59.2
Nepal	87.8	46.2	0.0		25.4	17.6
Pakistan	54.5	16.4	15.5	30.0		28.4
Sri Lanka	66.6	41.5	85.4	37.4	29.7	

Source: Weerakon and The nankeen 2008.

Note:

SAFTA = South Asian Free Trade Agreement;

SL = Sensitive list.

in negotiating a bilateral FTA with India. Bangladesh and Maldives will both stand to benefit from enhanced access to India with the proposed unilateral reduction of India's sensitive list by a further 264 items applicable to LDCs. This may still restrict some amount of trade, but it is being offered on a non-reciprocal basis and ahead of the scheduled four-year revision of sensitive lists.

Thus, bilateral market access to India for the smaller South Asian economies is evolving at a much more rapid pace than under the SAFTA framework. The net result of these alternative bilateral and regional agreements in South Asia with India playing a pivotal role may eventually become something approximating free trade within the region. However, Pakistan is conspicuously absent in the evolving network of such alternative agreements except an FTA with Sri Lanka in 2002 (PSFTA) — Pakistan is seeking its own trade arrangements with the East Asian region. It has signed FTA with China (2006) and Malaysia (2007).

Table 5.10
Bilateral and Regional Agreement except SAFTA

Country	*Bilateral*	*Country (Year)*	*Other*
Afghanistan	PTA	India (2003)	
Bhutan	FTA	India (1995)	BIMSTEC
Bangladesh	Trade Agreement	India (2006)	APTA, BIMSTEC
Maldives	Trade Agreement	India (1981)	
Nepal	FTA	India (1991)	BIMSTEC
Pakistan	FTA	Sri Lanka (2002)	
Sri Lanka	FTA	India (1998)	APTA, BIMSTEC

Source: Department of Commerce, available at www.commerce.nic.in
Note: APTA = Asia Pacific Trade Agreement;
BIMSTEC = Bay of Bengal Initiative for Multi Sectoral Technical and Economic Cooperation;
FTA= Free Trade Agreement;
PTA= Preferential Trade Agreement;
SAFTA= South Asian Free Trade Agreement.

Thus, there are obvious divergences of interests and strategic interest among SAARC countries. These developments pose internal challenges to the SAARC process and the future pace of regional economic cooperation under SAFTA. A multiplicity of alternative bilateral and regional arrangement among SAFTA members would not pose a major constraint, if the SAFTA process was keeping pace with such developments. Unfortunately, the current experience is that SAFTA is, in fact lagging.

India's attention on issues of regional trade initiatives is spreading rapidly beyond South Asia. India's more accommodative approach to SAFTA- such as the unilateral decision to enhance market access to LDC- as well as its bilateral agreements with South Asian countries can be read as a signal of its growing economic confidence, and a sign of its willingness to carry along the South Asian region as it links up with East Asia. The onus will be on the other South Asian economics to weigh the advantages and disadvantages of strategically linking with a fast expanding Indian economy and to take advantage of potential intraregional trade and investment linkages.

(c) South Asian Economic Union

The eleventh summit of SAARC at Kathmandu from 4-6 January 2002, provided further impetus to the regional economic cooperation to give effect to the shared aspirations for a more prosperous South Asia. At the summit, the leaders agreed to accelerate cooperation in the core areas of trade, finance and investment to realise the goal of an integrated South Asian economy in a step-by-step manner. They also agreed to the vision of a phased and planned process eventually leading to a South Asian Economic Union.[6]

(d) Introduction of a Common Currency

The growth of regional economic cooperation arrangement is one of the major developments in the post - World War II period. The formation of regional integration has been greatly successful in bringing historically hostile countries together. The European Union and the South East Asia are the classic examples where economic dimensions have brought long time foes in the same dais. The basic premise on which SAARC was founded was that by activating cooperative cultural identities and economic interests, political conflicts and tensions in South Asia could be moderated, if not completely eliminated. It looks advantageous if SAARC countries could adopt a single currency substantially enhancing their bargaining power together in the world market. A common currency's attraction is that it doesn't represent the currency of any single country. It is advantageous to deal with a lesser number of currencies since each time one converts a currency there is a huge loss. The common currency regime, when achieved, can present substantial benefits to the region.

With uncertainty about exchange rates removed, and transaction costs reduce trade and investment in the region can get a big boost. Also with money creation under regional guidelines, there would be better prospects of synchronisation of inflation, interest rate and GDP growth, all of which can contribute to accelerated growth and poverty reduction.

The Steps Involved in the Proposed Process are

(1) Creation of a parallel currency and associated agreements for its stability.
(2) Setting up of a reserve fund.
(3) Funding of regional public goods to promote trade and investment.
(4) Special and differential treatment of lagging parts of the region to help the convergence process in the region.
(5) Building of mutual trust and confidence among the partners in the region.

These steps with create conditions, which are usually necessary for a common currency area. SAARC Summit could take steps to set up a Working Group comprising of Central Bank Governors to evaluate the feasibility of the proposal and take it forward.

Nevertheless, after 20 years' of establishment, neither South Asian nations have been able to push the process of integration into full swing nor the organisation itself has become viable that could promote peace and harmony or prevent conflicts in the region. South Asia has emerged as a regional entity in the international political system with the creation of SAARC but it failed to strengthened regional cohesiveness. Regional cooperation in South Asia cannot be said to have evolved into a complete bloc in terms of regionalism and economic integration due mainly to the prevalence of conflict over the desire of peace and stability.

Hence, at this moment, SAARC countries have to improve their relationships and attitudes towards each other and they need to take initiatives to eliminate the existing conflicts among them. In order to introduce a common currency in the region, economical homogeneity is the prime factor, which has some deficiencies in the SAARC countries. Any move towards introducing a common currency for SAARC countries in recent time will not be viable unless a good neighbourly relationship and economic homogeneity in the region are achieved.[7]

Developmental Mechanism of SAARC

SAARC owes various mechanisms that help in the developmental functions of this organisation:

1. **The South Asian Development Fund (SADF)**

In 1996, a first funding mechanism was created in SAARC known as South Asian development fund by merging the SAARC fund for regional projects (SFRP) and the SAARC regional fund.

The King of Bhutan had mooted an idea of a South Asian Development Fund at Colombo SAARC Summit in 1991. The idea behind such a fund was to encourage the possibility of giving preference for regional investments in projects in SAARC countries. There was also a need to hold an investment survey to identify production capabilities and export promotion investment projects. The proposal of the King of Bhutan was finally endorsed in New Delhi Summit in 1995.

The Heads of State or Government underlined the urgent need to make the South Asian Development Fund operational by making utilisation of the existing funds. They also instructed the Secretary General to submit a proposal for seeking possible assistance from regional and international sources for the implementation of specific regional poverty alleviation priority projects.

The South Asian Development Fund (SADF) was formally launched in June 1996. Its aim is to promote projects which will benefit two or more member countries of the SAARC region. The SADF Secretariat is based in Dhaka.

The member's countries had donated by June 1996 a total of five million US dollars as the initial core capital of the Fund. The highest amount of US $1,605,000 was contributed by India. Pakistan contributed $1,192,500 and Bangladesh and Sri Lanka gave $567,500 each. Japan promised to provide 500,000 dollars to the fund. The two existing funds-SAARC Fund for Regional Projects and the SAARC Regional Fund- were merged with the SADF. It now has three windows. There is window for Identification and Development Projects, Window for institutional and Human Resource Development and the window for Social and Infrastructure Development Projects. The fund for regional projects has already identified and recommended 13 projects, mostly large-scale manufacturing projects for different South Asian countries.[8]

2. SAARC Development Fund

The Heads of state and Government of South Asian Association for regional cooperation (SAARC) established an institution known as SAARC Development Fund to promote the welfare of people of the SAARC region, to improve their quality of life and to accelerate economic growth, social progress and poverty alleviation in the region. This charter was signed on 3 August 2008, at Colombo, Sri Lanka.

The fund serves as the umbrella financial institution for SAARC projects and programmes, which are in fulfillment of the objectives of the SAARC Charter. It is aimed to contribute to regional cooperation and integration through project collaboration.

The Permanent Secretariat of the Fund is located in city and country. Membership of the fund is open only to the member state of the SAARC. The capital of the Fund is in terms of Special Drawing Rights (SDR). The Fund Possess juridical personality and, in particular, the full legal capacity:

(i) To contract.

(ii) To acquire, and dispose of, immovable and movable property.

(iii) To institute legal proceedings.

Function of the Fund

To implement its objectives, the Fund has the following functions:

(i) To identify, study prospects and approve projects.

(ii) To finance approved projects in SAARC member states.

(iii) To leverage funding, arrange and mobilise financing and co-financing projects.

(iv) To provide grants for projects of strategic importance to SAARC.

(v) To provide financial and technical assistance.

(vi) Management of the Fund.

The utilisation of the Fund monies are for projects emanating from the following windows:

(i) Social Window.

(ii) Economic Window.

(iii) Infrastructure Window.

(i) The "Social Window" is primarily a fund projects, on poverty alleviation, social development focusing on education, health, human resource development; support to vulnerable/disadvantaged segments of the society; funding needs of communities, micro enterprises, rural infrastructure development.

(ii) The "Economic Window" is primarily extend funding to non-infrastructural projects related to trade and industrial development, agriculture, service sectors, science and technology and in other non-infrastructure areas.

(iii) The "Infrastructure Window" is primarily be utilised to fund projects in areas such as energy, power, transportation, telecommunications, environment, tourism and other infrastructure areas.

(iv) The "Economic Window" is utilised for supporting and other projects which are not covered explicitly under the social and the infrastructure window.[9]

3. SAARC FINANCE

The SAARC FINANCE was established on 9 September 1998 as a regional network of the SAARC Central Bank Governors and Finance Secretaries. It meets twice a year concurrently with the IMF/WB Annual and Spring Meetings. Since its inception thirteen meetings were held till now. It is a permanent body, which got formal recognition of SAARC at the eleventh SAARC Summit, held in Kathmandu, Nepal in January 2002.

Each Central Bank established a SAARC FINANCE Cell in its Research Department to coordinate the activities of SAARC FINANCE. Member central banks also appoint a coordinator. The coordinator of the central bank of SAARC chairperson's country acts as the central coordinator.

The SAARC Payment Council (SPC) has also been launched by SAARC FINANCE in 2008. At its regular meetings, the SAARC FINANCE also undertakes exchange of views on the impact of currently global financial crisis on individual South Asian economies.

The following are the broad objectives of SAARC FINANCE

- To promote cooperation among central banks and finance ministries in SAARC member countries through staff visits and regular exchange of information.
- To consider and propose harmonisation of banking legislations and practices within the region.
- To work towards a more efficient payment system mechanism within the SAARC region and strive for higher monetary and exchange cooperation.
- To forge closer cooperation on macro-economic policies of SAARC member state and to share experiences and ideas.
- To study global financial developments and their impact on the region including discussion relating to emerging issues in the financial architecture, IMF and World Bank and other international lending agencies.
- To monitor reforms of the international financial and monetary system and to evolve a consensus among SAARC countries in respect of the reforms.
- To evolve whenever feasible joint strategies, plan and common approaches in international fora for mutual benefit particularly in the context of liberalisation of financial services.
- To undertake training of staff of the ministries of finance, central banks and other financial institutions of the SAARC member countries in subjects relating to economics and finance.
- To explore networking of the training institutions within the SAARC region specialising in various aspects of monetary policy, exchange rate reforms, banks supervision and capital market issues.
- To promote research on economic and financial issues for the mutual benefit of SAARC member countries.
- To consider any other matter on the direction / request of the SAARC FINANCE, Council of Ministers or other SAARC bodies.

Until now twenty three meetings of SAARC FINANCE have been held as of January 2012. Maldives is the current chairperson of SAARC FINANCE.

4. SAARC Chamber of Commerce and Industry: (SCCI)

In December, 1992, SAARC chamber of commerce and industry (SCCI) was recognised by SAARC as a Regional Apex Body. In February 1994, SCCI was formally inaugurated in Dhaka by the Prime Minister of

Bangladesh. Its headquarters was set up in the premises of FPCCI in Karachi, later it was shifted to Islamabad.

The SCCI consists of the following national federations and chambers of commerce and industry as

1. Afghanistan chamber of commerce and industry (ACCI).
2. Federation of Bangladesh chambers of commerce and industry (FBCCI).
3. Bhutan chamber of commerce and industry (BCCI).
4. Federation of Indian chambers of commerce and industry (FICCI).
5. Maldives national chamber of commerce and industry (MNCCI).
6. Federation of Nepalese chamber of commerce and industry (FNCCI).
7. Federation of Pakistan chambers of commerce and industry (FPCCI).
8. Federation of chambers of commerce and industry of Sri Lanka (FCCISL).

The Objectives of the "SAARC Chamber"

The objectives of the SAARC chamber are:

- To encourage trade, service, industry, small and medium enterprise, agriculture, intra-regional through creating strong business linkages amongst the entrepreneurs of the region of South Asia.
- To make recommendations to safeguard the economic and business interests of the SAARC.
- To serve as a consultative body of the private sector of the region to provide input and/or feedback on regional economic issues.
- To encourage member countries to accord preferential terms of trade to each other and finally strive towards the gradual realisation of the SAARC Economic and Monetary Union.
- To promote the exchange of commercial, technical, industrial management and scientific information, education and know-how amongst its members.
- To collate and disseminate statistical data and joint research and development among the SAARC member countries.

Focused Areas

The thrust areas for the SAARC CCI can be divided into five major areas:

1. Awareness building on key economic issues like; trade facilitation, NTBS, TBTs, harmonisation of customs procedures, intra-regional investment and others to promote economic cooperation at the regional level.
2. To develop global linkages as a part of its outreach strategy.
3. To provide services to its members and representatives of the private sector.

4. Work closely with governments, NGOs, CSOs to raise the concern on socio-economic issues.
5. To develop an institutional framework for supporting economic cooperation.

The present President is Mr. Annis-ul-Haq of Bangladesh.

5. Asian Development Bank (ADB)

The Asian Development Bank (ADB) is a regional development bank established on 22 August 1966 to facilitate economic development of countries in Asia. The 12th Summit meeting of the SAARC, held on 4-6 January 2004 in Islamabad, has opened new avenues of regional cooperation among the South Asian countries. The Islamabad Declaration identified several priority areas of potential cooperation among the SAARC countries. In view of the improved prospects for regional cooperation in South Asia, Asian Development Bank (ADB) and the SAARC Secretariat started the discussion for mutual cooperation to this end, and signed a memorandum of understanding on 12 April 2004. ADB and the SAARC Secretariat discussed possible ADB assistance to assess regional cooperation prospects in South Asia, and to identify specific programmes and projects that will foster closer economic linkages between the SAARC member countries. ADB has considerable experience in promoting sub regional and regional cooperation initiative in South Asia like, South Asia Sub-regional Economic Cooperation (SASEC).

Due to the unsupportive political and economic conditions in South Asia for pursuing regional cooperation agenda, ADB has been taking project-based and sub-regional approaches based on mutual economic interests and political will to work together among participating countries. Thus, ADB has been supporting the South Asian sub-regional economic cooperation (SASEC) programme, involving four SAARC countries-Bangladesh, Bhutan, India and Nepal. The four countries are grouped under the South Asian Growth Quadrangle (SAGQ) initiative, which identified five priority sectors for cooperation:

(1) Transport
(2) Energy
(3) Environment
(4) Tourism
(5) Trade and investment.

ADB approved SASEC Phase I and SASEC Phase II to assist the participating countries in:

(i) Identifying and prioritising sub-regional projects.
(ii) Developing action programmes.

(iii) Preparing a need-assessment, including human resource development, for implementing the action programme in the five priority sectors. Information and communication technology was added as the sixth priority sector under the SASEC Phase II.

ADB also approved two technical assistance grants to conduct technical feasibility studies of the Turkmenistan-Afghanistan-Pakistan Natural Gas Pipeline Project. In addition, other Sub-regional cooperation initiatives are being explored through two separate small scale technical assistance, for the Maldives and Sri Lanka.

South Asia Regional Cooperation Initiatives

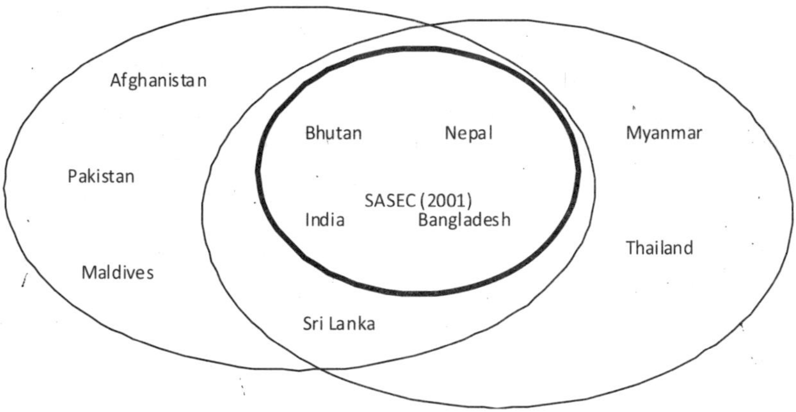

SAARC (1985) **BIMSTEC (1997)**

SAARC – South Asian Association for Regional Cooperation.
SASEC – South Asia Sub-regional Economic Cooperation.
BIMSTEC – Bay of Bengal Initiative for Multi-Sectoral Technical and Economic Cooperation.

Asian Development Bank can play a strong supportive and catalytic role assisting SAARC to realise some of the major regional cooperation agendas of the Islamabad Declaration, particularly in the areas where greater strategic impact is expected and Asian Development Bank has comparative strengths and substantial experience. While, the technical assistance will build and extend on the work undertaken with ADB support, such as the SASEC and sub-regional economic cooperation in South and Central Asia programmes (SECSCA).

Implementation Arrangement

Legend: - Guidance —Coordination — Supervision SAARC = South Asian Association for Regional Cooperation.

Table 5.11. Technical Assistance Framework of Asian Development Bank

Design Summary	*Performance /Indicators Targets*	*Monitoring Mechanism*	*Assumption and Risks*
Goal-Effective cooperation among all South Asian countries, enabled by the SAARC, helps to promote peace, stability amity and progress in the region, reaffirming the centrality of SAARC for promoting regional and emphasising the need to enhance its efficiency.	Implementation of cooperation activities including projects and training through a SAARC framework.	Reports by the SAARC Secretariat SAARC Standing Committee meetings.	
Purpose-Enhanced regional co-operation through the SAARC framework in implementing the regional cooperation initiatives in priority sectors in outlined in the Islamabad Declaration.		SAARC Standing Committee Meetings, other meetings and workshops to monitor the technical assistance implementation. Regular monitoring meetings between the Asian Development Bank (ADB) and the SAARC secretariat.	Macro economic and political conditions of the region.Commitment of the SAARC member states to regional cooperation under the SAARC framework
Establishment of better transport connectivity in South Asia, thereby facilitating services and people among SAARC members.	Increase in cross-border traffic volume and movements of people in an efficient manner in South Asian region without creating adverse impacts.	SAARC reports, feasibility studies for the identified projects/programmes and ADB project processing adminis-tration missions' back to back office reports.	Financial resources of the SAARC members states to implement the identified projects/programmes.

(Contd.)

(Contd. Table 5.11)

Design Summary	*Performance /Indicators Targets*	*Monitoring Mechanism*	*Assumption and Risks*
Effective planning, processing and implementation of the key regional cooperation agenda by the SAARC secretariat and its members.	No. of (i) trainings organised based on the capacity building program, and (ii) qualified participants in these trainings.	SAARC reports, progress reports by TA implementation advisor and ADB review mission.	Well prepared programmes and capable trainers and resource persons at the SAARC centres.
Institutionalisation of collaborative activities to strengthen coop-between SAARC and the ASEAN and other regional organisations.	Establishment of partnerships or strengthened cooperation between SAARC and regional organization and regular meetings with such organizations.	Programs of the conference/ workshop meetings, SAARC reports implementation advisor and monitoring of meeting between ADB and SAARC.	Commitment by SAARC and other organizations to the identified collaborative activities.
Outputs- SAARC Regional Multimodal Transport Study (SRMTS) report with a road map for improving regional transport connectivity, paying due considerations to (i) major institutional and physical constraints hindering smooth movement of goods and people in South Asia, and (ii) Social and environmental safeguards for the expanded/improved transport linkage/ connectivity.	To ensure quality, the first workshop discussion on the report and documents was submitted by ADB and the second workshop discussion on the final report was approved by SAARC standing Committee.	ADB TA teams' review the draft reports, ADB review mission and Standing Committee meetings.	Validity of recommendations.Quality of outputs from national and regional sector experts.

(Contd.)

(Contd. Table 5.11)

Design Summary	*Performance /Indicators Targets*	*Monitoring Mechanism*	*Assumption and Risks*
Enhanced capacity of the SAARC Secretariat in carrying out regional cooperation activities and the SAARC member countries' in stitutions in the priority sectors, through training targeted staff of these institutions.	The submission of the capacity-building programme by the SAARC Secretariat satisfactory to ADB, by the time of inception mission. Conducting training in line with the programme.	Reports from the SAARC secretariat and centres, and monitoring of meetings between the SAARC Secretariat and centres and ADB TA team.	Adequacy of the programmes. Better representation of the relevant officials and or stakeholders in the programmes from most of SAARC member states.
Output- Important lessons to be learned from other regional organizations as well as opportunities to enable the SAARC secretariat to be an efficient and effective institution in implementing cooperation activities in South Asia.	Identification of collaborative activities and implementation	Reports from the SAARC Secretariat and progress reports by TA implementation advisor.	Equal interest of ASEAN and other organisation in collaboration with SAARC.

(Contd.)

(Contd. Table 5.11)

Design Summary	*Performance /Indicators Targets*	*Performance /Indicators Targets*	*Assumption and Risks*
Effective TA implementation.	Coordination within ADB and among the SAARC Secretariat, SAARC centres, SAARC member states, ADB TA team and others to conduct each component of the TA as scheduled. (e.g. convening an inception workshop within 2004, and conducting capacity-building training in line with the program to be submitted by the SAARC secretariat)	Coordination within ADB and among the SAARC Secretariat, SAARC centres, SAARC member states, ADB TA team and others to conduct each component of the TA as scheduled. (e.g. convening an inception workshop within 2004, and conducting capacity-building training in line with the programme to be submitted by the SAARC secretariat)	Availability of a core counterpart in the SAARC Secretariat.
Activities: Conduct the SRMTS, focusing on multi-modal linkages/connectivity among South Asian Countries.	**Input:** Fielding of 24 person months of national sector experts to prepare the individual country reports, and 9 person-months of regional sector experts to synthesize the individual country reports and prepare the final report, and the engagement of a senior sector advisor to be recruited as the ADB TA team member for quality control of the SRMTS. ($43,000).	**Input:** Fielding of 24 person months of national sector experts to prepare the individual country reports, and 9 person-months of regional sector experts to synthesize the individual country reports and prepare the final report, and the engagement of a senior sector advisor to be recruited as the ADB TA team member for quality control of the SRMTS. ($43,000).	

(Contd.)

(Contd. Table 5.11)

Design Summary	*Performance /Indicators Targets*	*Monitoring Mechanism*	*Assumption and Risks*
Capacity building and training activities in the priority sectors in line with the programme submitted by the SAARC secretariat and endorsed by ADB.	$90,000		
Convene conferences, workshops, seminars and meetings.	$70,000		
Provision of logistic services and support by ADB TA team for effective and efficient TA implementation,	Recruit and retain a TA implementation advisor for 16 months and a programme analyst for 14 months. (?$73,000)		

Implementation Arrangement

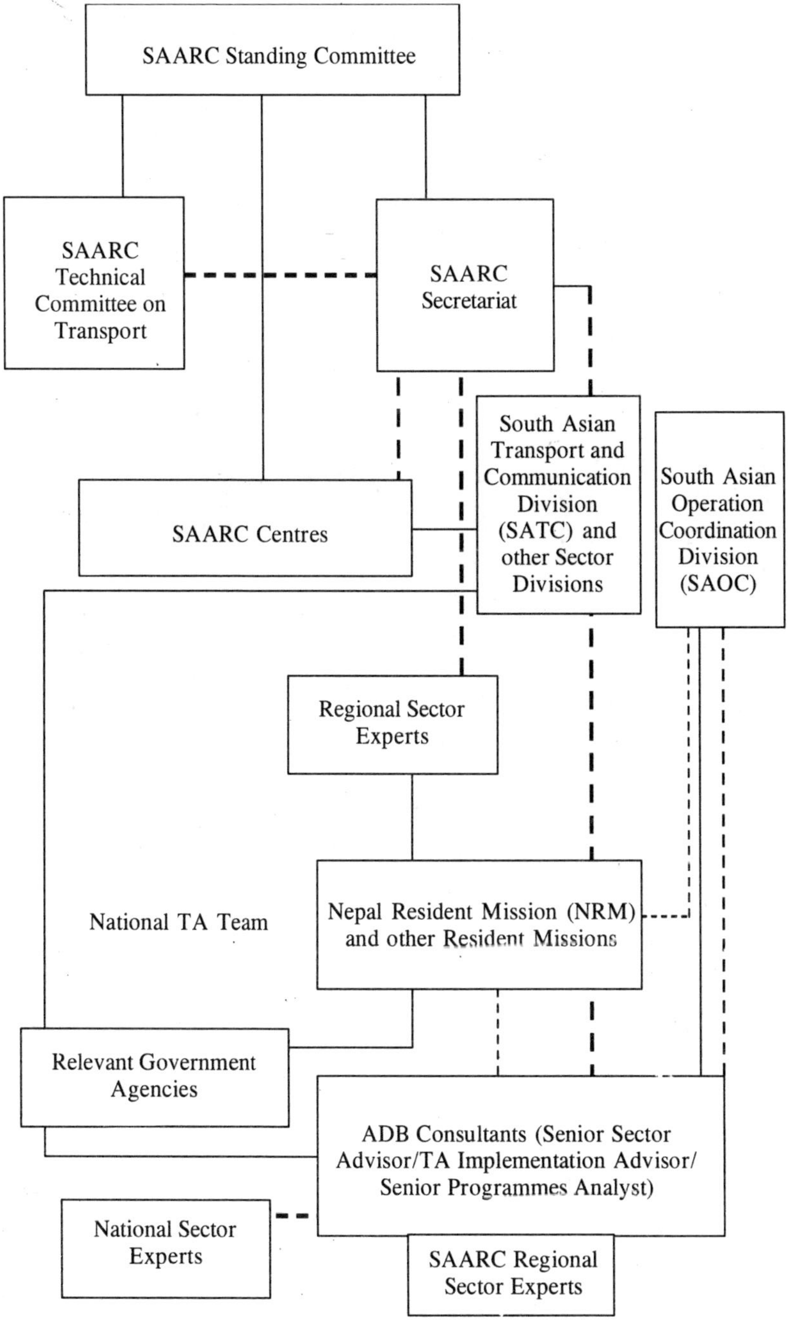

SAARC Member States.

Table 5.12 ADB lending Assistance to South Asia.

Countries	*Operation started (year)*	*Cumulative Assistance*	*Cumulative Technical Assistance*	*Major focus of sectoral operations*	*Key crosscutting issues*
Afghanistan	1973	$2.1billion inloans, grants, guarantees.	ADB administiered co financing and private sector investment.	Energy and communication agriculture and natural resources, governance sectors.	Additional strategic private sector investments, economic and social development, rule of low and human rights.
Bangladesh	1973	$8 billion for 148 projects.	$165 million -312 projects. 7 private projects-$1372.	Energy, transport education, urban health and water supply sectors.	Disaster mitigations, regional cooperation, gender and environment.
Bhutan	1983	$138 million for 19 projects.	$35 million for 94 projects.	Transport, rural electrification, urban development, finance and private development	Building institutional, policy and regulatory capacity of the sector policy making and executing agencies.
India	1986	$15 billion for 81 loans.	$ 116 million for 212 projects.	Transport, energy, urban services and infrastructure, rural finance development.	Fiscal consolidation, private sector operations agriculture and rural development, state level operations, regional cooperation, social development, environment, good governance.

(Contd.)

(Contd. Table 5.12)

Countries	*Operation started (year)*	*Cumulative Assistance*	*Cumulative Technical Assistance*	*Major focus of sectoral operations*	*Key crosscutting issues*
Nepal	1968	$2.2 billion for 109 loans.	$ 114 million for 247 projects.	Agricultural and rural development, education, infrastructure, water supply.	Internal conflict and political instability.
Maldives	1978	$91 million for 15 loans.	$ 19 million for 55 projects.	Energy, transport and communication, social infrastructure.	Tsunami recovery and economic reforms.
Pakistan	1966	$20-89 billion in 293 loans.	$192 million for 300 projects.	Power, energy, transport, national trade corridor and water resources.	Urban development, public-private partnership, economic reforms.
Sri Lanka	1968	$ 3.7 billion for 128 loans.	$ 92 billion for 220 projects.	Power, roads, education, infrastructure, private and public sector governance.	Civil conflict.

Source: Overview: Asian Development Bank Presentation: ADB in South Asia.

TA = Technical Assistance.
SAARC Standing Committee
SAARC Technical Committee on Transport

Asian Development Bank's Strategy for South Asia in Regional Cooperation Integration

- To facilitate dialogue with regional initiatives and entities.
- To strengthen region – wide cooperation through SAARC.
- To support ongoing sub-regional cooperation initiatives (South Asian Sub-regional economic cooperation).
- To promote inter-regional cooperation through Bay of Bengal Initiative for Multi-sectoral Technical and Economic Cooperation (BIMSTEC).
- To strengthen mechanisms to deliver cooperation projects through working groups.
- To strengthen coordination with other development partners.
- To improve connectivity, facilitate trade and investment, develop regional tourism, and facilitate cooperation in energy and to promote private sector development.
- To help South Asia to realise its full potential in economic and social development and enable it to play an effective part in wider Asian integration.

A separate study or codification of variations in the level of development of Capital Markets in SAARC Member States has also been commissioned with the assistance of Asian Development Bank as approved by the member states. This study was recommended by the colloquium on Management of stock exchange systems and regulations of stock markets in SAARC secretariat, Kathmandu, from 21-22 April 2008. The report of which was approved by the thirty-fifth session of the standing committee at Colombo from 29—30 July 2008.

A study on Economic Integration has been commissioned with the assistance of the Asian Development Bank.

A SAARC - ADB Inception workshop for the SAARC studies on trade, economics and finance was also held at the SAARC Secretariat on 23 - 24 June 2011.

6. SAARC Development Goals (SDGs)

At the thirteenth SAARC Summit held in Dhaka, Bangladesh, the Heads of state or government endorsed the SAARC Development Goals (SDGs), as recommended by the Independent South Asian Commission on Poverty Alleviation (ISACPA), and entrusted the commission to continue its advisory and advocacy role in this regard.

To facilitate the work of ISACPA, the SAARC Secretariat in collaboration with the UNDP convened a Regional Brainstorm in Nepal on 24-25 January 2007, where regional and international experts discussed at length on elaboration of SDGs, its monitor able indicators, and appropriate and cost saving monitoring and evaluation mechanisms at national and regional level.

In third meeting of ISACPA was held in Nepal on 25 January 2007, the commission fine-tuned the recommendations of the Regional Brainstorm and decided to prepare a report entitled "Taking SDGs Forward- on the elaboration done on the SDGs" recommends adoption of 75 indicators for the 22 SDGs. It is expected that adoption of these indicators will help to achieve the SDGs during next five years. Accordingly, this report recommends that all the national governments annually send monitor progress reports based on these 75 indicators to the SAARC secretariat, which will compile and analyse these reports and submits its findings in the annual meetings of the SAARC Poverty Alleviation Ministers.

This action reflected South Asian leaders' recognition of the regional imperative for galvanising a popular imagination of poverty free South Asia as well as the international imperative of achieving the Millennium Development Goals (MDGs) by 2015. Collective will of the SAARC leaders to go further and faster, beyond the MDG targets inspired the identification of the SDGs.

Table 5.13. SAARC Development Goals (SDGs) 2007 – 2012

Livelihood SDGs	
Goal -1	- Eradication of hunger poverty.
Goal -2	- Halve Proportion of People in Poverty by 2010.
Goal -3	- Ensure adequate nutrition and dietary improvement for the poor.
Goal -4	- Ensure a robust pro-poor growth process.
Goal -5	- Strengthen connectivity of poorer regions and of poor as social groups.
Goal -6	- Reduce social and institutional vulnerabilities of the poor, women and children.
Goal 7	Ensure access to affordable justice.
Goal -8	- Ensure effective participation of poor and of women in anti-poverty policies and programmes.
Health SDGs	
Goal -9	- Maternal health.
Goal -10	- Child health.
Goal -11	- Affordable health-care.
Goal -12	- Improved hygiene and public health.
Education SDGs	
Goal -13	- Access to primary/communal school for all children, boys and girls.
Goal -14	- Completion of primary education cycle.

(Contd.)

(Contd. Table 5.13)

Goal -15	-	Universal functional literacy.
Goal -16	-	Quality education at primary, secondary and vocational levels.
Environment SDGs		
Goal -17	-	Acceptable level of forest cover.
Goal -18	-	Acceptable level of water and soil quality.
Goal -19	-	Acceptable level of air quality.
Goal -20	-	Conservation of bio-diversity.
Goal -21	-	Wetland conservation.
Goal -22	-	Ban on dumping of hazardous waste, including radioactive waste.

The report – "An Engagement with Hope" on the SDGs was finalised in 2004 and it identified a set of twenty–two goals. Of these, eight SDGs are related to livelihood, four to health, four to education and six to environment.

As a follow–up of these directives, there was a realisation of a clear elaboration of SDGs : detailed identification of short-term and medium-term, monitorable and double indicators; benchmarking of these indicators, and projecting targets for the five years period; and developing a credible monitoring and evaluation framework.

The 27th session of the council at Dhaka from 1-2 August 2006 agreed that :

(a) SDGs would be achieved in the next five years starting from year 2007.

(b) A mid–term review on the attainment of SDGs would be undertaken towards the end of the third year.

The Millennium Development Goals (MDGs)

The Millennium Declaration of the United Nations on September 2000 contains development goals, which are similar to the International Development Goals set before. Later, the goals of these two sets were merged under the designation of "Millennium Development Goals" (MDGs). MDGs contain eight major goals, 18 targets and 48 indicator. Numerical targets have been set against the base of 1990 for each goal and most of the goals are to be achieved over a period of 15 year, ending in 2015. The MDGs were strongly reaffirmed by all United Nations member states at the Johannesburg World Summit on sustainable development in September 2002 and their progress was widely reviewed and assessed during the 60th session of the UN General Assembly in September 2005.

Regions as well as respective countries have made attempts to localise the MDGs. One of such attempts is the preparation of the SAARC Development Goals (SDGs) developed by the seven member states of the SAARC.

The goals essentially revolve around the MDGs. Similarly, efforts have been made at the country level to localise MDGs by revisiting targets suitable for the country, adopting the revised targets in their national plan and further breaking down and adjusting these targets at the sub-national level planning exercises.

Taking SDGs Forward

Attaining the SDGs in possible in SAARC countries. However, it would require preparing SDG based plan, localising the SDGs and their sustained follow up. As the monitoring is given least importance in the SAARC countries, it is necessary that it be given critical significance both in terms of priority and resource allocation for enhancing monitoring capability of the SAARC development goals. Above all, the attainment of the goals requires political will and commitment that translate the MDG-based plan into action.

The following actions would be required to attain in SDGs

- Attainment of the SDGs is primarily a responsibility of the individual member states. Therefore mainstreaming of these goals in the national policy planning and their implementation need to be done with the same dynamism and determination, as in the case of the MDGs.
- MDGs have been contextualised for South Asia through the SDGs, meaning that they are complementary to each other. Attainment of SDGs therefore is directly linked to the progress made towards achieving the MDGs.
- SDGs would require reprioritisation of resources, incentives for intimate engagement of all stakeholders at the national levels, clear delineation in the allocation of tasks and responsibilities, effective inter-sectoral coordination and enabling legal and regulatory frameworks.
- Putting in place the benchmarks against indicators as agreed and monitoring mechanisms must reflect the distinctiveness and specificity of a country and its regions, and as such are essentially national tasks, although harmonising indicators have to be done at the regional level.
- The indicators should be able to measure input, output and impact/outcome, but must be cognisant of the 'data-gaps' and carry the requirement of 'regionality'. They should also provide impetus to policy focus, both at the national and regional levels.
- The efforts towards harmonisation must be characterised by the intention to agree on a common set of workable indicators, based on availability of credible data, to facilitate comparison across the countries. Besides, the set of indicators agreed at the regional level should also encourage the countries to try to generate data at regular

intervals, which are not being collected in some countries at the time.

- The concerned countries should have the flexibility to add additional or proxy indicators where there is necessary to capture their specific requirements and situations.
- The countries would be required to decide on targets and benchmarks, through a truly participatory process to advance the attainment of the SDGs.
- In order to establish cost-effective monitoring methodologies, it would be prudent to principally rely on the mechanisms available for MDGs monitoring or their national equivalents, with necessary expansion of scope and mandate as well as appropriate strengthening.
- Data wherever applicable should be disaggregated by gender and by area.

All the actions suggested in this report have great potentials in enhancing regional cooperation. Some simply highlighted existing initiatives with the suggestion to develop or expand them while others would set the countries of the region off in new directions. National level determination and commitment, however is required to achieve the goals and maximise the benefits from regional cooperation. All these efforts can, however be greatly enhanced by concerted regional actions.

The SAARC Development Goals are expected to help member states to galvanise their development efforts, offering a space in which all sections of society can come together to debate national and regional priorities. But, they will only serve their purpose if the government pay due attention on the observed gaps, and on the changes needed to safeguard the rights of everyone, especially the poorest and most vulnerable groups. Advocacy for greater resources is already under way. But, these resources need to be complemented with appropriate institutional changes to ensure that all these goals are achieved.[11]

7. SAARC – Japan Special Fund

Japan has shown a keen interest in promoting both political stability and a cooperative environment in South Asia and is the only country, which has been supportive of regional integration in South Asia through an institutional interaction with SAARC. Since 1993, Japan has been supporting activities of SAARC through a special SAARC – Japan Fund. Due to its constructive engagements with the states in South Asia, at present, Japan is considered by all the states of the region as a friendly country, which has a more acceptable face for playing any meaningful role to help strengthen the SAARC framework, for security related cooperation through friendly persuasions.

Japan's support provided by the Japanese authorities to forged a cooperative relationship that encompasses both the government and the

Table 5.14. Present Status of SAARC Goals in South Asia

Country	*Year*	*Poverty (per cent) eradication*	*Universal (per cent) primary education*	*Gender equality (per cent) empowerment*	*Child (per cent) Mortality*	*Maternal health (per cent)*	*Environment Sustainability (per cent)*
Afghanistan	2002	59.3	34.3	7	257	12.4	32.0
	2011	62.3	37.3	67	257	14.3	30.0
Bhutan	2002	-	72.0	69	100	23.7	52.0
	2011	31.7	100.0	95	84	56.1	52.0
Bangladesh	2002	33.8	60.5	82	92	12.1	32.0
	2011	30.0	87.2	92	61	20.1	36.0
India	2002	42.3	72.3	71	89	42.5	23.0
	2011	31.0	85.7	78	72	46.6	28.0
Maldives	2002	-	98.0	96	54	70.3	58.0
	2011	17.3	99.0	96	30	84.0	59.0
Nepal	2002	34.4	72.8	56	86	11.9	20.0
	2011	24.1	76.5	86	55	19.8	27.0
Pakistan	2002	47.7	58.5	73	108	23.0	48.0
	2011	17.0	70.0	85	90	31.0	58.0
Sri Lanka	2002	3.8	95.0	93	19	96.0	81.0
	2011	5.8	97.6	95	21	96.0	86.0

Source: SAARC Development Goals: Commitments and Achievements. Taking SDGs Forward (2007-2012)

private sector. The private sector is considered as playing a vital role in the future cooperation between Japan and South Asia.

The SAARC – Japan Special Fund have contributed immensely towards achieving its stated objectives. This fund has been instrumental in evolving consensus among the masses of South Asia that the governments should rise above their petty political agendas and sincerely work towards the integration of the region, in view of the emerging challenges of globalisation and for the benefit of one fifth of humanity that resides in South Asia. At the same time, the Fund has helped in broadening an understanding between the Japanese and South Asian intelligentsia. It has helped the Japanese side to understand the political dynamics of South Asia.

Under the prevailing circumstances Japan can best help the SAARC by alleviating the level of SAARC – Japan Special Fund, especially through the component I objectives, facilitating investment in the region, expanding trade opportunities and transferring technical knowhow, for the uplift of South Asia. Also Japan needs to evolve a long term policy for South Asia, in commensuration with its emerging leadership role in Asia, which will facilitate greater interaction with institutions like SAARC.

Table 5.15. SAARC – JAPAN Special Fund in South Asian Countries

Country	*Total Grant and Aid Amount ($ millions)*
Afghanistan	$46.4 million
Bhutan	$32.6 million
Bangladesh	$394.7 million
India	$1942.6 million
Maldives	$7.8 million
Nepal	$11.2 million
Pakistan	$13.4 million
Sri Lanka	$34.1 million

Source: Japan's Support to SAARC – http://www.mofa.go.jp/

Japan's Support to SAARC

1. **Support for Promoting Regional Connectivity**
   (a) Improvement of infrastructure.
   (b) Promotion of inter-regional trade and investment.
   (c) Environment and Energy Conservation.
2. **Support for Enhancement of Regional Disaster Prevention and Disaster Reduction System**
   (a) Disaster risk reduction programme in wide area by SAARC – Japan Special Fund.

(b) Support for UNDP Earthquake risk reduction programme.
(c) Improvement of Disaster reduction system by bilateral cooperation.

3. **Promotion of Exchanges of Young People Funded by SAARC – Japan Special Fund**
    (a) High school student's invitation programme.
    (b) Invitation programmes for Japanese learners and teachers.
    (c) SAARC student's internship programme.
    (d) Invitation programme for science and technological human resources.
    (e) Asian young business person exchange programme.

Regional Economic Cooperation in Other Areas

The benefits of regional economic cooperation among SAARC countries can be enhanced if the member countries can cooperate in many other areas, which also impinge on the pace of economic growth in these countries. Although it is possible to envisage co-operation in a large number of areas, but in this chapter it is confined to five selected areas:

(a) Investment prospects in the region.
(b) Joint Ventures and technology transfers.
(c) Physical Infrastructure.
(d) Regional Projects.
(e) Development of Tourism.
(f) Energy Co-operation.

These areas can be considered as crucial for accelerating economic growth.

(a) Investment Prospects in the Region

A SAARC Investment Promotion and Protection Agreement that is pending since 2007 is going to be finalised in the 18th SAARC Summit in Nepal. The deal is expected to make the region attractive investment destination.

The guidelines for the protection and promotion of investment envisions opening of intra-regional investments with equal treatment of the investments in any of the SAARC countries by any other regional block member country like domestic without restriction and quota and marketing. The products of such investments will not be listed under the sensitive list to promote cross border trade and investment.

The investment promotion and protection in the regional block is expected to give boost to the intra-regional trade envisaged in the South Asian Free Trade Area Agreements (SAFTA) that came into force on six years ago. Greater free trade and investment among South Asian Countries could also help SAARC become opportunity to catalyse the potential with the region.

India has called for fast–tracking a regional investment treaty and creation of regional production chains to deepen economic linkages in the SAARC region. At the 17th SAARC Summit in the Maldives held in November 2011, India had announced elimination of its sensitive list for Least Developed Countries (LDCs)[12].

The SAARC Arbitration Council will also be linked to the regional investment agreement for harmonizing tax laws within the region to access the possibility of having a Regional Agreement for the avoidance of Double Taxation.

The South Asian region is one of the capital scarce regions of the world. Low capacity of the region to raise domestic resources and low inflow of FDI, have made the region a capital deficient region. In the 90s, the SAARC region's economies have initiated aggressive reforms to correct domestic distortions as well as creating conditions for attracting FDI. Despite aggressive policy switching, South Asia continues to be a marginal host of global FDI flows. A for Multinational Enterprises (MNEs) have chosen the region as a base to produce and export manufactured products to other parts of the world. In order to attract FDI at a large scale, the region has to prepare itself to compete with other vibrant FTAs around the globe.

Sri Lanka is the first country to start countrywide economic liberalisation in South Asia. The present investment regime in Sri Lanka is highly liberal than many countries in the region. Almost all sectors of the economy are opened for foreign direct investment (FDI), and foreign ownership is extended up to cent per cent level. The country has evolved a strong legal and regulatory procedure to resolve any dispute between contracting parties. Unlike many countries in the region, Sri Lanka has an Arbitration Centre in Colombo. India and Sri Lanka have engaged in close economic relations since the second half of the 90s. In 1997, both the countries have signed an important Agreement, known as Investment Protection Agreement.

Under the Indo-Nepal Trade and Transit Treaty in 1996, Nepal can export manufactured products without any customs duty. In order to serve the northern Indian market, several Indian companies have relocated their production bases to Nepal. For number of agro and herbal based manufacturing industries, Nepal is an attractive destination.

In recent years, there is a surge of investment activities between India and Bangladesh. Bangladesh has a large reserve of natural gas on this source of energy has attracted many countries of the region to work on diversified production sectors, particularly in energy – intensive ventures.

Bhutan has built hydro–electricity ventures by collaborating with India with buy-back facility. In Bhutan, the performance of the non–

Table 5.16
Foreign Direct Investment (FDI) Inflows to South Asian Countries ($ millions)

Country	*2001*	*2002*	*2003*	*2004*	*2005*	*2006*	*2007*	*2008*	*2009*	*2010*
Afghanistan	1	50	58	187	271	238	243	300	185	-
Bangladesh	355	328	350	460	845	793	666	1,086	716	-
Bhutan	-	2	3	3	9	6	73	30	36	23.0
India	5472	5627	4323	5771	7606	20336	25001	40418	34613	28.0
Maldives	12	12	14	15	9	14	15	12	10	0.011
Nepal	21	-6	15	-	2	-7	6	1	39	0.0
Pakistan	383	823	534	1,118	2,201	4,273	5,590	5,438	2,387	3.5
Sri Lanka	172	197	229	233	272	480	603	752	404	-

Source: Author based on UNCTAD'S FDI online database (2010).
World Bank South Asia Economic Update (2010).

manufacturing infrastructure such as energy improved during 2000. Electricity generation which was accounted for 0.2 per cent of GDP in 1990, increased its share to 12.6 per cent by 2000 while Pakistan and Maldives are respectively second and third°to India as investors.

The above trend indicates that bilateral FTA has picked up in the South Asia. The speedy trade liberalisation at the bilateral level has spur trade, investments and technology flows within region. This experience of South Asia indicates that bilateral cooperation complements regional integration in South Asia in a more effective manner.

Foreign direct investment to the SAARC region is predominantly from outside the region. The sectors that have attracted most foreign investment vary between countries. In the case of Bangladesh and Sri Lanka, the textile and garment sectors account for 28 per cent and 16 per cent respectively of FDI, whereas 56 per cent of FDI has gone into infrastructure projects in India. In case of Pakistan, 40 per cent of all FDI has gone into the power sector, while FDI from outside the regions has been far greater than intra-regional investments. In SAARC FDI from outside is more important than in intra-regional investment in most countries.

In South Asia there is no developed economy but if the intra-regional FDI inflow will be promoted it will be a starting point for United South Asia and in future this region will be as strong as EU and ASEAN.[13]

(B) Joint Ventures and Technology Transfer

To meet the investment requirements of the region, there is a need to promote regional joint venture to expand economic activities in other partner countries. This would help in transferring resources and technology as a part of regional cooperation. The promotion of regional Joint Ventures has not only improved production capabilities of host countries but also their export capabilities. Very often it is observed that increase in exports from such source have improved trade imbalances of regional partners. It may be noted that South Asia has in fact benefited by promoting regional Joint Ventures, and it is the outcome of regional trade liberalisation between the small and medium countries (SMCs).

The recent years have witnessed the emergence of joint ventures among developing countries in the area of manufacturing and services. These ventures represent a continuing form of co-operation between enterprises of two developing countries. They are considered important forms of regional cooperation because they mobilise much needed capital, technology, entrepreneurship and organisational resources of relatively more industrialised developing countries for the lesser developed ones in their fraternity thus, these ventures enable optimum utilisation of the capabilities and resources of developing countries for their maximum common benefit. Besides, they encourage regional trade and contribute to their collective self-reliance. They have been considered to be more advantageous for the receiving countries than foreign direct investments associated with the industrialised countries' multinational corporations.

The transfer of resources and technology through regional joint ventures is more appropriate and cost effective for the receiving country than similar transfers affected by MNCs based in the industrialised countries.

For instance, the technology transferred to joint ventures has been found to have been appropriately scaled down to smaller size, made more appropriate to factor endowments of developing countries and adapted to local raw materials and condition. They have been found to depend less on imported capital goods and raw materials and result in significantly lower foreign exchange outgo on account of servicing.

Joint ventures, especially with buy–back arrangements have generally been considered as an effective means of promoting regional co-operation. Joint ventures are also regarded to play an important role in accelerating the pace of industrialisation in the less developed countries since they usually involve transfer of technology as well.

The Joint Business Councils setup in the SAARC region have identified a large number of economic activities in various sectors as suitable areas for establishing Joint Ventures. These areas range from agro-processing activities to tourism promotion and consultancy services.

During the last decade, there is surge in the number of Indian Joint Ventures in several South Asian countries like Bangladesh, Nepal and Sri Lanka. These Joint Ventures are engaged with varieties of production activities indifferent parts of the region.

The favourable economic climate between India and Sri Lanka has promoted many Indian joint ventures to setup their production units in Sri Lanka. There are about 90 Indian joint ventures operating in Sri Lanka.

The duty free provision of Indo-Nepal Trade and Transit treaty 1996, has further induced Indian Joint Ventures to operate from Nepal. At present there are 72 Indian Joint Ventures.

In recent years, there is a surge of Joint Venture activities between India and Bangladesh. Bangladesh has a large reserve of natural gas and this source of energy has attracted many Joint Ventures to work on diversified production sectors, particularly in energy-intensive ventures.

Bhutan has built hydro-electricity ventures by collaborating with India with buy-back facility. With this arrangement India is now a net deficit country with Bhutan.

The governments of SAARC nations have simplified the procedures for establishing joint ventures. Separate "Board of Investment" has been set up in many member countries to attract FDI along with provision of tax concessions and other facilities. The entrepreneurs in the member countries have to take advantage of these opportunities to establish joint ventures within the region.

In addition to joint ventures, Indian enterprises have transferred technology through licensing and technical collaborations, export of turnkey projects, capital goods and machinery and consultancy services to many SAARC countries.

(a) Technical Collaborations

Indian enterprises has entered into technical collaboration agreements with firms in other countries of the region for transfer of technology for manufacture of a wide range of goods such as reactive and sun fast dyes, assembly of two wheelers and commercial vehicles engines. Bangladesh has received know-how for manufacture of bicycle and parts, and diesel engines. Several Nepalese enterprises have entered into technical collaborations with Indian firms for manufacture of paints, furniture, dry cell batteries, and automotive components. The National Research Development Corporation of India has transferred technologies developed in national laboratories for high draught kiln, spice-oleoresin, anti-fungal tablets and bleaching powder to Nepal and for buff coloured green pepper to Sri Lanka.

(b) Turnkey Plant Export

Turnkey projects are important means of transfer of technology for countries, which don't has indigenous base of capital goods manufactures, and engineering skills. In turnkey contracts, the contractor usually is responsible for supply and erection of plant and machinery and accompanying civil works, training of local personnel and sometimes operation for limited period. Indian firms have undertaken projects covering activities ranging widely form very simple technologies (textiles, transmission towers, small-scale industries) to intermediate level technologies (paints, pharmaceuticals, rubber, conveyors) and to very complex capital intensive and/or skill intensive technologies (power generation, basic drugs, machine tools, telephone exchanges, steel mills, railway engineering and petro-chemicals).

Indian enterprises has undertaken turnkey jobs for power stations and transmission lines and equipment in Nepal, its storage tanks in Sri Lanka and power transmission network in Bangladesh.

It is thus possible to identify many more areas for technology transfer from India to other SAARC countries. The entrepreneurs and most importantly, the specific industry level associations in the various member countries should take the necessary initiatives to commercially exploit the largely untapped potential of setting up Joint Ventures and technology transfer in the SAARC region.

(c) Physical Infrastructure

A major impediment to economic growth that is emerging or intensifying in the SAARC region is the inadequacy of physical infrastructure such as power supply, telecommunications and transport, including roads, railways and ports. It needs to be stressed that it would be difficult to stimulate intra-regional trade and investment without improving infrastructural facilities. Regional co-operation in the development of infrastructural faculties in the member countries could play a significant role in enhancing the level of regional economic cooperation. The development of efficient transport infrastructure has a strong influence on location of industries and on associated investment decision.

The need to improve the transport infrastructure and transit facilities in the region was recognised and the 11th session of the SAARC council of ministers in Colombo directed the committee on economic cooperation (CEC) to take appropriate steps in this regard. With a view to enhancing trade within and outside the SAARC region, the study was completed in 1994 and has made far-reaching recommendations.

1. Surface Transport

Railways remain by for the most important, though not the most dynamic, mode of on land transport in the SAARC region.

The performance of railways in Bangladesh, Pakistan and Sri Lanka has deteriorated very much during the 1980s as is evident from the sharp decline in the freight and passengers carried by the railways in these countries. In Bangladesh, the freight carried by the railways declined from 2984 tons in 1980-81 to 2350 tons in 1992-93. In Pakistan, the freight carried by the railways declined from 7918 million ton km in 1980-81 to 5939 million ton km in 1993-94, while in Sri Lanka the freight kilometrage declined from 281 million in 1978 to 168 million in 1993. The investment in rail transport in these countries has not been adequate enough to modernise its infrastructure to make it competitive with other modes of transport in terms of convenience and speed. Indian railways and also the private sector wagon building industry in Indian can help the railways in other SAARC countries in improving their performance. Serious attention has to be given to this aspect since railways provide a cheap mode of long-distance transport of freight and passenger. Moreover, in comparison to road transports, their energy consumption per ton/kilometer is about half that of road transport.

SAARC countries can be largely benefited by sharing their road/ rail links with neighbouring countries. For example, the North-Eastern region of India will be immensely benefitted if Bangladesh Government permits India to utilise the railway link of Bangladesh for carrying essential commodities to some of our North-Eastern states from other parts of India. It will reduce the transport cost and hence the high cost of living in those states.

2. Ports and Shipping

The development of seaports plays an important role not only in country's external trade but also in the provision of ship supplies and repairs, manufacturing, storage and warehousing activities. The private sector in different SAARC countries has substantial scope to invest in different areas of port infrastructure.

Coastal shipping can play a very important role in expanding intra-regional trade in the SAARC region. At present, cargo traffic between India and Maldives originals from Tuticorin ports. But Tuticorin often gets congested because of which the traffic is affected. There is also delay in the traffic. Because of the difficulties of import from India, Maldives import goods from Singapore the volume of which is estimated to be almost ten times that imported from India. If all the goods were imported from India, the consumers in Maldives would stand to gain as well as the shippers from India. Maldivian authorities feel that if the new port at Thiruvananthapuram could be expanded it would save a lot of time in cargo movement between India and Maldives. The coastal shipping companies of Bangladesh, India and Sri Lanka have to cooperate and evolve a suitable strategy for expanding coastal shipping facilities.

3. Containerisation and Multimodal Transport

Containerisation and multimodal transport system have assumed crucial importance in the present global scenario for developing an efficient transport system. The introduction of the container has revolutionalised the ways in which goods are moved in internal and external trade. Containerisation is a basic prerequisite for expanding the multimodal transport system. The major advantage of this system is that goods can be moved from one location to another through various modes of transport on surface and air under a single contract and single document and a through freight rate. Both the consignor and the consignee don't face any difficulties with respect to loading and unloading at various places during transhipment and the clearance formalities at ports. Thus, the major advantages of system are reduction in overall transportation cost and delays. Smoother and quicker movement of cargo and improvement in the quality of service. The consultancy firms of SAARC countries can play an important role in the expansion of infrastructural facilities in many areas like power, rail-transport, shipping, port development and management in the SAARC countries.

(d) Regional Projects

There are immense possibilities for implementing regional projects through co-operation among SAARC countries especially in the area of development of water and energy resources. There projects have the potential to confer various kinds of direct and indirect benefits to many SAARC countries in a sustained manner over a long period of time. Water resource play an important role in the agricultural and industrial development in many developing countries, and the SAARC countries are perhaps in greater need to develop water resources in order to create large employment opportunities for the large population of these countries still dependent on agriculture. The SAARC countries share commonly the great Himalayan Rivers like the Ganges, Brahmaputra and the Meghna. It is essential that all the riparian countries of the Himalayan rivers Bangladesh, Bhutan, India and Nepal, cooperate and formulate a general framework in the nature of "water resource treaty" to develop the water resources of the Himalayan rivers.

This framework would be useful for initiating work on specific projects and also in avoiding disputes on issues connected with the utilisation of water resource. Similarity, the riparian countries can also envisage generating electricity from hydro resources. In fact, discussions have been going on between India and Nepal for several years for development of water resources, but these have not materialised into concrete projects so far mainly because of the absence of a general framework for sharing the benefits.

. The public and private sector construction and consultancy companies in the SAARC countries can join together to establish consortiums for bidding and executing construction of projects in infrastructural areas like highways, airports, seaport, container terminals, improvement of rail network, inland water transport and expansion of telecommunication facilities, instead of entrusting such projects to firms from the industrialised countries. This would provide a lot of opportunities for the technically skilled manpower available within the SAARC countries to work together for the development of the region as a whole.

(e) Development of Tourism

Yet another area where regional projects could be undertaken for the common benefit of all the SAARC countries is the development of tourism. It is significant to note in this context that, realising the importance of tourism; the SAARC countries have appointed a SAARC Technical Committee on Tourism. This committee has also appointed an Expert Group consisting of representatives from Government and the private sector from the member countries.

The group has identified following areas where concrete action was needed on a long-term basis :

- Publicity in the potential targeted markets.
- Joint participation by SAARC countries for distribution of joint and national tourism packages.
- Encourage air carriers of SAARC countries in the sale and promotion of SAARC region as tourist destination.
- Use tourism offices of SAARC countries abroad for publicity.
- Establishment of SAARC tourism information centres.
- To bring out a SAARC travel guide.
- Familiarisation of tourist operators among SAARC countries on a reciprocal basis.

Tourism is a major foreign exchange earner in the SAARC countries especially Nepal, Sri Lanka, Bhutan and Maldives. Several Indian companies have got considerable expertise in building and managing world-class hotels and are managing hotels and restaurants in several countries. These companies could set up hotels and restaurants in different SAARC countries to contribute to the development of infrastructure for tourism promotion.

Thus, it is evident that, though a lot more to be done, regional cooperation in the field of tourism is progressing fast.

(f) Energy Cooperation

Energy is vital to the development process and is essential even at the subsistence level of the economy. The countries in South Asia are subjected to very sever foreign exchange constraints by the multiple increases in OPEC oil prices.

There are equally severed, but less well-known, problems even in the sector of traditional fuels, where deforestation and soil erosion are the main indicators.

The SAARC countries have some common energy problems. They are:

- Dependence upon imported oil resources.
- Dwindling forest resources with threatening environmental implications.
- Inadequate availability of physical exploration data and capability to process this data.
- Limited design and engineering technology, particularly for exploration.

There is vast scope for co-operation among the SAARC countries to overcome some of these common energy problems. In view of the limited capacities of these countries, initially the co-operation may be mainly in exchanging information and in training personnel. However, there are other potential areas for co-operation also.

Trade in Energy Resources

Some of the SAARC countries are rich in conventional energy resources, such as coal, natural gas, and hydropower. These can be traded among the SAARC countries which would benefit the buyer countries by way of reduction in transportation costs because of the geographical proximity of these nations and benefit the seller countries, in view of the extended market.

Information Exchange

All the SAARC countries are carrying on research into energy-related activities at some level or the other. But overcoming the energy problems is beyond the capabilities of individual countries due to the poor status of their economies. Information concerning research and operational experiences, therefore, should be exchange freely among the SAARC countries, so as to present duplication of efforts. This would result in more optimum utilisation of capital and data resources.

Joint Research and Development

Co-operation is a long-term concept and joint R & D should help in building up regional scientific and technological capabilities. Collective self sufficiency in the long-term can be achieved through joint research and development and technical co-operation in the field of energy.

Sharing of Technology

Some of the SAARC countries have achieved some amount of expertise in certain areas of energy technology. For instance, Nepal has successfully designed and managed mini and micro-hydel power stations. This technology can be transferred to other SAARC countries. In the field of new and renewable sources of energy, India has successfully installed and used solar photovoltaic cells, solar batteries, solar street lighting systems, solar signal systems, solar cooker and water heaters, wind mill based water pumps, and biogas plants. Transfer of such technologies to other South Asian countries would not only make these products available to the other countries but would also help in sharing and disseminating technologies for wider and more efficient use of new energy systems.

Training of Personnel

One of the potential areas of co-operation is in the field of training. Some countries like Pakistan, Bangladesh and India are relatively more advanced than the other SAARC Countries in energy technologies. These countries can train the personnel of the other countries in designing, manufacturing, installing and maintaining energy systems.

Possibilities of co-operation among the SAARC countries exist in undertaking combined efforts in developing energy conservation methods, research and development, demonstration and in adaptation of relevant technologies. Co-operation would also be possible in creating a comprehensive data bank for disseminating information and preventing duplication of efforts. The countries in the region also can cooperate for development of appropriate regional institutions for conducting applied research in the field of energy.

Energy cooperation is a drive for the SAARC process leading to durable peace in the region.

Securing sustainable energy supplies to meet energy needs at reasonable / affordable prices has become a major energy policy imperative of SAARC States. The sky-rocketing oil prices and increasing energy demand have put severe strains on resources of all SAARC countries. It has serious implications including slowing down of economic development, increasing inflation, deepening poverty and causing political and social instability in the region. The SAARC region is energy deficient as it does not produce enough oil and gas to meet its needs thus depend heavily on imports.

The process of regional cooperation in energy sector began in January 2000 with the establishment of a technical committee on energy. The Technical Committee on Energy met twice; there after recognising that this vital area required focused attention, the council of ministers approved the creation of a Specialised Working Group on energy in January 2004. SAARC Energy centre was created through Dhaka Declaration in 2005. The first meeting of the SAARC Energy Ministers in Islamabad was held on 1 October 2005, as the special purpose vehicle to realise the vision of SAARC leaders to establish an energy Ring in South Asia. It has started journey from 1 March 2006 in Islamabad. SAARC energy cooperation programme provides a major substantive element for economic prosperity of South Asia through meeting the energy demand of the countries. SAARC Energy Centre is converting energy challenges into opportunities for development. It is the platform involving officials, experts, academics, environmentalists and NGOs to tap potentials of cooperation in energy sector including development of hydropower, renewable and alternative energy, promoting technology transfer, energy trade, energy conservation and efficiency improvement in the region.

As directed by the thirteenth SAARC Summit, the Government of India organised South Asia Energy Dialogue on 5 March 2007 and made a number of recommendations to promote cooperation in this area.

SAARC Energy Trade Study (SRETS) has been completed with the assistance of Asian Development Bank. It has identified four trade options which will be considered by the relevant SAARC mechanism in order to make a road map for implementation. As a follow SAARC has commissioned a study on Regional Power Exchange. The study is likely to be completed in 2012. The study will explore the development of a regional power market involving SAARC Countries that already have interconnection, as well as those that have planned interconnection. It will also examine both economic and technical requirements of establishing a regional power exchange that would maximise the potential for power transfers among SAARC regions to reduce power shortages and take advantage of economic benefits.

As a follow up to the summit directive the expert group on electricity in its meeting held in January 2011 considered the concept paper on the road map for developing SAARC Market for Electricity (SAME) and the concept paper on SAARC inter-Governmental framework agreement for regional energy cooperation.[14]

Regional Economic Cooperation Among SAARC Countries

There is a considerable scope for enhancing the level of regional economic cooperation among SAARC countries which could prove mutually beneficial to all the member countries. The process of economic cooperation can help in accelerating the pace of industrialisation and economic growth in all the member countries without conflicting with their own national objectives and priorities. The SAARC countries have been experiencing relatively low rates of economic growth as compared to other developing countries in East and Southeast Asia. The people in the SAARC countries are having great expectations about improvement in their standards of living and welfare. Further delays in meeting the aspirations of the people can lead to socially disruptive situations which would affect both growth and welfare. Considering the constraints posed by the emerging tendencies in the world economy, regional economic cooperation among SAARC countries provides a viable strategy for the collective economic development of the region.[15]

Among the SAARC countries, India happens to dominate the economic scenario as its population accounts for 77 per cent, followed by Bangladesh 10.2 per cent, Pakistan 9.8 per cent, Nepal 1.7 per cent and Sri Lanka 1.6 per cent. Once again, India's hegemony is a lurking fear in the minds of other SAARC members. Hence, they are generally hesitant to commit themselves to cooperation in hard-core economic areas. But India can assist most of the other SAARC members in their developmental efforts by virtue of its diversified industrial base and relatively skilled manpower. For example, Nepal and Bangladesh could benefit in textiles and plastic products while Bangladesh and Pakistan could substantially improve iron and steel production with a little cooperation from India. Sri Lanka and India can also co-operate in exporting tea to the rest of the world through a properly evolved set of guidelines. But in reality, attempts to use SAARC as a platform from which to launch joint industrial or manufacturing ventures threatens the smaller states with further integration into India, while India itself remains reluctant to allow access to what is still an essentially protected domestic market. Pakistan has continued to restrict Indian trade because of strategic considerations, especially involving investments by private Indian firms that might displace Pakistani firms from lucrative market from emergent third markets in Central Asia, Moreover, most of the SAARC countries continue to remain primarily agricultural in nature and depend upon the developed world for their exports and imports of both manufactured as well as semi-manufactured products. The resources of the governments in SAARC countries are almost perpetually under severe strain in view of the ever increasing need for social amenities for the expanding populace. This also cuts into the funds originally allocated to various developmental projects. Therefore, lack of adequate financial resources is considered one of the major constraints in transforming the work of technical committees and other SAARC bodies into more effective action. One of the key outcomes of the Eighth SAARC summit that concluded in New Delhi on May 4, 1995 was an agreement among seven member states to initiate the South Asian Preferential Trade Agreement (SAPTA). The agreement came into effect from December 7, 1995, but after the signing of SAPTA, it was realised that SAPTA is a good beginning, but it is not enough. Politics and infrastructure were the major roadblocks to SAPTA's success. After sometimes in 2006 SAPTA was evolved as SAFTA (South Asian Free Trade Agreement) but most economists privately believed that SAARC can never achieve its full potential unless major political differences between members are settled. A major part of the problem in implementing the economic agenda stems from the near perennial Indo-Pak tension.

The informal talk between Indian Prime Minister and Pakistani President on 10th April 2012 in New Delhi have reinforced the growing conviction between India and Pakistan that peace in South Asia is a necessary condition to extricate Pakistan and India from its economic quagmire.

Pakistan's grant of MFN status to India is a starting point. Hence, if the Indo-Pakistan relations cannot improve until the Kashmir issue is resolved, then any encouragement of trade would be seen as a sell-out and tantamount to repudiating the governing national interest.

The growing emphasis on economic cooperation is significant in view of the fact that intra-regional trade among SAARC countries, as a percentage of their total world trade, is presently a low 3.4 per cent. This is because of trade policies pursued in these countries that, along with sour political relationships, have tended to discourage cooperation within the region.

Levels of trade between India and its neighbours are low because their economies do not complement each other in resource availability, the structure and content of production, the supply of services and cut-throat competitiveness. For example, Bangladesh, India and Nepal compete with their jute products in the United Kingdom, EC and Japan. India, Sri Lanka and Bangladesh compete with tea in the UK and EC. Similarly, there is a bitter rivalry between India, Pakistan and Bangladesh over the export of textiles to the US and EC, which has been compounded in recent years by complex rules and regulations regarding textiles in the international trading system.[16]

Thus, South Asian business groups have no powerful incentives to seek regional trade liberalisation.

The supporters of free trade agreements and RTAs, however, argue that despite the potential for trade diversion, SAFTA would bring significant benefits to small countries in the region and would facilitate unilateral trade liberalisation in South Asia.

Although South Asian countries have pursued economic liberalisation policies in the early 1990s, these policies have not led to deeper regional economic cooperation. One important reason for South Asian political leader's lack of deep commitment towards regional trade is limited potential of economic benefits from SAFTA arrangements. South Asian leaders remain largely unconvinced that SAFTA would facilitate their power-regaining objective. Instead it had been perceived inequity, that is larger economies like India would benefit more from SAFTA arrangements.

There is also lack of consensus about India's leadership in SAARC because of India's unwillingness to assume the role of a regional "paymaster" who can ease distributional problems associated with free trade practices for small countries in South Asia and also its reluctance to assume leadership has also made coordination of rules, regulations and policies regarding free trade issues difficult and time consuming.

Free trade arrangements and RTAs would make a great deal more sense and would be an essential underpinning of an emerging regionalism in South Asia. But the level of regional economic interdependence achieved so far and the pace at which South Asian countries are progressing their negotiation for free trade arrangements will leave South Asian countries at an appreciable distance from the goal of economic cooperation.[17]

Also the economic prosperity of India prompted the other SAARC members to seek resort to international trade as a platform for economic growth. Both Sri Lanka and Nepal have shown their interests to enhance intra-regional trade. Bangladesh is also following the same trend. With the increased intra-regional trading activities, the economic relationship among the SAARC nations is bound to be stronger in future.

Table 5.17
Intra SAARC Trade During (2000 – 2011)

Year	*Total Trade (US $ Mn).*
2000	5787.2
2001	6420.6
2002	7515.2
2003	10767.5
2004	13127.6
2005	17119.5
2006	20459.6
2007	19,652,581.16
2008	139,138,89.57
2009	559,161,799.92
2010	570,281,530.57
2011	1.3 US $ Billion.

Source: Direction of Trade Statistics Year Book, IMF.

SAARC Trade Fairs

On January 9, 1996 the commerce minister and leaders of delegations of all SAARC Member states jointly inaugurated the first SAARC Trade Fair in New Delhi from (January 9-14) 1996 as part of the commemoration of the first decade of SAARC. The Trade Fair was organised with the theme of **Cooperation for Growth**. They recognised that such trade fairs were a particularly effective instrument for direct promotion of intra-SAARC trade, as well as for raising the general awareness levels in the region of the importance of trade among their countries for their economic development and agreed to promote organisation of similar trade fairs regularly at various venues in all SAARC countries. Until now 11 SAARC trade fairs had been held. The next trade fair will be organised in Maldives in 2012.[18]

Impediments or Challenges to Further Enhancing Economic Cooperation

Sometimes, South Asia's economic prospects look grim. Pakistan is trapped in a cycle of violence. Bangladesh emerged from an Islamist government led by Khaleda Zia and successive caretaker administrations only three years ago. Sri Lanka is still recovering from the debilitating 27 year old civil war with the LTTE. Nepal and Maldives are in a political ferment. Afghanistan remains mired in war. South Asia is at a fork in the road. A wrong turn could set it back years in its battle against corruption, political mis-governance and political inertia. The converse could help it build into an economical power within a decade. Only India is the key to South Asia's emergence as one of the world's most powerful regional blocs. But, to ensure the present momentum of economic cooperation and development, we have to examine some impediments in the way of development of South Asian economy or SAARC as an organisation. To establish any organisation the stakeholders have to overcome many difficulties which can be considered as challenges for that organisation.

1. Low Education Level, Lack of Awareness and Weak Economy of Member States

The basic reasons which are creating hindrance in the development of SAARC are the low education level and weak economy of its member countries while education and strong economy are very much important for the success of regional organisation. As the member countries of SAARC are developing nations and the people of the South Asia are not well educated, so they are not aware of the role of such organisations and are not ready to cooperate with it.

2. Ethnic Conflicts and Social Differences

Ethnic conflicts, social differences and the superiority complex of India are the prime hindrances in the way of success of SAARC. As the main hurdles are the ethnic conflicts, social difference and the superiority complex of India, so most of their resources are spent on defense and every single penny is poured into the mouth of cannon. Due to this fact the member countries waste most of their potentialities and resources on weapons.

3. Economic Condition of South Asia

The economic conditions of South Asia is also one of the obstacles for SAARC because most of the governments of its member countries are very poor and depends largely on developed countries. Due to this reason the member countries of SAARC should also launch a single unit of money and should establish an open market amongst them to provide easy access to trade and overcome economic problems of the region.

4. US Influence in Asia

US influence in Asia does not allow the member countries of SAARC to work independently and make the progress of this organisation difficult. The basic reason for the slow progress of SAARC is the US attitude towards the subcontinent and advocate conflicts and war in the region and initiated the arm race in the subcontinent. The member countries are very much dependent on US for their economies and cannot work independently.

5. Low Level of Integration in South Asia

There several explanations for the low levels of economic integration in South Asia. The trade diversion, unequal sharing of benefits and the relatively high levels of protection in the region, In South Asia, economic gains from integration are perceived to be asymmetric and potentially adverse for the smaller members.

In South Asia, there is low level of gains emerging from regional cooperation is substantial from informal or border trade. The thriving illegal trade is mainly driven by difference in the tariff structures among the South Asian countries, as well as the incidence, of high transactions costs in the formal routes.

6. Too Small and too few with Similar Revealed Comparative Advantage

The SAARC comprises of only eight countries with a marked imbalance created by the dominance of the Indian economy. The North American Free Trade Agreement (NAFTA) has even less number of member countries than SAARC and is also dominated by a large country. However, a critical difference between the two regional formations has been the pro-active role played by the US in forging NAFTA compared to the passive and at times negative stance adopted in the past by India. An analysis of trade flows in South Asia indicates that the countries have almost identical pattern of revealed comparative advantage in a relatively low range of products and bilateral trade exhibits low levels of trade complementarities.

7. Fear of India

In some South Asian countries there is real fear of deindustrialisation if preferential market access is provided to the large and better established Indian manufactures. India's hegemony is a lurking fear in the minds of other SAARC members. Hence, they are generally hesitant to commit themselves to cooperation in hard-core economic areas.

Despite India's hegemonic position, there is no consensus among South Asian countries to recognise India as the region's undisputed leader. Additionally, most South Asian countries share a distrust of India's economic and military domination in the region. This distrust makes it difficult for SAARC countries to work towards common regional economic strategies. India also shows unwillingness to assume the role of a regional "paymaster" who can ease distributional problems associated with free trade practices for small countries in South Asia. India's reluctance to assume leadership has also made coordination of rules, regulations and policies regarding free trade issues difficult and time consuming.

8. Weak Port and Transport Infrastructure

The poor port and transport infrastructure is one of the major reasons for low-integration in the region (as well as an obstacle to growth for the region). Delays in transit due to road or port congestion and customs procedures (non-tariff barriers) raise the costs for exporters. The limitations are in both physical (lack of cargo / ship handling equipment) as well as non-physical infrastructure (excessive and cumbersome border procedures).

9. Persistence of High Level of Overall Protection

The SAARC region as a whole has been one of the more heavily protected regions in the world. In particular, India is considered to be the least open among the group in terms of trade – weighted average applied tariff rate 30.1 per cent, followed by Bangladesh with 21.3 per cent, Pakistan with 17.4 per cent and Nepal with 15.5 while Sri Lanka is the most open with an average applied tariff of 6.2 per cent. These high tariffs are expected to decline under SAFTA when it is fully implemented. However, a wide range of non-tariff barriers are also used by these countries to protect their markets. These are more difficult to remove and identify.

10. Restrictive Rules of Origin and Destination

Rules of origin in preferential or free trade agreements help determine the products for tariff preferences, but tighter rules of origin often reflect protectionist intention. The co-existence of high tariff barriers and tight rules of origin raises the risk of trade diversion. SAARC members specify the port of entry sometimes for all imports and often for selective products. While this approach has been implemented to curb illegal imparts, it also seems to be driven by inadequate administrative capacity. But the port specific restrictions have increased transactions costs of formal trade and bolstered the informal boarder trade.

11. Lack of Coverage and Commitment in the Merchandise Trade Agreement

The liberalisation in merchandise trade as envisioned in SAFTA is much less ambitious than what the South Asian countries have themselves been autonomously pursuing under the regime of the WTO. The SAFTA tariff liberalisation programme also allows members to retain a negative list of items that are not offered for concessional treatment. Almost 53 per cent of the total imports between SAFTA members have been subject to the negative lists of the respective countries. Among the large member countries India and Sri Lanka have restricted up to 38 per cent and 52 per cent respectively of their total imports by value from the SAFTA members under the sensitive list category. The negative lists thus continue to significantly limit the scope of the South Asian **"Free Trade"** regime.

12. Service are not Included in Regional Trade Agreement

The services sector accounts for more than half the GDP in most South Asian economies. However, trade in services is conspicuous by its absence under the SAFTA. This is paradoxical especially considering that the region as a whole is emerging as a strong exporter of commercial services worldwide. Most of the South Asian countries have been negotiating liberalisation of the services sector under the WTO, and a liberalisation exercise at the regional level would be a good testing ground for this dynamic sector.[19]

13. Policy Paralysis in South Asia

According to latest World Bank Report on 19 January 2012, in its **'Global Economic Prospects'** said that South Asia's economies are also confronted with **"domestic policy paralysis"** and uncertainty about regulatory reforms.

The weakening in activity reflects a significant moderation in domestic demand, led by a deceleration in investment activity that has faced head winds of rising borrowing costs, high input prices, slowing global growth and heightened uncertainty. Delays and uncertainty surrounding the implementation of policy reforms have also hindered investment and also development of the region.

14. The Political Economy of South Asia

SAARC is now in its twenty–fifth year. But the persistence of conflict within and between the states of SAARC is a single most potent factor that has prevented the region from forging an effective regional economic cooperative mechanism since the beginning. There is no particular explanation of the persistent conflict among the countries. They are embroiled in various complex issues and provide a disappointing picture from the political as well as economic perspective. The fact that the region is perpetually plagued with various inter-state and intra-state conflicts reflects the Lukewarm approach of the ruling elite has always been driven by the narrow considerations of caste, religion, ethnicity, language and community rather than the welfare and economic prosperity of the people. The persistence of multifarious problem both within and between the South Asian states therefore hampers the sustenance of an economic environment where the basis essentials of the common man are fulfilled. The success of SAFTA, however largely depends on normalisation of Pakistan – India relations. In case the relations between the two countries do not normalise, SAFTA's fate will not be different from that of its predecessor, SAPTA. However, it is with India that most other countries in South Asia had bilateral disputes.

Hence, developing and sustaining a sound economy and securing and protecting economic interests are the priority of governments' internal and external policies respectively.

Therefore, pragmatically, the best approach will be to address economic and political issues together.

15. Limited Scope for Mutually Beneficial Market Exchange

The main inhibiting factor has been a lack of complimentarity in exports of SAARC member countries. The four major SAARC nations exports a similar basket of commodities and often competes directly especially for textiles.

Furthermore, India's economic dominance and comparative advantage have resulted asymmetric trade relations hindering regional integration. Indeed, most of SAARC member's trade is with the United States and Europe rather than with their neighbours. Given the small size of markets of South Asian countries with India as an exception, there is limited scope for mutually beneficial market exchange among South Asian countries. Thus, South Asian business groups have no powerful incentives to seek regional trade liberalisation. Consequently demand for Free Trade Agreement (FTA) by business group is weak.

16. Multiplicity of Contracts Hinders the Growth of SAARC

Due to interstate differences and disputes there is a lack of movement at the multilateral level, member states are more inclined to take a bilateral course of creating bilateral free–trade areas. There are also trilateral (India–Bhutan - Nepal), quadrilateral (Bangladesh-India-Nepal-Bhutan) and multilateral arrangements. This is what the experts describe as "spaghetti", a multiplicity of contracts that hinders the growth at the SAARC level. There are also transregional trading arrangements including India – ASEAN FTA, BIMSTEC – FTA and Indian Ocean Rim Association for Regional Cooperation (IORARC), Pakistan remains actively involved in Economic Cooperation Organisation (ECO) and Organisation of Islamic Countries (OIC). India's involvement in a "noodle bowl" of bilateral trade agreements with Singapore, Thailand, Vietnam, Japan, China, South Korea, Sri Lanka, Nepal, Bhutan and Bangladesh, and her initiatives for the "spoke-spoke" pattern of economic cooperation among subgroups of South Asian countries, like the creation of South Asian Growth Quadrangle (SAGQ) with India, Bangladesh, Bhutan and Nepal are motivated in part by Pakistan's unwillingness to increase the speed of free trade negotiation with India. While these pattern of trade cooperation may provide some short-term solution to India's need for trade expansion and market access, given their lack of commonality and different rules of origin, it is not clear as to what extent these type of trade agreements will facilitate deeper economic cooperation.

Thus, there are divergences of interests and strategic interests amongst SAARC countries. These impediments pose internal challenges to the SAARC process and the future pace of regional economic cooperation.

Ways to Overcome Impediments

The following measures, some of which may be implemented as port of SAFTA, will contribute towards strengthening economies ties in the region thus help to overcome and to achieve the shared goal of development and prosperity.

1. Regional countries need to reduce high tariffs on the specific industries of each partner country which are applied to safeguard the interests of some of the local business communities at the cost of low completion and high domestic prices. In particular, high and specific duties on textile, clothing and agricultural products should be reduced to make available the cheaper goods in the domestic market, thereby improving consumer welfare. This will also lead to enhanced trade within the region. To reduce the complexity of the tariff structures, duties and exemptions provided to domestic producers need to be removed. Some studies have pointed out a tendency to use anti-dumping duties as a tool for restricting imports in some South Asian countries. There should be mutual revision of anti-dumping policies on a regional basis. At the same time small countries including Bhutan, Maldives and Nepal and need to build their capacity to deal with anti–dumping investigations on their exports and to improve their technical expertise on using safeguard measures.

   To minimise trade diversion and the attendant welfare loss, the preferential removal of trade barriers in the region to enhance regional integration may be accompanied by a long term plan for reduction in the level of external protection.

2. Reduction in tariffs alone is not sufficient to promote economic ties in the region. Improvements in the customs as well as tax and other administrations must complement tariff reduction policies. This process should be designed and implemented in close consultation with the stakeholders, business, farmers, investors, traders and other. What is needed is a regulatory environment that facilitates trade through reduction in the transaction costs associated with bringing goods and services across border.

   Trade facilitation involves a wide range of initiatives, including, for instance, reforms in the regulation and harmonisation of standards, promoting efficiency in customs and improvement in regional transport infrastructure. The regional countries need to adopt a coherent strategy to harmonise their policies, focusing in particular on transport and transit systems and customs procedures. Domestic regulatory procedures and institutional structures based on international best practice models can improve transparency and introduce professionalism in border clearance procedures.

3. Streamline regulation on technical barriers and liberalising transport and telecommunications regimes can also facilitate trade. Collective action to raise capacity in trade facilitation in terms of upgrading ports, and introduction of information technology for processing trade documents would lower transaction costs and expand trade across the region.
4. Confidence-building measures are needed to create the right atmosphere for greater economic ties in the region. Indeed, the region is dominated by two large economies India and Pakistan and these countries must lead the way towards regional economic integration in South Asia. Action of these economies has a strong influence on policies of other South Asian countries. Both countries need to work together to ensure smaller regional countries that their interests will be safeguarded and their apprehensions' about the domination of large economies will be addressed at the regional level.

   In this respect, SAFTA's provision to compensate the least developed member states for customs revenue loss promises to be useful mechanism for building the confidence of smaller member states.
5. Easing of travel and visa restrictions would also promote business contracts within the region, leading to ushering of new possibilities for economic cooperation. Finally, there is a need to create awareness about the potential benefits of regional economic cooperation initiatives more acceptable to the public thus making it easier for governments to engage in such initiatives.
6. The SAFTA agreement provides a useful framework for strengthening trade ties in the region and implementing many of the measures. However, effective implementation of SAFTA will require a strong willingness of all members for greater economic integration as well as a favourable political environment in the region, Also, continuous dialogues and interaction along with sincere efforts towards protecting the interest of smaller member states are essential for the success of SAFTA and other regional initiatives.
7. For sustained economic cooperation in the region, there is a need to explore potential in new areas. The importance of developing vertical specialisation through regional production sharing arrangements. These arrangements would allow the regional trading

partners to achieve economies of scale by concentrating on various segments of the value chain in a production process. Such arrangements would be facilitated through regional cooperation on foreign investment and competition policies.

8. Despite some recent changes, the Indian stance towards SAARC still remains somewhat equivocal and unclear. This is direct outcome of the perception that SAARC cannot really move forward because the Pakistani establishment will simply not let it progress.

   Therefore, it is argued that India's national interests are better served by supporting other initiatives like the BIMSTEC, the Indian Ocean Rim and the Swarnbhoomi initiatives. In spite of this India should give its fullest and proactive support to make SAARC successful.
9. South Asia's low level of regional integration is also reflected in the relatively low level of FDI inflows in the region. There is no doubt that a peaceful, stable and regionally integrated South Asia will attract greater volumes of FDI into South Asia and this will have significant positive implications for achieving rapid inclusive growth.
10. Increasing inequity fuels insecurity and cross-border terrorism. Thus, it is in India's interest to help improve the standard of living and reduce poverty in the smaller South Asian economies as she continues to pursue the path of high growth. India can hardly hope to remain an island of economic growth if the growth impetus is not shared with or transferred to neighbouring countries.
11. Regional integration will provide a larger market and also scope for intra-industry trade. Both features will benefit the South Asian industry to lower costs and become more globally competitive by exploiting economies of scale and scope. Even small and medium-sized South Asian companies will benefit by improving their global competitiveness in a phased manner by initially producing for SAARC markets and then striking out for a greater share in global markets.
12. The South Asian subcontinent is an integrated geo-ecological system. It can easily be seen that some public goods and services like energy, water management and conservation, prevention again endemics and maximising tourist earnings are achieved on a regional basis. As, India shares with all SAARC members, it is in her interest to ensure that a cooperative approach is taken to address these issues of the delivery of regional public goods and markets.
13. Channeling Asian Development Bank resources through South Asia Fund (SAF) can be a good option for implementing regional projects.
14. The experience from other parts of the world shows that smaller countries benefit from regional associations centred on an anchor

economy. For SAARC, India is such an economy. In creating a working economic and political region, South Asians will have to find the leaders from within their own organisation (SAARC). Without a workable South Asian economic region, the countries will lose out in a rapidly changing global economy. There are immense opportunities available but they will only come South Asia's way if the states in the region place economic benefits above national politics. They must understand that relations among nations are a plus-sum and not a zero-sum game.

15. SAARC countries are endowed with specific kinds of natural and human resources that could be efficiently utilised for the benefit of the entire region.
16. The efforts for forging closer economic cooperation in the SAARC region can succeed only by carefully examining and identifying the areas in which regional economic cooperation would prove most fruitful.
17. The process of functional economic integration should be based on free trade in goods and services, technology transfer, joint ventures, direct investment or equity participation all of which have to be facilitated by the normal working of the market mechanism. This process would then lead to expansion of intra-regional and intra-industry trade.[20]
18. It looks advantageous if SAARC countries could adopt a single currency – substantially enhancing their bargaining power together in the world market. A common currency's attraction is that it doesn't represent the currency of any single country. Its advantageous to deal with a lesser number of currencies since each time one converts a currency, there is a huge loss. The common currency regime, when achieved, can present substantial benefits to the region. With uncertainty about exchange rates removed, and transaction costs reduce trade and investment in the region can get a big boost. Also with money creation under regional guidelines, there would be better prospects of synchronisation of inflation, interest rate and GDP growth, all of which can contribute to accelerated growth and poverty reduction.
19. The removal of poverty and hunger is the most important objective, since it will only improve economic growth. The poverty reduction would require a holistic and consistent policy. There is a need to refocus and review the implementation of the Millennium Development Goals (MDGs) as they are lapsing into rhetoric, particularly in the education and health sector and programmes which impact the female and the girl child.

20. One economic hurdle which has impeded faster integration in the region has been similarity of products. It is suggested to start joint ventures and market themselves as large consumer and production bases to the rest of the world. The captains of industry, communication, energy, media and tourism should be given greater say, rather than the bureaucrats concerned, in pushing the economic and cooperation agendas forward.
21. Setting grandiose goals for intra-regional trade is likely to be counterproductive. Instead, over the next ten to fifteen years, SAARC countries should pursue modest trade objectives and seek joint development projects of modest scale. In this context, the SAARC countries should negotiate with the United Nations Development Programme (UNDP) and Asian Development Bank (ADB) for the development of joint projects. Development of joint projects with the assistance of ADB in smaller units can create new opportunities and help establish linkages with other regions.
22. Though there is direct relationship between the exchange rate depreciation and exports, SAARC countries could adopt cautious exchange rate policies as this may have adverse impact on the terms of trade.
23. Economic development of the region should not include just goods and services but the whole set of social and political institutions that are necessary for "human functioning".
24. Health is a major trigger that pushes people into poverty and keeps productivity at a low level in South Asia. Therefore provision of high quality preventive and curative health facilities would be a strategic intervention for poverty reduction, human development and economic growth in the region. For this purpose South Asia Health Foundation may be instituted.
25. Free trade in agricultural commodities will help stabilise seasonal price fluctuations and prevent the associated real income losses to farmers. Free trade in capital and intermediate goods will lower the incremental capital output ratios, thereby enabling higher GDP growth for given levels of investment. Free trade in consumer goods and services will mean substantial welfare gains particularly for the middle class, lower inflation rate and improved income distribution in South Asia could play a synergistic role in accelerating economic growth and the peace process.
26. Through private sector joint venture infrastructure projects, like facilitating private sector joint projects in building a network of motorways and railways, regional and global joint venture projects for developing new ports along both the western and eastern seaboard of South Asia and regional investment projects in building a network

of airports, cold storages and warehouses can lead to stimulate GDP growth and employment in SAARC nations and can create new economic inter-dependencies.

27. Economic growth of South Asian countries must not only be accelerated but restructured in such a way that its capacity to alleviate poverty is enhanced for given growth rates of GDP. For this purpose SAARC Fund for vocational training may be established. The purpose of this Fund should be to help establish a network of high quality vocational training institutes for the poor. Improved training in market demanded skills would enable a shift of the labour force from low skill sector to higher skill sectors and thereby increase the productivity and income earning capability of the poor. It would at the same time generate higher growth for investment by increasing factor productivity.

Moving the process of regional economic cooperation and regional trade integration forward requires concerted efforts aimed at reducing tariff barriers, trade facilitation, and building the confidence of small regional countries. SAFTA provides a useful basis for addressing many of these issues in South Asia, but strong and constant political will from all members will be needed to ensure effective implementation of this agreement.

More generally, South Asian and other countries need to adopt collective approaches to safeguard the interests of their region. Collective positions will help in improving the bargaining power of individual countries and can be very effective in multilateral negotiations forums such as WTO. Closer cooperation can also help the regional economy absorb external shocks.

However, over the last decade, all of the region's economies have been liberalising and generally growing at respectable rates, which would further facilitate deeper cooperation in the region. Within a few years of its establishment, SAARC launched dozens of initiatives for promoting regional cooperation in several priority areas, including region-level action on food security, poverty alleviation, energy development and trade.

The initiatives also aimed at creating SAARC Regional Centres, people-to-people contact programmes and a SAARC Development Fund. While some visible progress has been made, much of it remains on paper and comprises the repeated summit declarations of members' commitment to underlying objectives. The process of regional cooperation among SAARC countries is being achieved through what is known as the "Integrated Programme of Action" (IPA).

Achievements of SAARC (Economic Dimension)

The SAARC framework has also taken measures to promote economic cooperation. The SAARC as a regional body has taken initiatives to promote cooperation with inter-regional organisations. A memorandum of understanding (MOU) was signed between SAARC and UNCTAD Provides SAARC up-dated versions of the software, trade analysis and information system (TRAINS) which is computerised information system containing latest information on trade control measures prevailing in fifty developed and developing countries of the world. The SAARC Secretariat also provides similar information about trade control measures of SAARC member countries to the UNCTAD. This arrangement helps all the SAARC countries.

Similar agreements of cooperation have been signed with the Economic and Social Commission for Asian and the Pacific (ESCAP).

The SAARC member countries have signed a number of conventions and agreements in economic sphere:

(a) Agreement on the Establishment of South Asian Regional Standards Organisation (SARSO) (3 August 2008).
(b) Agreement on the establishment SAARC Food Security Reserve (November 1987).
(c) Agreement on Avoidance of Double Taxation (3 November 2005).
(d) Agreement on Custom matters (13 November 2005).
(e) Agreement on South Asia Free Trade Area (2004).

The SAARC has also carried out a number of studies and brought out reports. Since the 1988 summit, greater attention is being given to important areas of economic cooperation in the region. These included development planning, trade in manufactures and services, joint ventures and regional projects, energy, environment, disasters and ecology and basic needs and human resource development. The areas covered by SAARC reports include "Women in Development", "Trade, Manufactures and Services", "Disasters and environment" and "Poverty alleviation".

The study on poverty alleviation was carried out by the independent South Asian Commission on Poverty Alleviation (ISACPA) appointed by the SAARC leaders at their summit meeting in Colombo in 1991. The report of this study has recommended a concrete and practical "Agenda for Action" for eradication of poverty in the member countries.

The "SAARC study on Trade, Manufactures and Services" is also unique in the sense that the report was prepared by a group of coordinators and several experts from the member countries. The report has identified the various constraints to trade expansion – both in terms of goods and services – and in industrial cooperation in the SAARC region and has recommended several policy measures to overcome the same.

A major initiative towards promotion of regional economic cooperation was taken at the Dhaka summit in 1993 when the member countries agreed to introduce what is known as "SAARC Preferential Trading Arrangement" (SAPTA) and the introduction of SAFTA in 2006 is one of the most significant achievements of SAARC. The SAARC Secretary General observed in 2009 that SAFTA creates an enabling basis for regional trade in South Asia. It is path breaking in that sense. SAFTA has the potential to drive SAARC economies towards building a tariff–free trade regime in South Asia. Moreover, tariff liberalisation in goods trade under SAFTA can be expected to be accompanied by the similar liberalisation of trade in services and investment activities and in general contribute to accelerate deepening of cooperation and integration in South Asia.

It is also important to note that a "SAARC Fund for Regional Projects" (SFRP) has been setup for the development of regional projects. This fund is managed by a Regional Council of Development Financing Institutions of the SAARC member countries. A proposal to establish a South Asian Development Bank has also been made and it is being examined.

Another important development is the establishment of the SAARC Chamber of Commerce and Industry in which the apex chambers was inaugurated in 1994 with its headquarters being located in Karachi. The SAARC Chamber is an effective instrument to promote trade and economic cooperation among the member countries.

The SAARC FINANCE which was established on 9 September 1998 works as a regional network of the SAARC Central Bank Governors and Finance Secretaries. It had also launched SAARC Payment Council (SPC) which undertakes exchange of views on the impact of currently global financial crisis on individual South Asian economies is also one of the achievements of SAARC which can facilitate economic cooperation.

Another important achievement is the setting up of SAARC Development Goals (SDGs) which are expected to help member states to galvanise their development efforts, offering a space in which all sections of society can come together to debate national and regional priorities. It is also an international imperative of achieving the Millennium Development Goals (MDGs) by 2015. Collective will of the SAARC leaders to go further and faster, beyond the MDGs targets inspired the identification of the SDGs.

SAARC woes various funding mechanisms like SAARC Development Fund, South Asian Development Fund, Asian Development Bank, SAARC Finance, SAARC – Japan Special Fund that help in the developmental functions of SAARC which is not less than any achievement.

Various empirical result shows significant positive relationship between export flows and the size of the economy (either export or import) indicating the strong economic growth of the SAARC countries.

The total intra – SAARC trade have also increased from US$ 5787.2 million in 2000 to 1.3 US$ billion in 2011 which is also an achievement of SAARC as an organisation. Hence, all the above development can be expected to provide the necessary impetus to economic cooperation in South Asia.

SAARC and Other International Forums

In the changing regime of globalisation under WTO, it would be highly difficult for any nation to sustain the harsh conditionality of international trade and commerce. The unlimited access would only be available to limited nations who are well knitted with strong regional organisation. The strength of the regional organisation would determine and guarantee the socio-economic development of the member states and their status in international forum.

In the wake of highly successful ASEAN, EU, NAFTA and other such regional organisations as a single market, SAARC was also established in 1985, as a highly ambitious regional organisation of South Asia.

In order to analyse the economic dimensions of SAARC it is necessary to take its relations with other regional organisations into consideration. Through its comparative study with other regional organisation it would become easy to analyse its effectiveness and its future prospects.

1. SAARC and ASEAN (Association of South East Asian Nations)

South East Asia has the Association of South East Asian Nations (ASEAN) and South Asia has the South Asian Association for Regional Cooperation (SAARC). Both regional organisations were founded to minimize and settle disputes without the use of force and to maximise growth through economic development and trade. ASEAN was founded in 1967 whereas SAARC come into being in 1985.

In Asia's resurgence both South Asian and South East Asian regions are important in terms of natural and human resources. India is far ahead of the rest of the South Asia in terms of relationship with South East Asia. There are countries in the ASEAN like Singapore and Indonesia that worry about China's foray into the ASEAN and might like to interact with India more to balance that. As far as ASEAN – SAARC cooperation is concerned, the circumstances are different. Views of other South Asian countries regarding integration with South East Asia are in some respects different from those of India.

The ASEAN showed interest in South Asia only after India's growth. The ASEAN is interested in South Asia for :

- Gaining Market Access
- Two–way investment
- Attracting high–end tourists
- Exchanges in the field of education.

SAARC countries have been pursuing individual FTAs with ASEAN which ASEAN might find difficult to manage and may not turn out to be sustainable.

As India and Pakistan are dialogue partners of ASEAN, India, Pakistan, Bangladesh and Sri Lanka are also members of ARF (ASEAN Regional Forum) and India is a member of the East Asia Summit (EAS) process, this process has the potential to bring SAARC and ASEAN even closer together. The trade liberalisation initiatives in South Asia and Southeast Asia will create new opportunities to forge stronger economic and political ties.

In recent years ASEAN and SAARC have been stepping up their engagement. Officials from both sides have met to exchange information and best practices in areas ranging from trade to tourism, and to tackling HIV/AIDS and Avian Influensa. Looking ahead, we can expect cooperation to increase in scope and intensity as the two regional bodies continue to mature and develop as we find more areas of common interest.

ASEAN and SAARC are two pivotal regional platforms for actuating economic cooperation in South and South East Asia. A comparative study will reveal that despite a symmetrical sise why ASEAN has surpassed SAARC in terms of trade benefits and value addition to the overall regional economic growth.

- Both ASEAN and SAARC were setup because the members were embroiled in serious disputes. Perhaps ASEAN was more troubled because of its conglomeration of islands and unclear laws dealing with maritime frontiers. Yet, while ASEAN was able to avoid conflict, SAARC was not able to avoid such conflicts.
- Yet, ASEAN members had serious interstate disputes which they decided to forget. On the other hand, SAARC members insisted that disputes should be resolved first, before economic cooperation could start.
- ASEAN nations were inclined to be trading nations; whereas SAARC nations were inclined to be warlike. ASEAN moved to conflict-avoidance mechanisms but SAARC refused to discuss bilateral issues.
- On one hand ASEAN took no time in agreeing on two types of free trade areas (AFTA, 1997) while SAARC made heavy weather of its South Asian Preferential Trade Area (SAPTA) signed in 1993 and South Asian Free Trade Area (SAFTA) in 2004 but added to the agreement in Article (14) stating that nothing in this Agreement shall be construed to prevent any contracting state from taking action and adopting measures which it considers necessary for the protection of its national security.
- ASEAN's conflict – management approach falls in the conflict prevention category, by which is meant that disputes have not

escalated to the level where force is used. The ASEAN process is not a typical conflict-resolution mechanism, but it has evolved as a conflict-avoidance technique relying on softer elements like regional understanding and trust rather than on formalised, rules-based instrumentalities.

- In SAARC's case there are no comparable formal or informal methods to prevent or contain violent conflicts. All SAARC decisions are based on unanimity. SAARC charter expressly excludes bilateral and contentious issues from SAARC's ambit.
- One of the reasons for ASEAN's consolidation in its formative decade was a common threat perception. The concern about the speared of communism acted as a glue to bind the member states and subsequently gave international visibility to the association when it opposed Vietnam's occupation of Cambodia. This formed the bedrock of what is famously called the 'ASEAN way' of handling intra-state relations.
- By contrast, SAARC hold widely divergent views on many important issues and lack a common political culture. Even after twenty-seven years of belonging to a regional forum there is no consensus on fundamental norms and values. Despite sharing certain common civilisational links the member states do not agree on a common future. An oddity at a time when most regions could boast of some sort of formal arrangement relating to trade or security. This glaring anomaly was a major factor that pushed the South Asian states to create a regional body (SAARC).
- In ASEAN, Indonesia is the largest state but it lacks the affluence of its smaller neighbour, Singapore. So Indonesia may not appear as threatening as India might in South Asia where the power difference between the largest state and the others is very wide along all dimensions.[21]
- The factor which is responsible for the success of ASEAN Free Trade Agreement (AFTA) is the economic group consciousness which is completely lacked in SAFTA. Although SAARC has been working towards enhancing its regional trade, it certainly requires a structural revival. Finally, strengthening of economic relations can be used to reinforce improving political relations in the region, because the conflicting relationship among SAARC members is creating a big hindrance in its success which is not present in ASEAN, since beginning.

Hence, we can say that ASEAN is committed to the ASEAN Community where political cooperation is buttressed by a solid single market from economic integration and assisted by a salubrious socio-cultural milieu. South Asia can leverage on this to reach a new height in its own vision of peace, prosperity and people centered future sooner than later.

SAARC and European Union (EU)

SAARC was established in 1985 in Colombo by the union of seven South Asian States, Afghanistan joined this association later in 2007. On the other hand European Union (EU) is a political and economic community of 27 European states. It was formally formed in 1993, but its origin can be traced back to European Coal and Steel Community. The European Economic Community had bilateral cooperation agreement with four of its member states before the SAARC was born. As of today the EU has strategic partnership with India. Free trade agreement between the EU and India is on anvil. The EU has at present a bilateral agreement with five member states of the SAARC.

In 1988, the European Parliament had adopted a resolution welcoming the establishment of the SAARC and expressed readiness of the European Economic Community to establish cooperation with the SAARC. In 1996, the EU entered into a technical cooperation agreement with the SAARC.

Between 1994 and 2004, the European Union concluded five similar cooperation agreement with five countries of SAARC: India, Sri Lanka, Pakistan, Bangladesh and Nepal. The basis of all the agreements was to respect for human rights and democratic principles. The objective of this cooperation agreement was to enhance and develop the various aspects of cooperation between the parties. The agreement also establishes bilateral trade cooperation between the European Union and these SAARC nations. The economic cooperation measures were focused on improving the economic environment in SAARC member countries, promoting dialogue between economic operators and reinforcing mutual understanding of their economic, social and cultural environments. The parties recognise the importance of cooperation in environment problems, cooperation in science and technology, developing human resources, investment, industry and services, intellectual property, information and communications, energy and tourism.

As mentioned SAARC and EU were established to strengthen their economy and to increase the cooperation. Yet they face so many hurdles in their ways. By comparing the two organisation we can see why EU is more successful than SAARC as an organisation. The prime objective of the study is to analyse and compare the performance of SAARC and EU as an organisation to find out the challenging factor faced by SAARC on its way of success.

Comparison between SAARC and EU

EU is an organisation of developed countries and most of the population of that region is educated while SAARC contain most of the developing countries and people of the South Asia are unaware and not well educated. So they are not aware of the role of such organisations and are not ready to cooperate with it that's why SAARC is not able so far to achieve its basis objectives.

The US attitude towards the subcontinent, that it advocates conflicts and wars in the region and initiated the arm race in the subcontinent. Due to this fact the SAARC countries waste most of their potentialities and resources on weapons, while European countries resolve their conflicts through negotiations. The main reason of conflicts in South Asian countries are the differences in their religion and cultures as Europe is relation

The US attitude towards the subcontinent, that it advocate conflicts and wars in the region and initiated the arm race in the subcontinent. Due to this fact the SAARC countries waste most of their potentialities and resources on weapons, while European countries resolve their conflicts through negotiations. The main reason of conflicts in South Asian countries are the differences in their religion and cultures as Europe is relatively homogenous in religion.

As economic conditions are one of the prime hurdles for the SAARC organisation but EU take a successful step in this regard by launching a single unit of money (Euro) throughout their member countries.

The European Union, which is a successor body of European Community, embodies rich experience of over 61 years in the field of regional cooperation while SAARC is a fledging organisation less than 27 years old. It is the most populous regional grouping in the world and potentially a big market for industrial and new technologies.

There is a growing acceptance in the European Union of the view that adherence to unanimity would often result in stalemate. The SAARC charter has clearly stipulated that all decisions will be taken on the basis of unanimity and that all bilateral and contentious issues will be excluded from discussion.

There are opinion, policy and decision-makers in the EU who subscribe to dictum, that recognising the difficulties does not mean giving into them. A confident and determined approach marks the work of the European Union. On the other hand, many SAARC leaders have a tendency to highlight the difficulties and constraints particularly those arising from unresolved bilateral problems. There is after ambivalence in approach, prevarication in thinking and tergiversation in action.

The European Union has yet to ensure the visibility of the common foreign and security policy. The Commission has proposed the setting up of a Joint Analysis Unit, composed of experts from the member states and the commission, and has the incorporation of a permanent political committee in the existing machinery and the council for preparing decisions, so as to facilitate the formulation of common foreign policy.

On several key issues, the member states of SAARC have diametrically opposite foreign and security policies. Two of the SAARC members India and Pakistan, are nuclear state with perceptions of threats from each other. However, on several issues relating to social development and international economic cooperation SAARC countries have common interests and have not hesitated to articulate these, often through joint committees of ministerial meetings held on subjects such as environment, labour matters, WTO related matters, social development etc.

There are Trans European Union networks in the fields of transport, telecommunications, energy, environment etc. while there are no Trans-South Asian networks in these important areas. The important subject energy is yet be addressed seriously in a regional context.

Common commercial policy is at the heart of the functioning of the European Union. SAARC is yet to make serious headway in this area.

The subsidiary principle has been laid down as a formula for an appropriate distribution of powers between EU and its member states. In SAARC detailed attention has not been given to this matter. Recently the Independent Expert Group on IPA has recommended the principle of subsidiary as one of the factors that may be taken into account while selecting activities to be undertaken under IPA.

Both SAARC and EU were established to sustain the economic conditions of the member countries, to increase the collaboration, and to reduce conflicts amongst their member countries. In this regard EU is very successful in achieving their objectives but SAARC struggles realising the major problems of the region and taking some firm steps for resolving them. The basic reason is the economic stability of the working region of an organisation is important, most of the member countries of EU are developed and they have a strong economy.

One the other hand, SAARC is an organisation of developing countries and they have a very weak and unstable economy and most of the time they depend upon US and other developed countries to fulfill their basic needs. This is the one of the basic factor of slow progress of SAARC.

To strengthen their economy, SAARC should establish an open market and its member countries should cooperate in trade and business to stabilise and strengthen their economy. They should resolve their problems through negotiations and reduce conflicts amongst them. The member countries of SAARC should make strategies to reduce the conflicts amongst them to reduce defense budget and spent that money on economic development of their nation.

Table 5.18
EU's Trade Balance with SAARC
European Union, Trade with SAARC

Period	*Imports*	*Variation (per cent y-o-y)*	*Share of total EU Imports (per cent)*	*Exports*	*Variation (per cent y-o-y)*	*Share of total EU exports (per cent)*	*Balance*	*Trade*
2007	37415	12.4	2.6	35582	13.5	2.9	-1832	72997
2008	40990	9.6	2.6	38037	6.9	2.9	-2953	79027
2009	36788-	10.3	3.0	33676	11.5	3.1	-3112	70464
2010	46109	25.3	3.1	42140	25.1	3.1	-3969	88249
2011	55002	19.3	3.3	48299	14.6	3.2	-6702	103301
Average Annual Growth (2007-11)		10.1			7.9			9.1

Source: SAARC – EU Bilateral trade and trade with the world, DG Trade Statistics. 21-3-12.

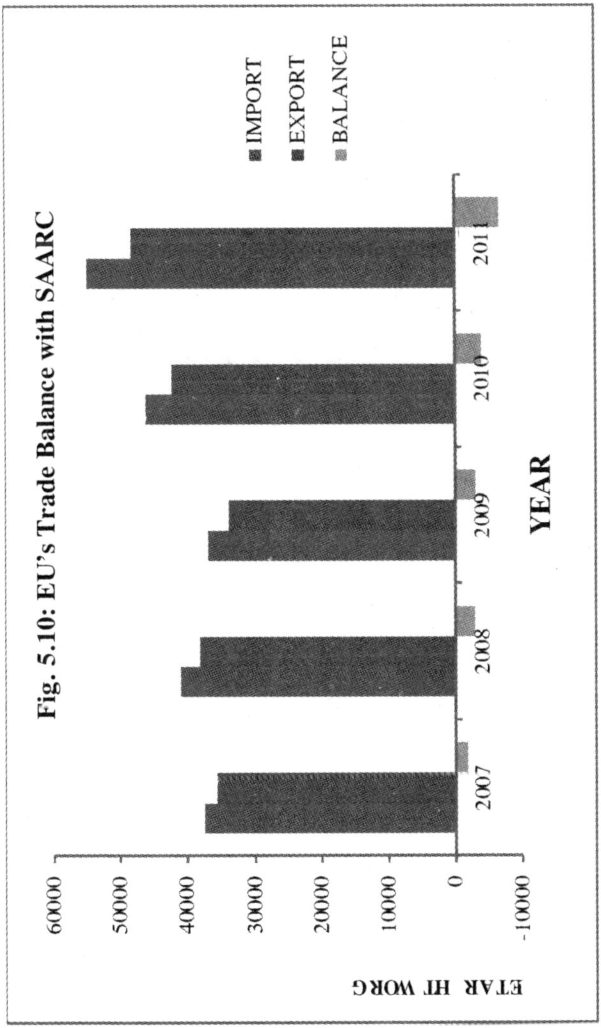

Fig. 5.10: EU's Trade Balance with SAARC

SAARC's Trade Balances with EU.
SAARC, Trade with the European Union

Period	*Imports*	*Variation (per cent y-o-y)*	*Share of total EU Imports (per cent)*	*Exports*	*Variation (per cent y-o-y)*	*Share of total EU exports (per cent)*	*Balance*	*Trade*
2007	39534	14.7	16.7	33910	12.7	24.2	-5624	73444
2008	35582	-10.0	14.1	35958	6.0	24.0	376	71540
2009	33397	-6.1	14.2	35285	-9.1	24.1	1888	68682
2010	39487	18.2	11.7	42852	21.4	21.3	3365	82340
2011	-	-	-	-	-	-	-	-
Average annual growth (2007-11)		-		-				-

Source : SAARC – EU Bilateral Trade and trade with the world - DG Trade Statistics, 21-3-12.

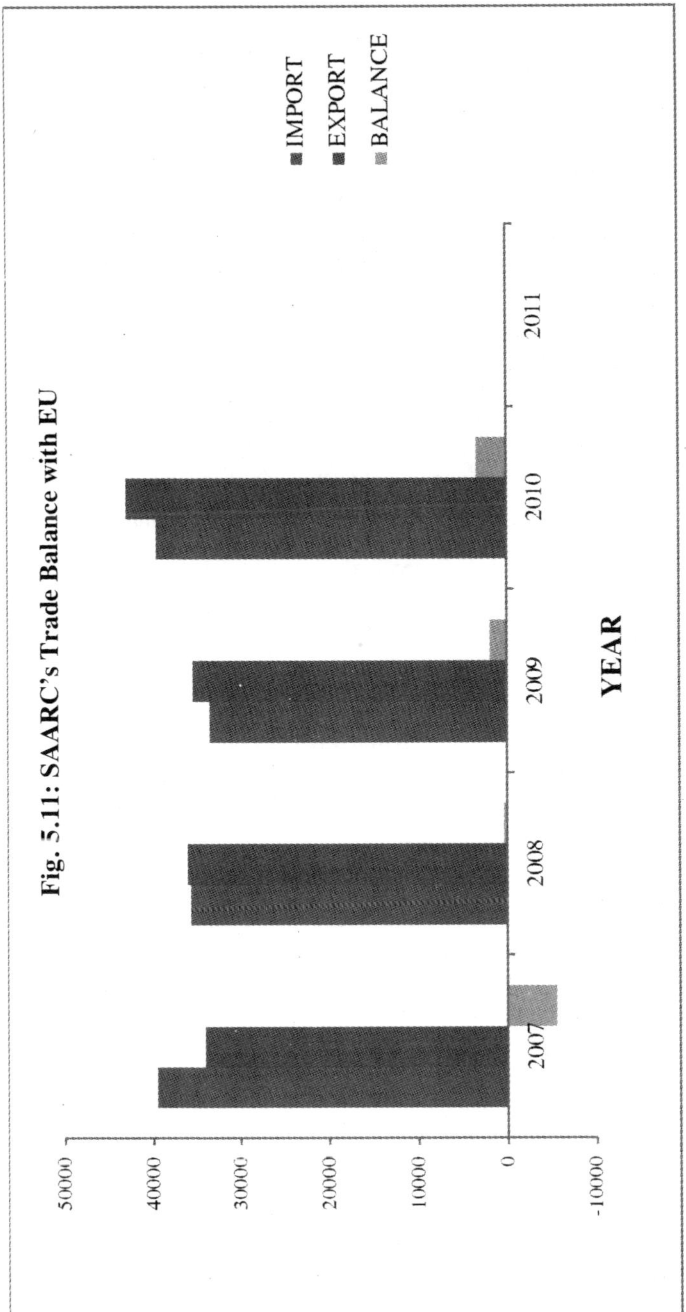

Fig. 5.11: SAARC's Trade Balance with EU

SAARC and BIMSTEC

Both South Asian Association for Regional Cooperation (SAARC) and Bay of Bengal Initiative for Multi–Sectoral Technical and Economic Cooperation (BIMSTEC) are forms of regional arrangements in Asia. While BIMSTEC was established in 1997 with a clear economic agenda, SAARC had its origin much earlier in 1985 that included economic agenda later though both are influenced by politico–strategic factors. Five of the members–India, Nepal, Sri Lanka, Bhutan and Bangladesh are common to both the groupings.

Countries of SAARC and BIMSTEC Groups

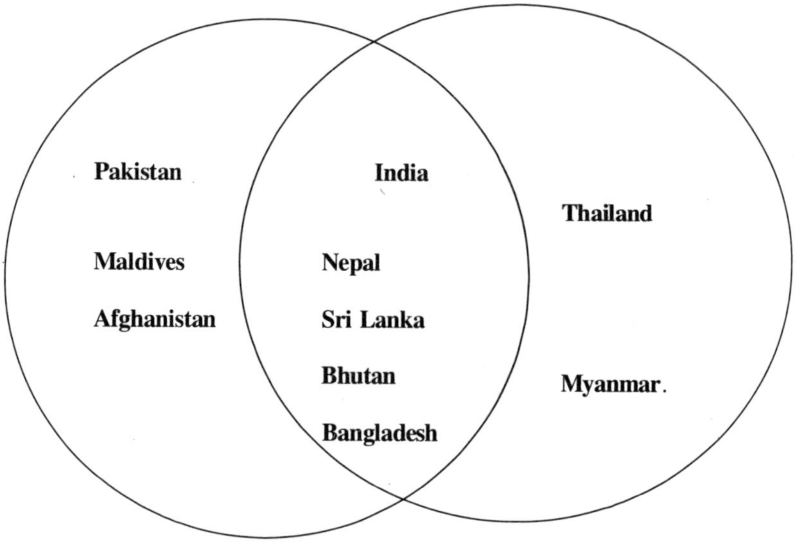

SAARC and BIMSTEC might be looked upon as one of the vehicles for socio-political stability and rapid economic progress. The unique characteristics of the process of sub-regional cooperation hold promise for both the groupings in terms of formulating projects and implementing them. Asian Development Bank's programme of South Asian Sub Regional Economic Cooperation (SASEC) through regional technical assistance grants which propose to identify cross regional projects in close cooperation and coordination with SAARC and BIMSTEC hold some hope of meaningful result–oriented cooperation in the future.

Both SAARC and BIMSTEC have their respective plans charted out with regard to energy cooperation. There is also proposal for all important tri-nation gas pipeline projects to carry Myanmar gas to India through Bangladesh. Some have suggested that the energy demand supply sectors in Bangladesh, India, Myanmar, Sri Lanka, Thailand, Nepal and Bhutan

Table 5.20
Some of SAARC's Activities

Areas of Cooperation	*Regional Centers*	*Working Groups on*	*Economic Activities*	*Security Issues*	*People to People contact*	*Other Activities*
Agriculture and Rural Development	SAARC agricultural and information centre (SAIC), Dhaka	Information communication technology	Committee on economic Cooperation	The police conference	SAARCH*	SAARC Decade of poverty alleviation (2006-15)
Health and population activities	SAARC meteorological research centre (SMRC) Dhaka	Biotechnology	Finance Ministers mechanism	SAARC regional convention on suppression of terrorism and its additional protocol	ADMISA*	SAARC Development fund
Women, youth and children	SAARC Tuberculosis centre (STC) Kathmandu	Intellectual property	Standing Group on standards	Convention on narcotics drugs and psychotropic substance	SAARC FUW*	SAARC chairs, fellowship and scholarship scheme
Environment forestry	SAARC Documentation centre (SDC) Delhi	Tourism	Group on custom cooperation		SAARC Cardiac Society	Establishing south Asian university.

(Contd.)

(Contd. Table 5.20)

Areas of Cooperation	*Regional Centers*	*Working Groups on*	*Economic Activities*	*Security Issues*	*People to People contact*	*Other Activities*
Science, Technology and meteorology	SAARC Human resource Development Centre (SHRDC) Islamabad.	Energy.	SAFTA Committee of Exports		SDEF*	Establishing SAARC Food Bank.
Human Resource Development	SAARC Coastal Zone management centre, Maldives				STF*	South Asia Growth Quadrangle (SAGQ)
Transport	SAARC information centre, Nepal.				FSWL* SAARC association of town planner.	
SAARC Energy centre Pakistan SAARC Disaster Management Centre, India			FSIO* RSSC* SSCS* SARAD* SAFMA* SCCI* SAARC LAW* SAFA*			

*Abbreviations

Table 5.21

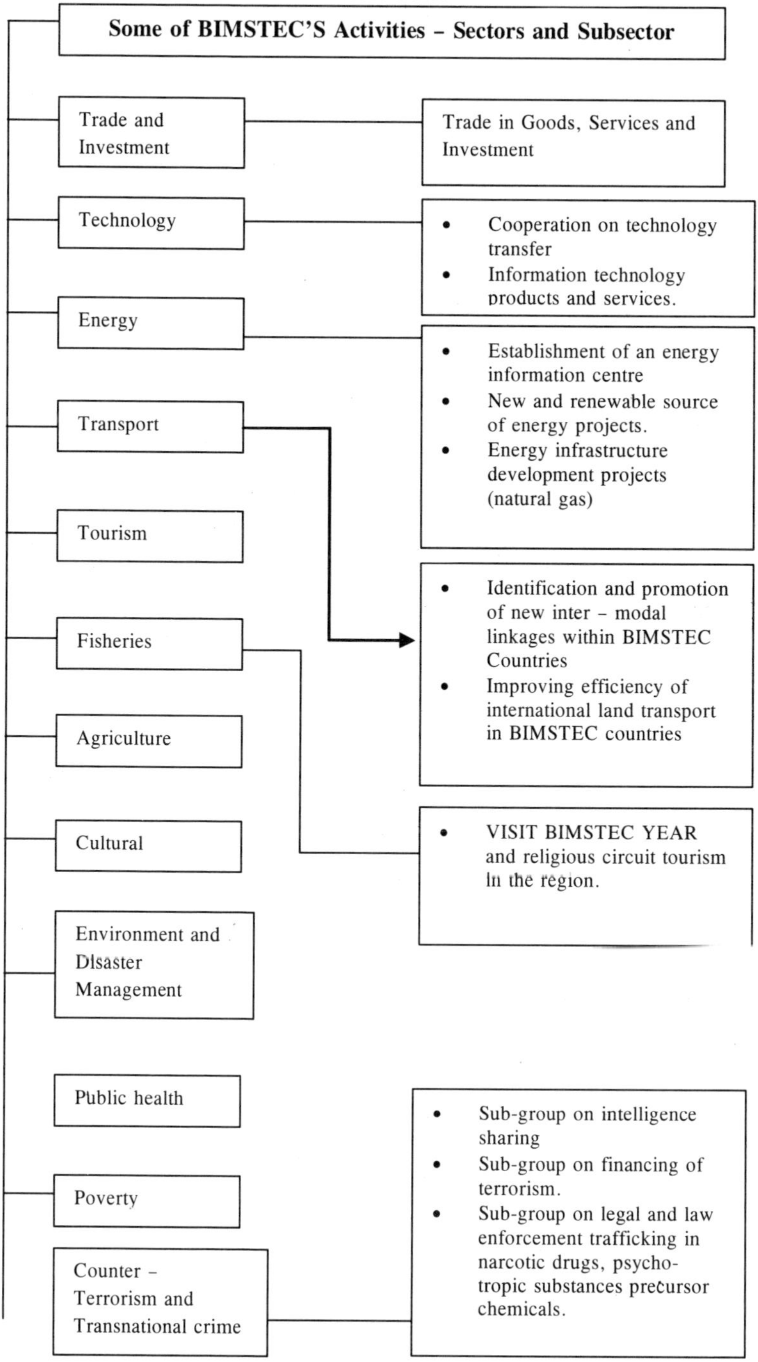
Some of BIMSTEC'S Activities – Sectors and Subsector
Trade and Investment
Technology
Energy
Transport
Tourism
Fisheries
Agriculture
Cultural
Environment and Disaster Management
Public health
Poverty
Counter – Terrorism and Transnational crime
Trade in Goods, Services and Investment
• Cooperation on technology transfer
• Information technology products and services.
• Establishment of an energy information centre
• New and renewable source of energy projects.
• Energy infrastructure development projects (natural gas)
• Identification and promotion of new inter – modal linkages within BIMSTEC Countries
• Improving efficiency of international land transport in BIMSTEC countries
• VISIT BIMSTEC YEAR and religious circuit tourism in the region.
• Sub-group on intelligence sharing
• Sub-group on financing of terrorism.
• Sub-group on legal and law enforcement trafficking in narcotic drugs, psycho-tropic substances precursor chemicals.

Table 5.22
A Comparison among European Union, SAARC, ASEAN, BIMSTEC

BASIC INFORMATION				
Establishment	European coal and steel community (ECSC) in 1951 = 61 years.	August 8, 1967 = 45 years.	December 8, 1985 = 27 years	1997 = 15 years.
Member	27 countries	10 countries	8 countries	5 countries
Religion	Christianity	Muslim, Hindu, Buddhist, Christian etc.	Hindu, Muslim, Buddhist, Christian etc.	Muslim, Buddhist, Hindu, Christian.
Environment	Democratic	Democratic, monarchy, autocracy.	Democracy, Monarchy, autocracy.	Democratic, monarchy.
Population	455 million	530 million	1.5 billion	1.3 billion
ECONOMY	*European Union*	*ASEAN*	*SAARC*	*BIMSTEC*
Nature of economy	Knowledge based service sector	Manufacturing and agriculture	Agriculture and manufacturing	Agricultures and manufacturing
Community and market	Single market and community	Single market and community is expected by 2020	Single market and community are future targets	Single market and community are future targets

(Contd.)

(Contd. Table 5.22)

ECONOMIC POLICY	*European Union*	*ASEAN*	*SAARC*	*BIMSTEC*
Fiscal policy.	Common fiscal policy.	No common fiscal policy	No common fiscal policy.	No common fiscal policy.
Monetary policy.	Common monetary policy	No common monetary policy.	No common monetary policy.	No common monetary policy.
SCIENCE AND TECHNOLOGY	*European Union*	*ASEAN*	*SAARC*	*BIMSTEC*
Attitude towards new technology	Driving for invention and innovation	Technology adoption rather than innovation	Technology adoption rather than innovation	Technology adoption.
Knowledge industry	Fully matured	Emerging	Emerging	Emerging
Spending on R & D	Around 3 per cent GDP.	About 1 per cent of GDP	About 2 per cent of GDP	About 3.1 per cent of GDP
National innovation system	Matured.	Emerging	Emerging	Emerging
INSTITUTION	*European Union*	*ASEAN*	*SAARC* :	*BIMSTEC*
Institution	Common institutions to guide association	No such common institution to guide the association	No such common institution to guide the association	No such common institution to guide the association
Attitude	Sacrificing national sovereignty for greater and united Europe	Reluctant to sacrifice sovereignty	Reluctant of sacrifice national sovereignty	Reluctant to sacrifice national sovereignty
Membership condition	A democratic govt. A good human rights record Properly functioning market economy.	No such condition	No such condition	No such condition

offer a potential for regional resource cooperation, which can go beyond trade relations and link the region in a Bay of Bengal Energy Community.

However, SAARC and BIMSTEC were formed in response to different domestic and international environment. But at present both are facing same socio-economic challenges which transcend national boundaries and wherein globalisation dictates the economic agenda.

South Asia's presence in BIMSTEC is prominent compared to only two members from South East Asia. Naturally, if either of the groupings was to function effectively, then the other would also be influenced positively. In this background, the argument for Indian foreign policy to overlook SAARC and focus on BIMSTEC does not have any merit. Both have their undeniable relevance and one cannot be substituted for the other.

At last, the regional cooperation in SAARC and BIMSTEC could actually take off as the members' countries, to sustain and carry forward the transformations, need a peaceful neighbourhood and rapid economic development within their countries. SAARC and BIMSTEC could be one of the appropriate vehicles to achieve it.[22]

SAFTA and NAFTA (The North American Free Trade Agreement)

The North American Free Trade Agreement is a comprehensive, ground breaking free trade and investment agreement which took effect on 1st January 1994. It involves the governments of Canada, Mexico and the USA.

It is an expansion of the 1989 Canada-US Trade Agreement (CUSTA) and is seen as a landmark in setting higher standards in a range of areas, including agriculture, investment, intellectual property and services.

The South Asia Free Trade Agreement (SAFTA) was agreed to among the eight South Asian Countries that form the SAARC: Afghanistan, Bangladesh, Bhutan, India, Maldives, Nepal, Pakistan and Sri Lanka.

SAFTA came into effect on 1st January 2006, with the aim of reducing tariffs for intra-regional trade among the eight SAARC members. Pakistan and India have to complete implementation by 2012, Sri Lanka by 2013 and Bangladesh, Bhutan, Maldives, Afghanistan and Nepal by 2015.

SAFTA replaces the earlier South Asia Preferential Trade Agreement (SAPTA) and may eventually lead to a full-fledged South Asia Economic Union.

Free trade agreements (FTAs) are becoming common and South Asia is not lagging behind either. SAFTA (South Asian Free Trade Agreement) has been relatively successful and is perhaps the only FTA which has served to reduced political asymmetry among the SAARC nations. Economic benefits apart, SAFTA would enrich political understanding among the members, something SAARC has found difficult to achieve. It is true that immediate impact of SAFTA is blurring as the member - nations are endowed with similar assets - abundant labour and natural resources. But barring India, there is a scarcity of technology and capital.

SAFTA members can reap economic benefits through enhanced cross-border trade. With better capital and technology, India would have a bigger role to play in SAFTA, just as the US in NAFTA.

Unlike the European Union, NAFTA was the first major Free Trade Agreement (FTA) between developed and developing nations. Mexico's per capita GDP is only a seventh of the US. In starting, the economic asymmetry between the countries roused concern over the likely success of NAFTA. But it has turned out to be a windfall for both the countries.

NAFTA emerged as a strong platform for Mexico to boost exports and supplement its economy, which was wobbling on a large trade deficit. NAFTA helped in Mexico's export recovery through duty-free trade with the US. Over the past decade, Mexico's export to the US has raised four-fold. And to the surprise of many, Mexico turned its trade balance with the US in its favour in the post-NAFTA period.

Mexico had succeeded on the NAFTA platform, despite being the only developing nation in the trilateral FTA by becoming a cheap workshop for many US multinationals by cashing in on investment, labour and service issues yet come under the WTO regime. These resulted in huge foreign direct investment (FDI) by US multinationals, which setup production units in Mexico and imported back the goods duty-free into the US.

A number of US firms established units setup with incentives from the government to make goods mainly for export (maquiladora) operations along the US - Mexican border. Maquiladora accounts for 53 per cent of Mexico's total export. NAFTA has become the spring-board for Mexico to export to the global market.

The issues relating to investment in NAFTA, which granted national treatment and exemption from export obligations, domestic procurement and transfer of technology prompted the US to invest heavily in Mexico. The latter had to accept the FTA on these terms, as its rather rudimentary legal system was turning out to be a barriers in attracting FDI. Therefore, NAFTA helped Mexico spur not only investment but also investment related exports to the world's biggest economy.

This shows that a developing nation in a multilateral FTA bloc can reap benefits and not have the fear of developed nations having the upper hand.

But unlike NAFTA, the issues covered under SAFTA are not comprehensive; the scope is confined only to trade in goods. Cross-border trade among member countries would get energised only if issues such as

Table 5.23
SAFTA and NAFTA (Integration Indicators)

Indicator	*SAFTA (2010)*	*NAFTA (2010)*
Export Growth (per cent)	41.43	33.2 per cent
Import Growth (per cent)	50.05	25.6
Foreign Direct Investment (US $) billion	N/A	357.7 billion
Trade Balance (per cent)	45.88	26.8

Source : Asia Regional Integration Centre.

treatment of foreign investment, movement of labour and trade in services are included in SAFTA.

WTO Negotiations and SAARC

Individual countries don't possess enough bargaining clout at multilateral forums. Group effort and cooperation on negotiating table can undoubtedly enhance the bargaining strength. Issues like labour or environmental standards or rules like anti-dumping and anti-subsidy investigations are areas where SAARC can stand together. And it is already happening. SAARC Commerce ministers meeting held at Islamabad in 1998 April 29-30 took decision to setup coordinating group of SAARC ambassadors at WTO. This was fruitful as before Seattle and the Doha summits they could adopt common positions.

SAARC nations took a joint stand against world trade organisation (WTO) talk in Doha, Qatar. They unanimously resolved that a new round of WTO talks should not be held until previous trade commitments were met.

The developing nations had been assured that the opening their doors could bring them trade opportunities ranging between $ 250-450 billion, but in reality there have been hardly any worthwhile gains for developing nations. The tariffs were unfairly stacked up against primary products like agricultural produce and the mainstay of their export.

The SAARC countries noted with disappointment the visible indifference of the advanced countries to addressing the concerns of the developing countries that have remained in jeopardy ever since the Uruguay Round of talks. As little change has been seen in the plight of the developing countries and the least developed nations despite WTO commitments to the contrary, the commerce ministers of the SAARC countries warned that any further delay in addressing their accumulated predicament could erode the credibility of the multilateral trading system among the developing and developed countries. Making appointed reference to the denial of greater market access for exports from the developing and least developed countries, the joint statement had been issued to ask the developed countries to desist from imposing restrictions on products in which the developing countries have acquired comparative advantage.

All the SAARC nations expressed the common concern over the hectic efforts of the developed countries to expand the WTO's trade agenda. It had been pointed out that, it would be essential to fulfill the obligations earlier agreed upon before rushing for fresh commitments.

The SAARC insistence on the actuality of considerable imbalance in the WTO agreements and stress upon the need of timely correction should serve as an unmistakable indication of the disillusionment of the developing countries with the ongoing process of globalisation.

The developing and less industrialised countries feel that in such a free trade atmosphere they would not be able to compete with highly industrialised countries who are besides having better technology and quality of production, also enjoying economics of large scale production. They apprehend that whatever little industrial base they have acquired will be destroyed, if trade restriction are removed in such a short time as demanded by WTO. The developing countries demanded that rich countries should provide material help to the developing nations to improve their competitiveness to ensure that they get their due share in the free international trade.

The joint statement by the SAARC on fourth WTO ministerial conference at Doha issued on 23 August 2001, agreed on the relevant provisions of the TRIPS (Trade related intellectual property rights) agreement relating to the meaningful transfer and dissemination of technology to developing and least-developed countries should be effectively operational.

Under the Agreement on Trade Related Investment Measures (TRIMs), there should be a positive approach to requests for further extension of the transition period for developing countries. There should also not be any expansion in the list of the measures covered by the disciplines of the TRIMs Agreement. Greater flexibility and appropriate amendments in the TRIMs Agreement are necessary for SAARC nations to enable them to pursue their goals for development and rapid industrialisation including indigestion.

SAARC ministers have resolved that urgent focus is needed on specific issues of particular interest to them, such as greater market access for exports of developing and least developed countries by addressing issues of tariff peaks, tariff escalation; operationalisation of special and differential provisions for developing countries, more meaningful integration of the textile and clothing sector; flexibility and clarity in the interpretation of the trade-related intellectual property rights agreement to prevent piracy of traditional knowledge, higher levels of protection in the form of geographical indication for products of export interest to the SAARC region and addressing public health concerns of the poor countries to ensure affordable access to essential drugs.

In agriculture, SAARC ministers have stressed the need for substantial reductions in tariffs and tariff escalations, substantial cuts in domestic support and elimination of all forms of export subsidies given by developed countries in order to facilitate greater market access for agricultural products of the developing countries.

In services, it had been decided to seek market access from the developed countries especially in terms of movement of natural persons.

Therefore, we can say that these deliberations would help the SAARC countries in forgiving a common front in present globalising world scenario.

SAARC and United Nations Organisation

SAARC had also signed various agreements with United Nations. SAARC - UNCTAD (United Nations Conference on Trade and Development) Memorandum of Understanding on the Trade Analysis and Information System (TRAINS) was signed in February 1993.

Under this agreement, UNCTAD provides the SAARC Secretariat and updated copy of TRAINS CD-ROM containing latest data on trade control measures prevailing in developed and developing countries. The SAARC Secretariat in turn updates trade control measures prevailing in the SAARC member states on a regular basis and forwards the same to UNCTAD Secretariat in the updated versions of TRAINS - CD-ROM.

A cooperation agreement between SAARC and UNICEF (United Nations International Children's Emergency Fund) was signed on 10 December 1993. The Agreement envisages cooperation in implementing the relevant SAARC decisions relating to children through an annual agenda which includes joint studies, exchange of documentation and monitoring of implementation. In pursuance of the cooperation Agreement, the SAARC secretariat and the UNICEF regional office for South Asia have been holding regular consultations, which have covered progress in the implementation of summit directives on children and the recommendations of the council of ministers, standing committee and the relevant Technical Committees.

A Memorandum of Understanding (MOU) between SAARC and UNDP (United Nations Development Programme) was signed by the SAARC Secretary - General and Administrator of UNDP in July 1995. The MOU embodies a general agreement for broad-based collaboration with the aims and purposes of promoting sustainable human development for attaining poverty elimination, preservation and protection of environment, regeneration of natural resources, employment creation and the goals of women in development; undertake periodic consultation for joint activities; publishing studies on priority concerns and exchanging relevant reports.

The SAARC Secretariat in collaboration with UNDP prepared the final version of Regional Poverty Profile (RPP) bringing out the regional dimension based on the country level profiles. The twelfth Summit in Islamabad, Pakistan, in 2004 declared that the SAARC Secretariat should periodically update and submit the RPP.

The social mobilisation strategy as envisaged by the first Independent South Asian Commission on Poverty Alleviation (ISACPA) had been put into practice across South Asia (except Bhutan) through UNDP sponsored South Asian Poverty Alleviation Programme (SAPAP), which was launched in early 1996 and completed in March 2003.

SAARC recognises that issues related to gender and empowerment of Women needs to be addressed to promote social development. In this regard, it has a MOU with the United Nations Development Fund for Women (UNIFEM) signed in December 2001 for cooperation in the promotion of gender issues.

SAARC Secretary - General and United Nations International Drug Control Programme (UNDCP) also signed an MOU on 18 Aug 1995 to coordinate their efforts in combating drug trafficking and drug abuse in the region. The memorandum envisages mutual consultation and exchange of information between the two organisation.

Thus, the agreements signed between SAARC and various United Nations agencies have proven successful in the social and economic development of SAARC.

So, there may be lessons to be learnt from the experiences of other regional groupings such as ASEAN and European Union that how they have been tackling such of their problems as may have similarities to those faced by SAARC, how they are dealing with international organisation like WTO and UNO and how they have been planning and implementing action programmes for their regional development.

This chapter has attempted to address the core issues of economic cooperation in South Asia through trade and investment linkages. The issue of cooperation among countries of South Asia has been the subject of widespread attention and interest, not only in South Asia, but in international fora as well. South Asia, while being one of the less rapidly growing regions of the world, characterised by widespread poverty, low human development indicators, and low level of growth, has also been at the centre of constant inter-state frictions, upheavals and political turmoil's. Economic cooperation through trade and investment link was seen in this context, as an effective way of forging relations, which would also act as a potent confidence building measure among these nations.

The evolution, formalisation and survival of SAARC was seen as a landmark achievement in the history of cooperation in South Asia. The establishment of SAPTA in 1995 and SAFTA in 2006, was a step further in attaining objective of free trade and moving towards greater cooperation in trade.

Investment links being perceived would be for easier to forge, under the circumstances and would help to act as effective confidence building measures among the SAARC members. Therefore, greater attention needs to be directed towards this end. The potential and prospects of intra-regional investments are enormous, given the natural resource base of these countries, and their latent comparative strengths. The need is to focus on core areas, and translate these potentials into meaningful business ventures. A crucial area is infrastructure development, which merits priority attention with constraints in public resources, and the paradigm shift towards market driven economies, the onus of development has come to rest more with the private sector.

The role of foreign assistance and funding also assumes critical importance. Official Development Assistance (ODA) loans could play an important part in shaping the intra-regional investment projects for future.

In view of the halting progress of SAARC, a new concept in the form of a South Asian Growth Quadrangle (SAGQ) has also been envisaged which by effectively bypassing the issue of Indo-Pakistan political tensions, would help to hasten the process of regional integration and capitalise on neighbourhood synergies in the region comprising of the north eastern states of India, the countries of Bangladesh, Nepal and Bhutan. The recent Asian Development Bank (ADB) initiative of SASEC with its onus on private and public partnership project driven approach for the SAGQ countries had been a further step forward.

In SAARC, India is destined to play a central role in the process of regional integration. By virtue of its diversified production base, larger exportable surplus, and its state of economic development relative to its neighbours, India is in a better position to open up its economy, extend concessions, and take the lead in forging investment alliances. Maintaining harmonious relations with its smaller neighbours may be the only available option to India, in a world increasingly dominated by regional blocs. For the smaller states, economic cooperation may be the only solution and imperative for survival.

SAARC should also learn from its own experiences and from the experiences of other regional organisations like ASEAN and EU in order to overcome impediments in its way of progress.

The new global order (WTO) dictates that economic survival and prosperity of any nation crucially hinges on its ability to successfully integrate with other economics. The compulsions and prospects for regional integration in South Asia are tremendous. There are obvious obstacles and political differences. Nevertheless, it is high time that governments as well as people of the region realise that economic cooperation is the only option available, which could eventually lead to the building of a more prosperous and socio-politically cohesive region.

References

1. Kumar Rajiv - SAARC : Changing realities, opportunities and challenges, Discussion paper - 11/2009, p. 2, http://www.die-gdi.de.
2. Muni S.D., Jaithly Rajshree- SAARC: the changing Dimensions, 2008, p. 7, institute of South Asian Studies, Singapore.
3. Weerakon Dushni, SAFTA-current status and prospects, p. 74, Institute of policy studies of Sri Lanka - www.ips.lk/saes/conference../dushni_weerakon.
4. Khanna. V.N., Foreign Policy of India, Vikas Publishing House, Delhi-2005, p. 249.
5. Khan Rafi Shaheen, Moeed Yusuf, Tanveer Aska - Regional Integration, Trade and Conflict in South Asia, International Institute of Sustainable Development, Jan-2007, p. 18. Project of International - development research centre. http://www.iisd.org.
6. Export- Import Bank of India - SAARC: An emerging trade bloc, p. 11, Quest Publication, June 2008.
7. Chaudhary Anup, Chaudhary Paul Suman, BRAC University Journal, Vol. V, No. 2, 2008, p. 76, Prospect and Possibilities of introducing a common currency in SAARC Countries.
8. Khanna. V.N., Foreign Policy of India, Fifth edition, Vikas Publishing House, Delhi-2005, p. 250.
9. Report - Charter of the SAARC Development Fund (SDF).
10. Nagata M., Report - Asian Development Bank, Technical Assistance for Promoting South Asian Regional Economic Cooperation, Sep - 2004, p. 2.
11. Report - SAARC Development Goals (2007-2012), Taking SDGs Forward, Independent South Asian Commission on Poverty Alleviation, March - 2007.
12. Business and Economy Journal - SAARC Investment Promotion and Protection Agreement to give boost to intra-regional trade, 9 Feb. - 22, 2012.
13. Alam Sayeed. M, Intra-regional foreign direct investment, Prospect in SAARC region, International Journal of Economics and Finance, Vol. 2, August - 2012, www.ccsenet.org/ijef/.
14. SAARC Report, http://www.SAARCEnergycentre.htm/
15. Raghvan S.N., Regional economic cooperation among SAARC Countries, Economic Cooperation in SAARC, p. 19. Economic and Scientific Research Foundation, Institute of Economic Growth.
16. Malhotra Nitasha, South Asia - Political and economic region, the association of geographical studies, New Delhi, p. 28. Working paper.

18. SAARC Report, http://www.sarc-sec.org/. SAARC Trade Fairs.
19. Kumar Rajiv – SAARC: Changing Realities, Opportunities and Challenges, discussion paper, German Development Institute, 2009, pp. 7-9.
20. Raghavan S.N. – Regional Economic Cooperation among SAARC Countries, Regional Economic Cooperation, Allied Publisher Pvt. Ltd., New Delhi, p. 11.
21. Sridharan Kripa – Regional organisations and conflict management: Comparing ASEAN and SAARC – working paper – March 2008, p. 10, www.crisisstates.com
22. Murthy Padmaja, Briefing paper, SAARC and BIMSTEC – understanding their experience in regional cooperation-2008, //http://www.cuts-international.org.

6

Overview

Regional integration offers several benefits, for instance greater economic integration, frequent and easier people to people contact, sustainable peace and development at the regional level. Regional cooperation in South Asia, initiated under the platform of the SAARC. Since its inception in 1985, SAARC has become a forum for addressing a wide variety of issues pertinent to the region. Member states met at annual summits, while foreign ministers are supposed to meet at least twice annually.

Over the years, SAARC's agenda has expanded considerably, exhibiting the intent and capability to work collectively on issues of agriculture and rural development, health and population; women, youth and children; environment and forestry; human resource development information and communications technology; biotechnology and energy amongst others.

The SAARC forum has made significant attempts towards economic cooperation and social cohesion. With the overall aim of economic integration, the SAARC chambers of commerce and industry was setup in 1992 to promote regional cooperation in the areas of trade and economic relations. A breakthrough came with the SAARC Preferential Trade Arrangement (SAPTA) Agreement which was signed in April 1993 and entered into force in December 1995; opening the way for a certain expansion of intra SAARC trade. At the January 2004 summit meeting, the SAARC countries' foreign ministers signed the South Asian Free Trade Area (SAFTA) agreement.

Ratified and entered into force in January 2006, the objectives of SAFTA include; elimination of all sorts of barriers in trade and facilitation of free and fair movement of products; promoting fair competition and free trade environment in respect of the existing economic conditions which will ensure the maximum benefit and establish an institutional frame to promote and expansion of regional cooperation.

One of the key elements of SAFTA is the compensation for revenue losses for smaller regional economies like Nepal, Bhutan, Bangladesh and Maldives in the event of tariff reductions. By the end of first two years of SAFTA's implementation, 2006-07 the developing countries in South Asia that is, India, Pakistan and Sri Lanka, were demanded to bring their duties down to 20 per cent. In the final five year ending in 2012, the 20 per cent of duty will be reduced to zero in a series of annual cuts, and on the other hand, the least developing country group in South consisting of Nepal, Bhutan, Bangladesh and Maldives, get an additional three years to reach zero duty, they have time till 2017.

Furthering SAARC objectives, in the 14th SAARC summit held in New Delhi in April 2007, member states agreed to launch the SAARC Development Fund (SDF), establish the South Asian University, create a SAARC Food Bank and set up the SAARC Arbitration Council. SAARC-Japan special fund was also launched for the further development of SAARC. In a significant move, Afghanistan was formally invited to take its place in the comity of SAARC the People's Republic of China, European Union, Republic of Korea and the United States of America-nations crucial to regional cooperation were invited as observers to enrich the agenda of SAARC with their input and experience. There are suggestions to include China and Iran as SAARC member states, so to make it more effective. In March 2007, Iran had formally requested for a grant for observer status in the SAARC.

Established with a vision to forge a South Asian identity, SAARC has been unable to fulfill this promise and has often been criticised for its failures and shortcomings. Some constraining factors that can be identified in the SAARC framework are: its inability to tackle inter-state conflicts that has often made it hostage to bilateral conflicts and the nationalistic interests of member states. Apart from this, an Indo-centric strategic perception exists both among India's neighbours as well as among the big players in global diplomacy. Lack of trust among South Asian elites: SAARC was born with disabilities and constraints, which were essentially self-imposed. It adopted a functional approach of cooperation in non-controversial areas like social and cultural fields, hoping that if successfully carried forward, opportunities for cooperation in more vital areas could open up. Moreover, SAARC follows the principles that all decisions have to be made unanimously and that no bilateral and contentious issue can be on the SAARC agenda. This clearly exhibits a weaker inter-state relationship toward equitable participation in policy making for South Asian people.

The lack of trust among member states has often manifested itself in the ineffective administration of several of the initiatives taken by the SAARC. A prime example is that of the SAFTA. Though the seven signatory nations of SAFTA implemented the first tariff reduction from July 1, 2006, Pakistan and India have not yet allowed each other to be facilitated under this agreement. Under the SAFTA agreement, the **free trade area** operates on the basis of the **sensitive list**. In this India accused Pakistan of backing away from its commitment under the multilateral SAFTA agreement.

However, this is not the only example of the two countries adopting confrontational postures towards each other at the SAARC platform. There have been several such occasions with both countries debating contentious issues and delaying the actual implementation of very important regional instruments for peace and economic integration.

Apart from the continuing India Pakistan conflict, a concern that has often come up at SAARC forums is the dominant position of bigger states, particularly India, in the regional set-up. The discrepancy of size and power between India, a nation of over one billion people, and all its neighbours, leads to natural concerns among the later about India's dominance in the region and potential interference in their affaires. At different times this has been a significant strand in the policy thinking of states such as Bangladesh, Nepal and Sri Lanka; and has led them to seek security assistance first and foremost from outside South Asia when they need it. Cooperative policies of SAARC are influenced by the fear among some of the smaller states around India that interdependence will lead to the erosion of their political autonomies and therefore undermine their advantage for securing "honourable" settlement of bilateral disputes with India.

This can be witnessed by the motivations of several member states in becoming a part of this regional body. Nepal joined SAARC hoping that this platform will provide it with opportunities to voice its most important concerns, most of which are related to India. Also Nepal wanted multilateral cooperation rather than a bilateral arrangement with India, especially in water related conflicts. At the time of conception of SAARC, Bangladesh had serious concerns over the issue of sharing Ganges water with India, therefore Bangladeshi leadership of that time hoped to seek solutions of Ganges water and similar issues through the SAARC platform. Sri Lanka was initially hesitant to joint SAARC, considering it's greater and favourable economic ties with South East Asian nations. However, Sri Lanka's internal conflict compelled her to join SAARC with the hope of getting help from SAARC towards alleviating its fears from India.

Pakistan joined SAARC to further strengthen its ties with other South Asian states, which would, in the long run, help to counter India's influence in the region.

Increasing military modernisation in SAARC member states could be seen as one of the indicators to assess the seriousness of commitments of SAARC member states towards an efficient regional cooperation mechanism in South Asia. Constant rise in military expenditure shows an unhealthy environment for human development and also for the peaceful interstate relationships; as even on the platform of SAARC the member states have manifested lack of trust in countries with which they have a dispute or conflict. Increasing defense spending will not only aggravate the countries internal and external disputes but also exacerbate human security in the region and increase poverty. According to statistics from the International Institute of Strategic Studies, the defense expenditure of five of the SAARC nations are as follows:

India	-	US$21.7 Billion.
Pakistan	-	US $ 4.14 Billion.
Bangladesh	-	US$840 Million.
Sri Lanka	-	US$686 Million.
Nepal	-	US$139 Million.

The continuing conflict between India and Pakistan has also led to ever-increasing investments in arms and ammunitions to counter each other's military capability. Both states continue to invest huge amounts of their financial resources in buying weapons from the USA, China, Russia, Sweden and France.

While, there has not been a single direct attempt from SAARC to deal with any of the above mentioned disputes, there have been bilateral dialogues between the SAARC member states to soften their contentions. There is an ongoing series of dialogues between India and Pakistan; and most recently, Pakistan and Afghanistan organised Peace Jirgas to resolve their tensions through this traditional conflict resolution mechanism. Pakistan has also recommended the creation of a conflict resolution mechanism in SAARC to deal with all intra-regional bilateral conflicts.

Globalisation has also been influential in South Asia, especially inters of its impact on intra-regional politics and economics. On some occasions there has been pressure on South Asian states to show seriousness towards exploring possibilities for cooperation and the peaceful resolution of conflicts.

Dispute resolution has recently found a place in the SAARC framework. At the 2005, SAARC summit in Dhaka, the member states agreed to establish a SAARC Arbitration Council in Pakistan. The council is aimed at creating favourable conditions for supporting greater investment by investors of one member state in the territory of another member state. This initiative is geared towards creating a South Asian forum for settlement of commercial disputes by conciliation and arbitration. However, SAARC is yet to take serious steps to fully tackle the issue of interstate conflicts between its member states.

Prevalence of several inter-state conflicts in South Asia is because the stake holders in conflicts are not highly motivated towards a productive peace - building process, involving bilateral dialogues, third party mediations, back channels, track II diplomacy etc. The involvement of South Asian states, in peace-building initiatives is evident in its long term participation in the UN peacekeeping operations. It is ironical, therefore that the same global peacekeepers continue to put deadlocks in several conflict resolution process within their own region.

For a country or an organisation to act as a facilitator in a regional setting to resolving bilateral conflicts it has to be accepted as a neutral player. In the case of SAARC, due to its socio-cultural linkages and political history, it is difficult to consider any country as neutral. India, considering its economic strength and geographical advantage, could play the role of a facilitator in resolving intra-regional conflicts. But that is not possible because India is a party too many inter-state South Asian conflicts. Second, the option could be taking benefit from the SAARC observers (EU, USA, China, South Korea, Japan and Iran) towards resolving bilateral conflicts in South Asia, but even among the observers there are ongoing tensions, for instance the troubled relations between the USA, Iran and China.

Apart from the conflicts between member states, there is also disagreement among them on the need for a South Asian conflict resolution mechanism to deal with bilateral disputes. India, Nepal and Sri Lanka are not in favour of conflict resolution as a domain of the SAARC.

Despite the criticism, the SAARC forum has enabled a constructive space for dialogue between member states. A significant success of SAARC has been the relationship - building it has allowed at the sidelines of its formal meetings.

Apart from the official institutions established under the ambit of the SAARC, there also exists an unofficial channel of communication and interaction among member states. It is evident that in the past two decades, there has been unprecedented rise in interaction and networking among various institutions, agencies and civil society organisations in South Asia. This unofficial cooperation exists on various issues, especially for the promotion of human rights, conflict resolution, health, business, performing arts etc.[1]

Apart from tensions between India and its neighbours, other SAARC members have by and large, maintained free relations. Since SAARC was initiated, there have been no noticeable conflicts between any member states except India.

Since, last three to four years, a drift in India's approach towards SAARC have also come to an end. India is gradually realising that its credibility and acceptance as a rising Asian power will remain under cloud if it fails to carry its immediate neighbour along. Without all boats rising in South Asia at the same time, India can neither prosper nor be secure. Due to this fact India has been promising to transform its regional role from being a reluctant participant to a dynamic leader, by indicating greater commitment to SAARC in recent years.

Within the region almost all the SAARC countries are experiencing satisfactory growth trajectories, notwithstanding international economic pressers and turbulent domestic politics.

In terms of politics, domestic turbulence is driving the South Asian countries in the direction of greater democratisation, opening political space and encouraging greater grassroots participation in it.

One of the banes of SAARC's stultified growth, the India-Pakistan hostility and Pakistan's insistence on not moving in the direction of cooperation until the Kashmir issue is resolved seems to be softening. Pakistan has also been agreed to provide MFN status to India.

From a structural point of view, SAARC has expanded not only by including Afghanistan as a new member, but also by opening its space to new members from outside the region.

SAARC, as the only regional instrument available to carry South Asian nations along cannot be neglected or undermined; instead it has to be endowed with greater vigour and a sense of purpose.[2]

After analysing the economic dimensions of SAARC the countries belonging to the South Asian Association for regional cooperation have in recent years attached increasing importance to regional economic cooperation for accelerating the pace of economic development and raising the standards of living of people in the member countries. If political differences among countries can be ignored, South Asia offers several desirable features for regional cooperation. And over the last decade, all of the region's economies have been liberalising and generally growing at respectable rates, (See chapter 5, Economic profile of SAARC nations), which should further facilitate deeper cooperation in the region.

However, many impediments like poverty, population, unemployment, illiteracy, etc., are posing threat to the economic development of SAARC region but since 1990's SAARC countries have experienced unprecedented growth, averaging close to 6-8 per cent per annum. This growth is impressive because many developing countries grew more slowly during this period.

As, it is well known that SAARC economies are basically rural in nature. Agriculture plays a vital role in SAARC region. Except for Pakistan and Sri Lanka, where service sector play a major role than agriculture, in all the other countries, the contribution of agriculture to GDP is the highest. However, over the last few decades, it can also be observed that there is a fall in the relative importance of agricultural contribution to GDP in SAARC members, except that of Nepal where agriculture's role has not changed significantly.

It is accepted that economic development entails an expansion of the secondary sector of the economy. SAARC partners have adopted various strategies for the expansion of their industrial sectors, or the diversification of their economies, from production of primary products, to that of manufactured goods. As for as Bangladesh, Bhutan and India are concerned, industrial sector and services sector have gained at the loss of agriculture. But, in the case of Nepal and Pakistan, role of industry has improved at the cost of agriculture and services sectors. The prominent trading and commerce activities in Sri Lanka have made the service sector vital than the agricultural and industrial sectors of its economy.

However, the members of SAARC felt their way towards putting the issue of economic cooperation on the association's agenda. The SAPTA was signed in 1993 and entered into force in 1995 with a view to pave the way for increased economic integration in the region. The agreement increased cooperation in the area of customs tariffs duties and established the important goal of providing more support for the least developed member states. SAPTA was successful in a respect that it opened the doors to achieve real economic integration.

Following on from this, SAFTA was signed at the 2004 summit of foreign ministers in Islamabad and entered into force on January 1, 2006. By signing this agreement, the governments of the member nations committed to follow a concrete roadmap towards facilitating the cross–border movement of goods, to harmonising product testing procedures and to increase cooperation on the question of cross–border transport infrastructures.

Apart from SAPTA and SAFTA, South Asian Economic Union and introduction of common currency also included in economic agenda of SAARC. The eleventh summit at Kathmandu, Nepal from 4-6 January 2002 provided further impetus to the regional economic cooperation to give effect to the shared aspirations for a more prosperous South Asia. At the summit, the leaders agreed to accelerate cooperation in the core areas of trade, finance and investment to realise the goal of an integrated South Asian economy. They also agreed to the vision of a phased and planned process eventually leading to a South Asian Economic Union.

An economic union involves the common currency, harmonisation of member's tax rates and a common monetary and fiscal policy. However it looks advantageous if SAARC countries could adopt a single currency substantially enhancing their bargaining power together in the world market. It is advantageous to deal with a lesser number of currencies since each time one converts a currency there is a huge loss. The common currency regime, can present substantial benefits to the region. With uncertainty about exchange rates removed, and transaction costs reduce trade and investment in the region can get a big boost. Also with money creation under regional guidelines, there would be better prospects of synchronisation of inflation, interest rate and GDP growth, all of which can contribute to accelerated growth and poverty reduction.

In order to fulfill economic agendas of SAARC, it has provided various funding mechanisms and economic institutions like South Asian Development fund in June 1996 and SAARC Development Fund in August 2008 to improve the quality of life and to accelerate economic growth, social progress and poverty alleviation in the region. These funds are serving as an umbrella financial institution for SAARC projects and programmes, which are in fulfillment of the objectives of the charter; SAARC finance was established on 9 September 1998 in order to promote cooperation among central banks and finance ministers in SAARC member countries through staff visits and regular exchange of information; SAARC–Japan Special Fund since 1993 for security – related cooperation through friendly persuasions and to help strengthen the SAARC framework; Asian Development Bank (ADB) Support in South Asia since 1968 is helping South Asia to realise its full potential in economic and social development and enable it to play an effective part in wider Asian integration. It helps in improving connectivity, facilitating trade and investment, developing regional tourism, facilitating cooperation in energy and promoting private sector development; SAARC Chamber of Commerce and Industry (SCCI) in December 1992 was established to create strong business linkages among the entrepreneurs of the region of South Asia, to safeguard the economic and business interests of the SAARC and to promote the exchange of commercial, technical, industrial management and scientific information, education and know how among its members and the SAARC Arbitration Council was setup in November 2005 to work on investment, arbitration and Avoidance of Double Taxation in SAARC region. The recent ADB (Asian Development Bank) initiative of South Asian Sub Regional Economic Cooperation (SASEC) with its onus on private-public partnership and project driven approach for the SAGQ (South Asian Growth Quadrangle) countries has been a further step forward.

SAARC Trade

The acceleration of economic growth is a charter objective of SAARC but there are various problems facing the countries in the SAARC region that hinders the economic and trade development in the region. Perhaps the root of all these varied problems is overpopulation. Total population of SAARC region as on 2010 was recorded to be more than 1.5 billion, which constitutes 24 per cent of the total population of the world. Clearly, the population levels of these countries exceed the resources present. With the world's largest population, total GDP volume of SAARC region was determined to be approximately US$ 3228.97 billion in 2010.

Total Economic Indicator of SAARC Region

Indicators	*Amount (2010)*
Total Population - 2010	1579469720.12 billion
GDP - (2010)	3228.97 US$ billion
Average GDP per capita	7.8 per cent
Total Import	51.29 per cent
Per cent share in World Import	2.84 per cent
Total Export	49.87 per cent
Per cent share in total export	3.97 per cent
Total Trade	21132.64 US $ billion.
Total share in World Trade	3.27 per cent
Intra-regional trade share	4.46 per cent
Intra-regional trade intensity index	1.91 per cent

Source: Asia regional integration centre.

Although SAARC region is facing various problems but there is considerably increase in the total GDP, import-export rate and percentage in total world trade since last five years (2005-2010) which signifies the good future prospects of SAARC. In HDI area, SAARC countries are in developing profile. This can be made clear from the figure given below:

Human Development Index of SAARC Nations

Country	*HDI (2010-2011)*	*HIGH / LOW*
Afghanistan	0.398	Low
Bangladesh	0.500	Low
Bhutan	0.522	Medium
India	0.547	Medium
Maldives	0.661	Medium
Nepal	0.458	Low
Pakistan	0.504	Low
Sri Lanka	0.691	Medium
South Asia	0.548	Medium

So, we can see, that human development index in South Asia in the year 2010-2011 is 0.548 which is medium. Among eight SAARC countries four of them are having medium human development index and the countries which low in profile is also not for from medium development index.

In SAARC region fruitful investment linkages through collaborative ventures could be forged. Some of these areas are infrastructure development (energy, roads, ports, railway projects) mineral based industries, IT and software, project and management consultancy, tourism, healthcare, biotechnology, education and human resource development. The financial implications of these projects are substantial. Investment links if it is being perceived would help to act as effective confidence building measures among the SAARC members. Therefore, greater attention needs to be directed towards this end. The role of foreign assistance and funding also assumes critical importance, in this context. ODA loans could play an important part in shaping the intra-regional investment projects for tomorrow.

The South Asian economies propelled by the changing international environment and the success stories of NAFTA and EU in the West and ASEAN closer home, realised albeit a little late that meaningful economic cooperation may be the only option ahead to ensure a greater say in international outcomes as well as create conditions for overall growth. Observers' states of SAARC see great potential in the BIMSTEC project because unlike SAARC, the organisation includes Thailand and Myanmar but does not include the crisis ridden countries of Pakistan and Afghanistan.

Regional communities such as the European Union and ASEAN have flourished due to a number of integrative factors. The concept of **Cooperative Security and Comprehensive Security**, were used in ASEAN for designing the basic objectives of this forum. These objectives were to foster constructive dialogue and consultation on political and security issues of common interests and concern, and make significant contribution to efforts towards confidence building and preventive diplomacy in the region. It set up a three stage process consisting of Confidence Building Measures (CBMs), Preventive Diplomacy and Conflict Resolution. Similarly, the purpose of European Union was to strengthen the economy of Europe and cooperate in security as in ASEAN. EU is so successful because their members countries make a combine defense community and they solve their internal problems through negotiation, which SAARC countries should follow to achieve full economic and political cooperation.

The new global order dictates that economic survival and prosperity of any nation crucially hinges on its ability to successfully integrate with other economies. The compulsions and prospects for regional integration in South Asia are tremendous. There are obvious obstacles and political imbroglios. Nevertheless, it is high time that governments as well as people of the region realise that economic cooperation is the only option available, which could eventually lead to the building of a more prosperous and socio-politically cohesive region.

Besides, a wide commonality of factors also exists in South Asia. But the attitude of Pakistan towards India and hostility in Indo-Pak relations is a major stumbling block. It is essential for any meaningful regional economic cooperation that it should be done both at inter-governmental level as well as at people-to-people level. There are a number of bilateral problems is South Asia. They must not be allowed to come in the way of regional cooperation. Development without detriment to their integrity and sovereignty is in the national interest of all the South Asian countries.

The birth of SAARC was not related to bloc politics it was considered a basic, inescapable, and prerequisite for ensuring better living standards for millions of people. It was a bold political experiment involving seven nations with different political systems. It was an honest attempt at self-improvement accepting the reality as start point.

Regional cooperation which is being promoted everywhere will be immensely useful in South Asian also. SAARC nations can enhance their bargaining power, with the developed nations and reduce their dependence on it. It will also create a new set of equitable relations within themselves in the region. Being more inward looking, the SAARC nations can exploit the regional resources more effectively in an environment of mutual trust and cooperation. But bilateral issues are largely responsible for slow progress in SAARC. There is also some sort of hidden fear about India's position in the region. Attempts should also be made for ethnic and religious harmony. True spirit of regional cooperation demands fruitful bilateral dialogues to resolve differences and promote development through cooperation. Distrust must be replaced by mutual understanding. There is ample scope of regional cooperation which can go a long way in promoting peace and progress in the entire world. In strengthening SAARC and making it more effective, the most important role has to be played by India while all bilateral relationships are important, the most important and relevant in the future evolution and success of SAARC would be a rapprochement between India and Pakistan.

Regional cooperation in South Asia will eventually strengthen non-alignment. It will provide ineffective forum to deal with the rest of the world. It will consolidate the common desire to live and let live, strengthen the friendship, reconcile or minimize differences and safeguard their independence and sovereignty. It will be the beginning of a new economic and political order in South Asia.

While lessons from the EU and ASEAN prove the benefits of regional integration, there is still a need to shape institutions that are asked to compete and yet cooperate in the neo-liberal political economy. Durable peace must therefore include the resolution of domestic and long standing difference. Growth of economic integration will depend on how individual nations deal with contentious issues and remain committed to regional cooperation peace also needs to include resolution of the Kashmir issue, border problems, distribution of natural resource and of the corrosive politics that divides Hindu, Muslim, Sikh etc along with the other religious minorities.

Political analysts have proposed the creation of a SAARC Parliament to offer new types of political interaction that would be an important condition for increasing transactions, linkages and coalitions. This might go beyond the bureaucratic – technical parameters of SAARC and introduce political, moral, cultural and civilisations dimensions of regionalism. Such a parliament could address conflict in the region, take advantage of civil society, incorporate the principle of unity in diversity, conflict could be managed through three stages: from input **(Source: latent and manifestation of identified conflict)** to management understandings, containing and negotiating problems and finally to output **(consequences defined and outputs generated and drafted).**

Shared management of renewable resources such as water can be leveraged within the region as a focal point for peace-building efforts.

SAARC could and should serve as a regional vehicle for extending resource management across the region. While such agreements do enhance people to people contact, they have not been capable in and of themselves of mitigating conflict and easing tension.

SAARC security discourses should also be expanded to include political, economic and social perspectives in order to achieve sustainability. Joint law enforcement, intelligence and linkages with international organisations could suppress violence if linked with broader development objectives that take into account the root cause of violence and the injustices that fan the flames of conflict.

The introduction of SAFTA in 2006 is one of the most significant achievements of SAARC. SAFTA is creating an enabling basis, hitherto non-existent, for regional trade in South Asia. It has the potential to drive SAARC economies towards building a tariff free trade regime in South Asia.

Thus significant progress towards trade liberalisation and economic cooperation can be expected in South Asia in the near future. However, such progress will likely come mostly in a fragmented manner from SAARC members working individually or in sub-groups, rather than together under SAARC's auspicies. Nonetheless, as the only entity capable of bringing the region's leaders together, SAARC is in a unique position to play a very important role by actively soliciting consideration of regional issues that can only be resolved with the cooperation of several or all members. By acting as an objective intermediary, the SAARC secretariat can present an issue directly to the region's leaders and fast track the processes of consideration and in principle endorsement at the highest level.

As SAARC completes more than 25 years of existence, to weigh the predicaments and prospects of the regional body prudent. The history of SAARC could be divided into four phases. The first phase 1985-90 was marked by great deal of enthusiasm to make, the second phase 1990-95 was marked by an economic agenda dominating the SAARC's proceedings; in the third phase 1995-2000, the pace of regional body slowed down as bilateral tension gripped the SAARC. The current and the fourth phase find SAARC getting rejuvenated again.

However, South Asia is at a historic moment of transforming the economic conditions of its people. In bringing the aspects of their culture to bear in facing contemporary challenges, the people of this region could bring a new consciousness and institutions to the global market mechanism.

In the rapidly changing global environment, regional integration in South Asia has assumed a new strategic significance. Not surprisingly, the potential political economic and strategic gains from SAARC for all member countries have increased significantly and this is a necessary condition for the region and its member countries to fully exploit their potential and achieve their objective of rapid, sustainable and inclusive economic growth.

Summing up, if South Asia is to play a leadership role in the new world that is taking shape, then it must undertake specific initiatives within a new policy paradigm for pursuing peace and overcoming poverty. However this requires that government move out of a mind-set that regards an adversarial relationship with a neighboring country as the emblem of patriotism, affluence of the few at the expense of the many, as the hallmark of development, individual greed as the basis of public action and mistrust as the basis of inter-state relations. We have arrived at the end of the epoch when we could hope to conduct our social, economic and political life on the basis of such a mindset. Now, the people of South Asia have recognised that they have a new tryst with destiny. They are affirming that their security and well being lies not in inter-state conflict but in peace and cooperation for the bright future of SAARC and South Asia. There is a need to promote South Asian regional cooperation to promote common goals, meet common needs and resolve common problems is highly desirable. The establishment of SAARC itself is a very significant achievement, against the background of the tumultuous interstate relations in the past among the major countries of the region. But the establishment of SAARC cannot be an end in itself. There are already too many fora in the world, if that were the intention, to keep the political and bureaucratic functionaries, consultants and academicians busy and for exchange of pleasantries. SAARC can become significant only in terms of the impact it may make or has made in achieving its goals, which indeed are laudable.

It is too early to judge the efficacy of the association, on the basis of its achievements. The activities of SAARC have hither to largely remain confined to seminars, workshops and training courses. This has been recognised in both the Bangalore and Kathmandu Declarations the former called for 'progressive movement towards more concrete and action-oriented projects and programmes to ensure more tangible benefits from SAARC to the peoples of the region, while the latter observed that the interest and enthusiasm so far demonstrated by the increased interactions and exchange of information at the inter-governmental level should be capitalised and translated into tangible programmes and project.

Review of Literature

1. Banerjee Dipankar- SAARC in the twenty-first century towards a cooperative future-India Research Press, New Delhi-2002. This boot contains contributed papers presented at the conference on 'SAARC in 21st century' held in December 2001 at Kathmandu.
2. Baylis John, Steve Smith and Owens Patricia- The globalisation of world politics, Oxford University Press, Washington-2009. This book provides a coherent, accessible and engaging introduction to the globalisation of world politics.
3. Chatterji Manas and Jain B.M., Conflict and Peace in South Asia, Vol. 5, Emerald Group Publishers, U.K.-2008, author in this book has explained about the South Asian region, as is turning out to be the most dangerous place in the world, represents a breeding ground of bloody terror and radical extremism. This book looks at these countries in a historical context from inter-regional and international perspectives.
4. Dahl Devraj and Nishchol. N. Pandey- New life within SAARC, Institute of foreign affairs and Friedrich-Ebert-Stiftung, New Delhi-2005. This book highlights the importance of SAARC into South Asian region, despite their common perception on many issues including trade and other matters which are beneficial to them, they are yet to benefit and materialise them. Although they have recently endorsed the SAFTA, the countries in the region still have differences on how to implement them.
5. E. Sudhakar- SAARC: Origin, growth, future, Gyan Publishing House, New Delhi-1994. The author explains that South Asia consist of states with divergent political system and perception and yet with social, cultural and ethnic affinities. While good neighbourly relations among the main actors of the region have been elusive still the desire for collective self-reliance and development has brought these states together and though belatedly resulted in the evolution of SAARC. The success and future of SAARC depends on various complex factors both internal and external governing the intra-regional relations of South Asia. This book is a modest and sincere effort to access the role, performance and future prospect of the ambitions regional organisation.
6. Export-Import Bank of India, SAARC and emerging trade bloc, Quest Publications, 2008, The aim of this book is to examine the

emergence of SAARC as a trade bloc, to present the brief profile of SAARC countries, to analyse trade, investment, and recent developments in the SAARC region, to empirically examine the trade potential in SAARC region, to recommend relevant policy suggestions and to examine the trade opportunities and challenges of the SAARC trading block.

7. Ghosh Parthasarthy- Cooperation and Conflict in South Asia, Manohar Publishers, New Delhi-1995, Writer in this book has explained that the forces of cooperation are overshadowed by those of conflict in South Asia-mainly because of the tenor of domestic politics of the region which thrives more by exploiting the regional discords than by underplaying them.
8. Goel O.P. – India and SAARC Engagements, Vol. 1 and 2, Isha Books, Delhi-2004. This book elaborately describes the development of South Asia and particularly India. Details of SAARC summits and regional conventions are also induced. History and evolution of SAARC finds description in detailed manner. India's relations with SAARC nations are analysed. The author aims at presenting the Indian policy perspective in South Asia in a larger context of the phenomenon of regional integration across the world. India's security concerns are associated with its relationships towards its SAARC neighbours. Their mutual cooperation can lead to peace, freedom, social justice and economic prosperity in the region.
9. Hassan Munnir, South Asia: Emerging Issues, The ICFAI University Press, Hyderabad-2006. This book explains that the South Asia is coming up as one of the most potent regions in the world. But due to political and economic problems, the real fruits of growth and development of South Asia have not materialised. The hostility among the countries of South Asia is the great barrier.
10. Khanna V.N. – Foreign policy of India, Vikas Publications, New Delhi-2005 describes about the fast moving international event have not only influenced India's foreign policy, but also the dynamic policy adopted by India has itself succeeded in adjusting the behaviour of other countries. India's relations with Pakistan and India's coming closer to ASEAN, EU and APEC were welcome developments. India's look east policy gave a new thrust to its diplomacy. All these and other major events, policies and diplomatic initiatives are reflected in this book.
11. Khan Rafi Shaheen- Regional Trade Integration and Conflict Resolution, Routledge Publications, New York-2009. This book addresses the growth of regional trade agreements which have mushroomed since the 1990s, and considers their potential as a tool for reducing inter and intra state conflict. This book maps the

extant RTAs in the region, analyses the factors which hinder or promote regional trade integration and considers their economic and political impacts.

12. Laursen Finn-Comparative Regional Integration-Theoretical Perspectives, Ashgate Publication, England-2003. In this book writer has explained various theoretical perspectives on integration.
13. Lawrence Saez- The South Asian Association for Regional Cooperation (SAARC), Routledge Publications, New York-2001. This book aims at the institutional structure, objectives and effectiveness of the SAARC in its role as South Asia's leading regional institution.
14. Mohanan, B- The Politics of Regionalism in South Asia, Atlantic Publishers, New Delhi-1992. This book is a modest attempt to apply the integration theory to the analysis of trends and shifts in interdependence in South Asia.
15. Mujtaba Ali Syed- Soundings on South Asia, New Dawn Publications, UK-2005, author has described in this book that the unity in diversity that makes South Asian culture unique is discussed. The region is marked by an asymmetry of power structure, different systems of governance, and interstate conflicts but at the same time exhibits a great deal of harmony in ethnic composition, language, values and norms.
16. Muni S.D. – The emerging dimensions of SAARC, Foundation Books, and June-2010. In this book author has made an attempt to look at the changing dynamics of South Asia and to learn whether SAARC will take regional cooperation and integration in their various dimensions closer to reality.
17. Mattli Walter- The logic of regional integration- Europe and beyond, Cambridge University Press, U.K. – 1999. This book examines regional integration in Europe and other regions, providing a new framework for the study of international cooperation. It also presents the first analysis of integration across time and across regions. Using the tools of political economy he considers why some integration schemes have succeeded while many others have failed.
18. Pandey Aditya – Conflicts of South Asia, Vol. 2, Isha Books, Delhi-2005. Author has described about the democratic peace in South Asia in the recent years and the problems and prospects of democratic peace have lowered the probability of war.
19. Panth Pushpesh – International Relations in 21st Century, Tata McGraw Hill, New Delhi-2011. This book explains the various theories of international relations and also the establishment of SAARC when the erstwhile President of Bangladesh Zia-ur-Rehman made the first.

20. Phillipe de Lombarde – Assessment and measurement of regional integration, Routledge Publications, New York- 2006, In this book an author aims to contribute to the advancement of assessments and measurement tools for monitoring regional integration processes in the world.
21. Raghvan S.N. – Regional Economic Cooperation among SAARC countries, Allied Publishers Ltd, New Delhi-1995. An author has explained an approach to regional economic cooperation among SAARC countries. There is considerable scope for enhancing the level of regional economic cooperation among SAARC nations which could prove mutually beneficial to all the member countries.
22. Salman M.A. and Uprety Kishore – Conflict and cooperation on South Asia's International Rivers: A legal perspective, Kluwer law international, Washington-2002. This book traces the development of international water law. The focus is on the hydro politics of four countries in the South Asian region: Bangladesh, India, Nepal and Pakistan. It analysis the problems that these countries have encountered as riparian's of international rivers and how they have addressed these problems.
23. Sareen T.R. and Bakshi S.R. – Socio-Economic and Political Development in South Asia, Vol. 1, 2, 3- Isha Books, Delhi-2004. This book in three volumes analyses the developmental action in South Asia from different dimensions. First volume deals with the progress and challenges of social developments are seen as major hindrance in the way of development. Second volume deals with the economic development of South Asian countries. Volume three looks at development from political point of view. This book revolves around the India's role and interest in all these spheres.
24. Schiff W. Maurice and Winters L. Alan- Regional Integration and development, World Bank and Oxford University Press, Washington-2003. The analysis presented in this book assesses the effects of regional integration arrangements on trade and competition. This book placed greater emphasis on the analytical and intellectual structures that can be used for exploring the effects of regionalism.
25. Sen Ayanjit – India's neighbours – Problems and prospects, Haranand Publications, New Delhi-2001. Author in this book has described about India's contemporary relations with its neighbours in the backdrop of historical factors. These factors have helped shape the regional power structure as well. India's bilateral relations with these countries have witnessed ups and downs. Internal politics of these countries, militancy and bound any disputes have formed core issues concerning relations between India and these countries. This book gives a detailed description and analysis of these events

as it attempts to explain how these events have unfolded before the world.

26. Singh Gopal, South Asia - Democracy, Discontent and Societal conflicts in South Asia, Anamika Publications, Delhi-1998. It contains articles by eminent scholars in different disciplines. Politics society, economy and gender issue constitute different sections of this book. Focus of an author is on the theory and practice of democracy in different countries of South Asia and the discontent and conflict caused by democratic processes. At present almost every state of South Asia is facing turmoil and conflict of one type or the other which is reflected in this book.
27. Sharma Mohanlal, Peacock Olive and Gopal Krishnan- Globalisation, democracy and governance in South Asia-Issues and alternatives, Kalinga Publications, Delhi-2003. In this book authors have explained about the issues and problems of governance in the South Asian countries have increasingly come under the gaze of social scientists and political activists. Ethnic conflicts, political movements, socio-religious conflicts and other violent upsurges on the one hand and widespread corruption, criminalisation of politics, soft regimes, bureaucratic inefficiency and red - tapism on the other hand are some of the more important manifestations of the problem constraining the systematic performance and retarding the development processes.
28. Syed M.H.- Encyclopedia of SAARC Nations, Vol.3, Gyan Publishing House, Delhi-2003. This book is a complete encyclopedia of SAARC nations. In this book there is a complete description of profile of SAARC nations. The theme has been well-weaved into several chapters having deep bearing on numerous problems of the member countries of SAARC.
29. Trivedi Ramesh- India's relations with her neighbours, Isha Books, Delhi-2008. This book gives fair account of bilateral relations between India and her neighbours. Further it discusses about the trade and treaties, agreements and accords, political and economic cooperation.
30. Wigharaja Poona and Hussain Akmal – The challenge in South Asia : Development, democracy and regional cooperation, Sage Publications, New Delhi – 1989. Author reflects the crisis of development, the associated crisis of state and its impact on regional cooperation in South Asia in this book.

References

1. Bhatnagar Stuti. and Ahmed Zahid – Interstate conflicts and regionalism in South Asia : Prospects and challenges, 2008, p. 5.
2. See chapter 4.

Bibliography

Books

1. Banerjee Dipankar – SAARC in the twenty- first century towards a cooperative future, India Research Press, New Delhi, 2002.
2. Baylis John, Steve Smith and Owens Patricia – The globalisation of world politics, Oxford University Press, Washington, 2009.
3. Chatterji Manas and Jain B.M.-Conflict and Peace in South Asia, Vol. 5, Emerald Group Publishers, U.K., 2008.
4. Dahl Devraj and Nischol-N. Pandey. Institute New life within SAARC, Institute of foreign affairs- Friedrich – Ebert-Stiftung, New Delhi, 2005.
5. E. Sudhakar – SAARC: Origin, Growth, Future, Gyan Publishing House, New Delhi, 1994.
6. Export-Import Bank of India – SAARC an emerging trade bloc, Quest Publications, 2008.
7. Ghosh Parthasarthy – Cooperation and Conflict in South Asia, Manohar Publishers, New Delhi, 1995.
8. Goel O.P. – India and SAARC Engagements, Vol. 1 and 2, Isha Books, Delhi, 2004.
9. Hassan Munnir, South Asia : Emerging Issues, The ICFAI University Press, Hyderabad, 2006.
10. Khanna. V.N. - Foreign Policy of India, Vikas Publications, New Delh, 2005.
11. Khan Rafi Shaheen- Regional Trade Integration and Conflict Resolution, Routledge Publications, New York, 2009.
12. Laursen Finn – Comparative Regional Integration: Theoretical Perspectives, Ashgate Publication, England, 2003.
13. Lawrence Saez – The South Asian Association for regional cooperation (SAARC), Routledge Publications, New York, 2011.
14. Mohanan. B, The Politics of Regionalism in South Asia, Atlantic Publishers, New Delhi, 1992.
15. Mujtaba Ali Syed – Soundings on South Asia, New Dawn Publications, UK, 2005.

16. Muni S.D. - The Emerging Dimensions of SAARC, Foundation Books, June, 2010.
17. Mattli Walter - The logic of regional integration : Europe and beyond, Cambridge University Press, UK, 1999.
18. Pandey Aditya- Conflicts of South Asia, Vol. 2, Isha Books, Delhi, 2005.
19. Panth Pushpesh - International relations in 21st century, Tata McGraw Hill, New Delhi, 2011.
20. Phillipe de lombarde- Assessment and measurement of regional integrations, Routledge Publications, New York, 2006.
21. Raghvan S.N. - Regional Economic cooperation among SAARC countries, Allied Publishers Ltd., New Delhi, 1995.
22. Salman M.A. and Uprety Kishore - Conflict and cooperation on South Asia's International Rivers: A legal perspective, Kluwer law international, Washington, 2002.
23. Sareen T.R. and Bakshi S.R. - Socio-Economic and Political development in South Asia, Vol. I, II, III, Isha Books, Delhi, 2004.
24. Schiff W. Maurice and Winters L. Alan-Regional integration and development, World Bank and Oxford University Press, Washington, 2003.
25. Sen Ayanjit - India's neighbours - Problems and prospects, Har Anand Publications, New Delhi, 2001.
26. Singh Gopal - South Asia: Democracy, discontent and societal conflicts in South Asia, Anamika Publications, Delhi, 1998.
27. Sharma Mohanlal, Peacock Olive and Gopal Krishnan-Globalisation, Democracy and governance in South Asia: Issues and alternatives, Kalinga Publications, Delhi, 2003.
28. Syed M.H.- Encyclopedia of SAARC Nations - Vol. 3, Gyan Publishing House, Delhi, 2003.
29. Trivedi Ramesh - India's relations with her neighbours, Isha Books, New Delhi, 2008.
30. Wigharaja Poona and Hussain Akmal- The challenges in South Asia: Development, Democracy and regional cooperation, Sage Publications, New Delhi, 1989.

Articles and Reports:

1. Alam Sayeed.M- International Journal of Economics and Finance-Vol. 2, Intra regional foreign direct investment, prospect in SAARC region, August, 2010.
2. Ahmed Rashid-NIPA-Karachi, Vol. 7, Should SAARC be wound up? December, 2002.
3. Aska Tanveer, Yusuf Moeed, Shaheen Faisal Haq, Khan Rafi Shaheen-Institute of Sustainable Development publication, Regional

Integration, trade and conflict, mapping regional trade agreements and conflicts, January, 2007.

4. Bangladesh Country Note: Promoting regional integration in South Asia.
5. Burki Javed Shahid-ISAS-working paper, South Asia: Overcoming the past, meeting the challenges of present and availing opportunities of future-June, 2009.
6. Business and Economy Journal-SAARC Investment, Promotion and protection agreement to give boost to intra-regional trade-February 2012.
7. Charter of the SAARC Development Fund-Report.
8. Chaudhary Anup, Chandhary Paul Suman, BRAC University Journal, Vol. 5, Prospects and possibilities of introducing a common currency in SAARC countries, 2008.
9. Dr. Prasad Kiran, The digital divides: implications of ICT's for development in South Asia, International and global communication, 2008.
10. Dr. Malhotra Nitasha, South Asia: Political and Economic region, the association of geographical studies, 1999.
11. Dr. Kapila Subhash- South Asia Analysis Group-South Asia and the Impact of Afghanistan events, 2001.
12. Dixit Aabha, SAARC: Towards Greater Cooperation, 2001.
13. Dash Kishore- Thunderbird Quarterly Review-Issue-2, Towards free trade in South Asia: Political and Economic Dimensions-Spring 2009.
14. European commission-External Cooperation Programmes-Report.
15. Fawn Rick, International Affairs Journal, Vol. 85, International relations theory, globalisation- the regionalising the globe, September, 2009.
16. Ganguly Sumeet, Counterterrorism cooperation in South Asia: History and prospects, National Bureau of Asian Research, 2009.
17. Hettiarachchi Chaminda- Role of Information and Communication Technologies in human development in South Asia, University of Moratuwa, Sri Lanka April, 2011.
18. Hussain Akmal, Indian Journal of Politics and International Relations, a vision for South Asia, Vol. I, Jan-June, 2008.
19. International Studies Journal, Vol. 41, Regional Trading Arrangements in the Era of Globalisation : an Indian perspectives, 2004.
20. Iqbal Jamshed Muhammad-Pakistan Journal of History and Culture, Vol. 27, SAARC: Origin, growth, potential and achievements, Feb, 2006.

21. Joseph Teresa- The enduring rivalry in South Asia: The India-Pakistan Conflict, Cambridge University Press, New York, 2005.
22. Kishore C. Dash-Pacific Affairs, Vol. 69, The political economy of regional cooperation in South Asia, 1996.
23. Kumar Anand, South Asia Analysis Group, Making a beeline for SAARC, April 2006.
24. Kumar Rajiv, SAARC: Changing realities, Opportunities and challenges –November, 2009.
25. Mundell – Uncommon Arguments for common currencies, 1973.
26. Muni S.D. – South Asian Journal, Vol. 1, South Asia as a region, Aug-Sep. 2003.
27. Mohanty K. Sanjeev-The Indian Journal of Political Science, Vol. (iv) The quarterly review, South Asian Conflicts, Oct-Dec, 2009.
28. Muni S.D. and Jaithley Rajshree – SAARC: The Changing Dimensions, UNU-CRIS working papers, Institute of South Asian Studies, Singapore, 2008.
29. Murthy Padmaja-Briefing paper, SAARC and BIMSTEC-Understanding their experience in regional cooperation, 2008.
30. Nagata M. Asian Development Bank, Technical Assistance for promoting South Asian Regional Economic Cooperation, September, 2004.
31. Qazi Abdullah-General information about Afghanistan-Report, 2006.
32. SAARC Reports – SAARC Documentation Centre, Delhi.
33. SAARC Development Goals (2007-12), Taking SDGS Forward, Independent South Asian Commission on Poverty Alleviation-March, 2007.
34. Sridharan Kripa – Working paper, Regional Organisations and conflict management: Comparing ASEAP and SAARC, March, 2008.
35. Upreti B.C., South Asian Studies, Bi-annual journal, Vol. 41 contemporary concerns and the road ahead, September, 2008.
36. Weerakon Dushi – SAFTA: Current status and prospects, Institute of policy studies of Sri Lanka, 2008.
37. W.T.O. Annual Report-Regional Integration, Part-II, III, 8 December, 1997.

Year Book/Periodicals/Journal Names:

1. Asian Development Review.
2. Asian Recorder.
3. Annual Report.
4. BRAC University Journal.
5. British Journal of Political Science.
6. Business and Economy Journal.

7. International Affairs Journal.
8. Indian Journal of Political Science.
9. International Journal of Economics and Finance.
10. International Studies Journal.
11. NIPA-Karachi Journal.
12. Pacific Affairs Journal.
13. Pakistan Journal of History and Culture.
14. Sage Journal Online.
15. South Asian Journal.
16. South Asian Studies, Biannual Journal.
17. Thunderbird Quarterly Review.
18. The Indian Journal of Politics and International Relations.

Webpages

1. Regional Integration agreement.
   http://www.regionalintegrationagreement.htm./
2. Bangladesh country Note.
   http://www.siteresources.worldbank.org/
3. European Cooperation Programs.
   http://ec.europa.eu/europad/saarc.en.htm/
4. Saarc Documentation Centre.
   http://www.sdc.gov.in/
5. SAARC.
   http://www.southasianassociation for regional cooperation.htm/
6. National bureau of Asian Research.
   http://www.nbr.org/
7. General information about Afghanistan.
   http://www.afghan-web-com/
8. Saarc Reports.
   http://www.sarrc.sec.org/
9. Online-International news network.
   http://www.onlinenews.com/-2006.
10. India and SAARC.
    www.scribd.com.
11. Unit 24, SAARC.
    http://www.egyankosh.ac.in/
12. Central Chronical.
    http://www.central chronical.htm/
13. South Asia Analysis Group.
    http://www.making a beeline for saarc.htm/
14. Wikipedia, Online Encyclopedia.
    http://www.regional integration.htm/

Magazine/Newspaper

1. Financial Daily.
2. The Economic Times.
3. Hindustan Times.
4. Times of India.
5. Outlook.
6. Frontline.
7. Competition Success Review.
8. Times Magazine.
9. India Today.
10. The Indian Express.

Confidential

SAARC: ORGANISATION-AWARENESS INSTRUMENT

Constructed and Standardised by:

Prof. Nisar-ul-Haq, Head of Department,
Department of Political Science
Jamia Milia Islamia, New Delhi.

Nidhi Sharma, M.A. (Pol.Sc.), Research Scholar (Pol.Sc.)

Personal Information Name

Education **Age** **Occupation**

Income **Rural/Urban**

Address

Instructions

1. The instrument is meant for research work. Your answer will be kept strictly confidential. Please answer every question without any fear and hesitation.
2. There are some statements and each one has three alternate answers.
3. Carefully read the question, and then on the basis of your choice put a (.) mark on allotted space on any three alternate answers or fill the blanks provided.

1. What is SAARC?
   (a) A regional organisation.
   (b) An international organsation.
   (c) A military alliance.
2. SAARC is an organisation of which region?
   (a) Central Asia.
   (b) South East Asia.
   (c) South Asia.

3. How many countries are member of SAARC?
   (a) 4
   (b) 10
   (c) 8
4. Which country has become a new member of SAARC?
   (a) Bhutan
   (b) Nepal
   (c) Afghanistan.
5. When was SAARC established?
   (a) 1995
   (b) 1985
   (c) 2005
6. SAARC is an organisation of which type?
   (a) Political
   (b) Economic
   (c) Both.
7. What is SAFTA?
   (a) SAARC free trade agreement.
   (b) South Asian Free Trade Agreement.
   (c) South Asian Foreign Trade Agreement.
8. Where is SAARC headquarter located?
   (a) Islamabad, Pakistan
   (b) Kathmandu, Nepal
   (c) Delhi, India.
9. How many states are observers of SAARC?
   (a) 5
   (b) 9
   (c) 10
10. How many SAARC summits have been held until now?
    (a) 15
    (b) 14
    (c) 17
11. Do you think SAARC is an effective organisation for Peace-keeping and economic development of South Asia?
    (a) Yes
    (b) No
    (c) Don't know
12. In which year SAARC got its new member?
    (a) 2006
    (b) 2005
    (c) 2004

13. How often do the foreign secretaries of the member countries meet in a year?
    (a) Once
    (b) Twice
    (c) Thrice
14. Where is the SAARC Documentation centre located?
    (a) Delhi, India.
    (b) Colombo, Sri Lanka
    (c) Islamabad, Pakistan
15. When was the last SAARC meeting held and at which place?
    (a) 10-11 November, 2011, Addu, Maldives.
    (b) 12-13 August, 2011, Colombo, Sri Lanka.
    (c) 2-3 November, 2011, Kathmandu, Nepal.
16. Which country is not a member of SAARC?
    (a) Bhutan
    (b) Afghanistan
    (c) China
17. What is SDF?
    (a) SAARC Development Fund.
    (b) SAARC Disaster Fund.
    (c) Don't Know.
18. Who is the present Secretary General of SAARC?
    (a) Sheel Kant Sharma (India).
    (b) Abdul Saleem (Maldives).
    (c) Fathimath Dhiyana Saeed (Maldives)
19. Where was the first SAARC summit held?
    (a) Dhaka, Bangladesh.
    (b) New Delhi, India.
    (c) Colombo, Sri Lanka.
20. Who mooted an idea of the establishment of SAARC?
    (a) Zia-ur-Rehman (Bangladesh)
    (b) Zia-ul-Haq (Pakistan)
    (c) Rajiv Gandhi (India).
21. What was the former name of SAARC?
    (a) SARC
    (b) SAR
    (c) SAC
22. When was SAFTA Signed?
    (a) 2005
    (b) 2006
    (c) 2007
23. Which country is following 'look-east' policy in SAARC?
    (a) Afghanistan
    (b) Maldives
    (c) India.

24. Do you agree that "Political Problems are overshadowing economic development of SAARC"?
    - (a) Yes
    - (b) No
    - (c) Don't Know
25. What is MFN status?
    - (a) Most favoured nation.
    - (b) Most forward nation.
    - (c) Most failure nation.

Index

A

Achievement of SAARC, 164
Achievements-SAARC, 174
ADB lending Assistance to South Asia, 216, 218
Afghan Jihadis, 152
Afghanistan
  entry in SAARC, 139
  and South Asia, 139-140
Afghanistan-Growth rate, 180
Afghanistan-profile, 105
Agreement on Avoidance of Double Taxation, 109
Agreement on South Asian Free Trade Area (SAFTA), 108
Agricultural commodities Free trade in, 250
And South Asia, 139
Anti-flooding structure, 162
APEC, 23
ASEAN and SAARC, 255
ASEAN three-step strategy and SAARC, 159
Asia Pacific Telecomm Unity (APT), 86
Asian Development Bank (ADB), 208, 286
Asian Development Bank Technical Assistance Framework of, 210
Asian Development Bank's Strategy for South Asia, 218
Asian Free Trade Area (AFTA), 22
Association of Management Development Institutions (AMDISA), 83
Association of SAARC Speakers and Parliamentarians, 80
Association of South East Asian Nations (ASEAN), 47, 88

B

Bangkok Agreement to an FTA, 199
Bangladesh-growth rate, 181
Bangladesh-profile, 102, 137
Bay of Bengal Initiative, 199
Bhutan-growth rate, 184
Bhutan economic growth in, 226
Bhutan history of, 100
Bhutan-profile, 102
Bilateral Trade Restriction SAFTA, 200
Bilateral and Regional Agreements, 201
Bilateral FTA, 228
Bilateral Issues, 148
BIMST-EC, 154, 264
BIMSTEC (1997), 209
BIMSTEC creation of, 146
BIMSTEC evolution India's role, 153
BIMSTEC formation, 54
BIMSTEC'S Activities, 267
Board of Investment, 229

C

Canadian International Development Agency (CIDA), 88

Casella, Alessandra, 46
China, 171
China and SAARC, nations, 171
China's territorial dispute, 156
Citizen's Commission for South Asia (CCSA), 164
Colombo Plan, 88
Colombo Plan of Action, 124
Club rules, 25
  enforcement, 27
Commitment mechanism, 32
Common Currency-Steps involved, 202
Comprehensive Security, 288
Communication and Transport among SAARC nation, 73
Comprehensive Test Ban Treaty (CTBT), 161
Concession under SAPTA, 192
Confidence Building Measures (CBMs), 288
Confidence-Building Measures, 161
Conflict resolution process, 283
Context-successful integration, 38
Containerisation and Multimodal Transport-SAARC, 232
Convention and Agreements SAARC, 252
Cooperative Security, 288
CTBT, 97
Council of Ministers-SAARC, 63
Customs Union Theory, 40

D

Declaration of Fifteenth SAARC Summit Colombo, 128
Declaration of the Eighth SAARC Summit, New Delhi, 121
Declaration of the Eleventh SAARC Summit, Kathmandu, 123
Declaration of the Fifth SAARC Summit, Male, 119
Declaration of the First SAARC Summit, Dhaka, 116
Declaration of the Fourteenth SAARC Summit, 127
Declaration of the Fcurth SAARC Summit, Islamabad, 118
Declaration of the Ninth SAARC Summit, Male, 122
Declaration of the Second SAARC Summit, Bangalore, 117
Declaration of the Seventh SAARC Summit, Dhaka, 120
Declaration of the Sixteenth SAARC Summit, Thimpu, 129
Declaration of the Sixth SAARC Summit, Colombo, 119
Declaration of the Tenth SAARC Summit Colombo, 123
Declaration of the Third SAARC Summit, Kathmandu, 118
Declaration of the Twelfth SAARC Summit, Islamabad, 124
Declaration of Thirteenth SAARC Summit, Dhaka, 125
Defense expenditure of SAARC nations, 282
Democracy in South Asia, 166
Development of SAARC Factors Leading to, 165
Dhaka Declaration, 116
Dhaka Summit (1985), 60
Dispute resolution, 282
Diverse Political Culture, 155
Domestic policy paralysis, 244
Drift in India's approach, 283
Drift in India's approach to SAARC, 146

E

Economic Agenda of SAARC, 190, 286
Economic and Social Commission for Asian and the, 252
Economic Commission (EC), 87
Economic Cooperation Challenges, 240
Economic development, 285
Economic growth, 251
Economic Indicator of SAARC Region, 287

Economic Indicators of SAARC Countries for India, 187
Economic liberalisation policies South Asian countries, 239
Economic Profile of SAARC Nations, 180
Economic union, 285
Eminent Persons Group and the SAARC report, 134
Energy Committee SIPA, 72
Environment, 75
Environment, Meterology and Forestry Committee SIPA, 75
Energy conservation methods-in developing, 236
Energy Cooperation, 234
Energy problems SAARC Countries, 234
Energy Resources Trade in, 235
Entry in SAARC, 139
Environment, 75
ESCAP, 86
Euro, 258
European Coal and Steel Community (ECSC)
European Union, 52, 258
European Union and SAARC, 257
European Union, SAARC, Asean, BIMSTEC Comparison, 268
European Union, Trade with SAARC, 260
European vision formation, 22
EU's Trade Balance with SAARC, 261
Exchange rate policies, 250
Extra Regional Security, 30
Extra-regional Linkage, 153

F

Facing SAARC Political Challenges, 146
Fear of India, 242
Federation of State Insurance Organisations of SAARC countries, 84
Fiscal federalism theory, 45
Foundation of SAARC Writers and Literature (FSWL), 84
Free Trade Agreement (FTA), 184, 245
Free Trade Agreements (FTA) provision, 193
Free trade agreements (FTAs), 270
Free Trade Area of the Americas (FTAA), 23
FTAs in South Asia Comparative Negative Lists, 195
Functional spillover, 37
Functionalism, 35

G

Ganges water sharing, 281
GDP volume of SAARC region, 286
Globalisation, 56, 282
Government and The Tamil LTTE, 152
Gujral Doctrine, 143

H

Health, 250
High Level of Overall Protection, 243
Human development index, 179
Human Development Index of SAARC, 287
Human Resource Development Centre SAARC, 76
Human Resource Development Centre in Pakistan, 122
Human rights, 27

I

Impediment to economic growth, 231
Impediments, 284
Impediments overcoming ways/ suggestions, 157
Impediments-overcoming, 246
Implementation Arrangement SAARC, 215

Independent South Asian Commission for Poverty Alleviation (ISACPA), 125, 218, 275
India and Afghanistan, 140
India and Bangladesh, 137
India's Look East Policy, 153
India and its neighbours, 283
India and its neighbours trade, 239
India and Nepal, 138
India and Pakistan, 136
India and SAARC Members Cooperation Trouble, 142
India and Sri Lanka, 136
India and Sri Lanka economic exchange, 229
India challenges, 98
India GDP, 179
India in SAARC, 141
India Pakistan relations, 92
INDIA-growth rate, 185
India-Pakistan Relations - improvement in, 167
India-profile, 103
Indian military intervention in Sri Lanka, 143
India's Look East Policy, 153
India's Renewed Commitment, 169
Indo-Pak Relations Effects on, 141
Indo-Pak train service, 168
Indo-Pakistan conflicts factors, 148
Informal political consultations, 163
Information and Communication technology (ICT), 94
Information Exchange, 235
Integrated Programme of Action (IPA), 60, 71
Integration, 19
Inter–state, 283
Inter governmentalism, 36, 39
International Telecommunications Union (ITU), 88
Intra –SAARC trade, 253
Intra Regional Security, 30
Intra-regional trade, 250
Investment Diversion Effect, 24
Investment Protection Agreement, 226
Iran and SAARC, 172
Islamabad Declaration, 155

J

Japan and SAARC nations, 171
Japan Fund, 171
Japan special fund, 280
Japan Special Fund-SAARC, 222
Japan's Support, to SAARC, 224
Jigme Singye Wanchuck, 100
Joint Research and Development, 235
Joint venture infrastructure projects, 250
Joint Ventures and Technology Transfer, 228

K

Kargil conflict, 99
Kashmir Issue, 147

L

Lahore Declaration, 136
Least Developed Countries (LDC), 54
Liberal Inter-governmentalism, 40
Liberalisation, 94
Lobbying for Integration, 32

M

Maldives, history of, 101
Major conflict in South Asia-Chronology, 149
Maldives - growth rates, 182
Maldives, political system, 166
Maldives-profile, 104
Male, 101
Male summit, 163
MECOSUR Formation, 47
Merchandise Trade Agreement Commitment in, 243
Meteorology, 75
Mexico's export recovery NAFTA role, 271
MFN status to India, 238
Military modernisation SAARC member, 282

Millennium Development Goals (MDGs), 220, 253
Most Favoured Nation (MFN) status on India, 143
Multi sectoral Technical and Economic Cooperation, 199
Myanmar's interest in South Asia, 172

N

NAFTA, 32
Narcotic drugs and psychotropic substances, 116
Negotiation costs, 29
Neighbours "ganging up" against India, 146
Neo-functionalism attributes, 36
NEPAL-growth rate, 180
Nepal and Bangladesh, 157
Nepal history, 99
Nepal-profile, 104
New Delhi Declaration, 60
New Delhi Declaration issued, 122
Non-governmental Organisations (NGOs), 80
Non-Tariff Measures (NTMs), 186
North American Free Trade Agreement (NAFTA), 242

O

Observer Nations Role of, 170
Observers to SAARC, 128
Official Development Assistance (ODA) loans, 276
Optimal Currency Area, 42
Optimal Currency Area Theory, 42
Optimal Currency Theory
  with internaional risk sharing system, 43
Organisation of Petroleum Exporting Countries, (OPEC), 31
Other regional grouping, 157

P

Pakistan and Afghanistan, 140
Pakistan and SAARC, 281
Pakistan history of, 98
Pakistan-growth rate, 182
Pakistan-profile, 104
Pakistani war of 1971, 99
Para Tariff Measures (PTMs), 186
People to people contact, 79
Political integration problem, 52
Political spillover, 37
Poor port and transport infrastructure, 243
Ports and Shipping-SAARC Countries, 232
Poverty alleviation, 119
Poverty removal, 249
Producer groups, 33
Produce crops
  and regional integration, 33
Project Cooperation, 31
Promoting People to People Contact, 79

R

Radiological Society of SAARC Countries (RSSC), 85
Railways in the SAARC region, 231
Region, 19
Regional Economic Cooperation, 225
Regional Economic Cooperation Among SAARC Countries, 237
Regional groups, 32
Regional integration advantage and disadvantage, 51
Regional integration, 20, 291
Regional integration,
  Agreements, 25
  Aims objectives, 21
  Economic approach, 34
  Economic vs Political, 29
  Moves towards, 22
  Political motives, 20
  Political approaches, 34
  Political implication, 25
Regional Integration and Globalisation, 47
Regional integration benefits, 279
Regional integration and Role of WTO, 48

Regional integration theory, 33
Regional integration economic approaches, 40
Regional integration agreements recent, 46
Regional organisations, 59
Regional Poverty Profile (RPP), 275
Regional Projects, SAARC, 233
Regional Trade Agreement, 244
Regional Trading blocks rise of, 56
Regionalism, 93
Resource Development Issue, 156
Road/rail links SAARC, 231
Rules of law, 27
Rules of origin, 243
Rules of origin (ROO), 193
Rules of Origin of FTA in South Asia, 194
Russia and SAARC, 172

S

SAFTA, 54
SAARC, 109
SAARC Audio-visual Exchange (SAVE) programme, 79
SAARC association of Tour Planners, 84
SAARC, Finance-objectives, 205
SAARC, Trade, 286
SAARC – JAPAN Special Fund in South Asian, 224
SAARC (1985), 209
SAARC (Economic Achievements of Dimension), 251
SAARC (Political Dimension) Achievements of, 162
SAARC Agreement on Mutual Administrative Assistance in custom matters, 109
SAARC Agreements, 108
SAARC agreement on avoidance of double taxtation, 109
SAARC Agricultural Information Centre (SAIC), Dhaka, 67
SAARC Agriculture Information Centre (SAIC), 119
SAARC and ASEAN, 254
SAARC and BIMSTEC, 264
SAARC and ESCAP, 86
SAARC and EU Comparison, 258
SAARC Dcoumentation Centre (SDC), 69
SAARC and European Union (EU), 257
SAARC and other International Forums, 254
SAARC and UN, 274
SAARC and UNICEF, 86
SAARC and United Nations Organisation, 274
SAARC Arbitration Council, 226
SAARC Arbitration Council-establishment of, 107
SAARC birth of, 289
SAARC Assembly could be, 161
SAARC Association of Town Planners, 84
SAARC Audio-Visual Exchange (SAVE), 119
SAARC Audio-Visual Exchange (SAVE) Committees social development Programme, 74
SAARC Audio-Visual Exchange Programme (SAVE), 164
SAARC
  Charter, 61
  Objective, 62
  Principles, 62
  Meetings, 62
SAARC Cardiac Society, 84
SAARC Chamber of Commerce and Industry (SCCI), 81, 123, 206
SAARC, Charter, 151
SAARC Coastal Zone Management Centre, Maldives, 69
SAARC Convention, 113
SAARC Convention on Mutual Assistance in Criminal Matters, 114
SAARC Convention on Narcotic Drugs and Psychotropic Substance, 116

SAARC Convention on Preventing and Combating Trafficking of women and Children for, 114
SAARC Convention on Regional Arrangements for the Promotion of Child Welfare in South Asia, 115
SAARC countries are resources, 249
SAARC Country Shares of Regional GDP, 186
SAARC Crisis of Trust, 156
SAARC Cultural Centre, 124
SAARC Cultural Centre, Sri Lanka, 71
SAARC Decade of the Girl Child, 119
SAARC Decade of the Right of the child, 124
SAARC Development Fund (SDF), 128
SAARC Development Fund (SDF) Charter of, 111
SAARC Development Fund-functions, 204
SAARC Development Goals (SDGs), 218, 253
SAARC Development Goals (SDGs) actions, 220
SAARC Disaster Management Centre, New Delhi, 71
SAARC documentation centre, 79, 119
SAARC economies nature, 284
SAARC efficacy of, 291
SAARC Energy Centre (SEC) Islamabad, 129
SAARC Energy Centre, Pakistan, 70
SAARC Energy Trade Study (SRETS), 236
SAARC Environment Action Plan, 126
SAARC Expansion, 169
SAARC Federation of University Women (SAARCFUW), 83
SAARC Forestry Culture, Bhutan, 71
SAARC Finance, 205, 253
SAARC Food Bank, 112
SAARC forum economic, 279
SAARC Fund for Regional Projects" (SFRP), 82, 203, 253
SAARC FUNDS, 82
SAARC Goals in South Asia, 223
SAARC Historical Burden, 153
SAARC Human Resource Development Centre (SHRDC), 69
SAARC Information Centre, Kathmandu, 69
SAARC-institutional setup, 63
SAARC Integrated Programme of Action (SIPA), 71
SAARC Investment Promotion and Protection Agreements, 225
SAARC Japan Special Fund, 82
SAARC LAW, 81
SAARC Market for Electricity (SAME), 237
SAARC market for electricity (SAME), 130
SAARC member Coutries-size, 152
SAARC Member States, 102
SAARC Members Relations between, 140
SAARC meteorological research centre, 76
SAARC Meteorological Research Centre (SMRC), Dhaka, 67
SAARC Nations Political System in, 144
SAARC Nations Political Conflicts and Relationship, 135
SAARC Observers, 169, 280, 283
SAARC Parliament, 161, 290
SAARC political issues, 151
SAARC Poverty Alleviation Fund (SPAF), 125
SAARC Preferential Trading Agreement SAPTA Principle of, 54, 108, 120, 190, 252
SAARC origin of, 60
SAARC principles, 280
SAARC Regional Centers, 67
SAARC Regional Convention on Suppression of Terrorism, 113
SAARC regional fund, 203
SAARC Recognised Bodies of, 83
SAARC Regional Fund (SRF), 83

SAARC Regional Multimodal Transport Study (SRMTS), 127
SAARC Scheme for Promotion of Organised Tourism, 79
SAARC Secretariat, 90
SAARC security discourses, 290
SAARC Standard, 111
SAARC
  Standing Committee, 64
  Technical Committees, 64
SAARC
  Action Committees, 65
  Secretarial, 65
  Financial arrangements, 65
SAARC study on Trade, Manufactures and Services, 252
SAARC Summit at Kathmandu, 75
SAARC Summit in 1990 at Male, 75
SAARC Summits Declarations, 116
SAARC Surgical Care Society (SSCS), 85
SAARC Teacher's Federation (STF), 84
SAARC Technical Committee on Tourism, 233
SAARC Trade Fairs, 240
SAARC, Trade with the European Union, 262
SAARC tuberculosis centre, 119
SAARC Tuberculosis Centre (STC), Kathmandu, 68
SAARC Visa Exemption Scheme, 80
SAARC Youth Volunteers Programme (SYVOP), 79
SAARC- Japan special fund, 280
SAARC- UNCTAD Memorandum of Understanding on the Trade, 85
SAARC-Japan Fund, 171
SAARC's Activities, 265
SAARC's Trade Balance with EU, 263
SAFTA, 54, 94, 125, 198, 201, 285
SAFTA (South Asian Free Trade Agreement), 238
SAFTA agreement, 281
SAFTA and NAFTA, 270, 272
SAFTA elements of, 280
SAFTA framework agreement provisions to, 197
SAFTA, implementation of, 185
SAFTA introduction of, 290
SAFTA ministerial council, 129, 199
SAFTA objectives of, 279
SAFTA Trade Restriction under, 196
SAFTA-Bilateral Trade Restriction, 200
SAFTA-Challenges and Prospects, 199
SAPTA, 94, 122, 285
SAPTA Rules of Origin, 191
SAPTA to SAFTA, 94, 192, 198
SAPTA-Principles of, 190
SASEC initiative, 276
SAVE programme, 163
Science and Technology Committee-SATC, 76
Secession in Pakistan, 93
Shelter information network SHELTERNET, 120
SIPA Technical Committees under, 72
Silver jubilee year' of SAARC, 129
Single currency, 249
South and Central Asia programmes (SECSCA), 209
South Asia, 92, 178
South Asia and Nuclear Conflicts, 154
South Asia and other Regions Comparative data, 106
South Asia Business Forum, 54
South Asia challenge, 93
South Asia Cooperative Environment Programme (SACE, 90
South Asia Economic Condition, 241
South Asia Fund (SAF), 248
South Asia Historical Background of, 97
South Asia and Nuclear Conflicts, 154
South Asia is Political Challenges, 147
South Asia Political Economy of, 244
South Asia Preferential Trade Agreement (SAPTA), 270
South Asia Regional cooperation, 289
South Asia Regional Cooperation Initiatives, 209

South Asia,
  Regional Integration, 53
  Religion, 53
South Asia religion, 53, 93
South Asian Association for regional cooperation Role of, 53, 83, 133, 178
South Asian Association for Regional Cooperation (SAARC) Countries, 59
South Asian Association for Regional Cooperation-Character of, 61
South Asia Business Program, 54
South Asian Countries Political History, 98
South Asian Development Fund, 82
South Asian Development Fund (SADF), 203, 204
South Asian Economic Union, 202
South Asian Festivals, 80
South Asian Free Trade Agreement (SAFTA), 192
South Asian Free Trade Area Agreements (SAFTA), 225
South Asian Free Trade Area (SAFTA), 108
South Asian Growth Quadrangle (SAGQ), 54, 276
South Asian Growth Quadrangle (SAGQ) initiative, 208
South Asian Preferential Trade Agreement (SAPTA), 238
South Asian Regional Standards Organisation, (SARSO), 110
South Asian Sub Regional Economic Cooperation (SAS, 286)
South Asian sub-regional economic cooperation (SAS, 208)
Southern Africa Development Community (SADC), 47
Sri Lanka economic liberalisation in, 226
Sri Lanka Ethnic violence in, 137
Sri Lanka-growth rate, 183
Sri Lanka-profile, 105
Sri Lankan, 152
Sri Lankan-history, 100

T

Tariff Concession under SAPTA, 192
Tamil LTTE fight, 152
Technical Collaborations, 230
Technical Committee on Agriculture and Rural Development SIPA, 72
The Maldives-profile, 104
TLP – Tariff Liberalisation Programme, 193
Tourism Development of, 233
Trade creation effect, 23
Trade diversion effect, 23
Trade facilitation, 246
Trade Related Investment Measures (TRIMs), 273
TRAINS CD-ROM, 85
TRIPS (Trade related intellectual property rights), 273
Turnkey Plant Export, 230

U

UNCTAD, 85
UNICEF, 86
United Nations Development Programmes (UNDP), 87
United Nations Environment Programme (UNEP), 89
United Nations Fund for Women (UNIFEM), 89
United Nations International Drug Control Programme, 87
United States of America and SAARC, 173
Upgrading common interests, 38
Uruguay Round, 50
US influence in Asia, 241
US interest in SAARC, 172
US policy for South Asia, 173

V

Vajpayee Atal Bihari, 143
Viner's Custom union union theory, 41

W

War on Terror, 151, 167

Working group on energy (WORGEN), 77
World Health Organisation (WHO), 89
World Trade Organisation (WTO) Provisions on Regional Integration Arrangements, 49
WTO Agreements, 94
WTO Negotiations and SAARC, 272

Y

Year of Green South Asia, 126, 127
Young People exchange provisions, 225
Young People Exchanges of, 225